Deformed and Destructive Beings

Deformed and Destructive Beings

The Purpose of Horror Films

GEORGE OCHOA

McFarland & Company, Inc., Publishers
Jefferson, North Carolina, and London

LIBRARY OF CONGRESS CATALOGUING-IN-PUBLICATION DATA

Ochoa, George.
      Deformed and destructive beings : the purpose of horror films /
   George Ochoa.
            p.   cm.
      Includes bibliographical references and index.

      ISBN 978-0-7864-6307-7
      softcover : 50# alkaline paper ∞

      1. Horror films—History and criticism.   2. Monsters in
   motion pictures.   I. Title.
   PN1995.9.H6O25   2011
   791.43'6164—dc22   2010052836

British Library cataloguing data are available

© 2011 George Ochoa. All rights reserved

No part of this book may be reproduced or transmitted in any form or by any means, electronic or mechanical, including photocopying or recording, or by any information storage and retrieval system, without permission in writing from the publisher.

On the cover: Poster image from the 1988 remake of *The Blob* (TriStar/Photofest)

Manufactured in the United States of America

McFarland & Company, Inc., Publishers
   Box 611, Jefferson, North Carolina 28640
      www.mcfarlandpub.com

To Martha and Melinda

Table of Contents

Preface — 1

Part I. The Horror Film Analyzed

1. Purpose — 5
2. Knowing — 18
3. DDB Profile — 28
4. Structure — 38
5. Essential Elements — 47
6. Ethics — 61
7. Meaning and Significance — 72
8. Evaluation of a Good Horror Film — 83
9. Evaluation of a Bad Horror Film — 96

Part II. The Horror Film in Context

10. Genres — 107
11. History: Beginnings to the 1950s — 117
12. History: 1960s to the Present — 131
13. Reputation — 143
14. Taxonomy — 151
15. Techniques — 168
16. Directors — 181
17. Stars and DDBs — 194
18. Other Directions — 201

Notes — 209
Bibliography — 215
Index — 219

Preface

This book introduces a new theory of the horror film: that the primary purpose of the horror film is to make the audience know the monster. Prima facie, monsters are so visible in horror films that this may seem obvious, and yet it is commonly overlooked or neglected. For example, Noël Carroll, in *The Philosophy of Horror*, writes that the locus of audience gratification from horror is "not the monster as such but the whole narrative structure in which the presentation of the monster is staged."[1] But why should the locus of audience gratification *not* be the monster as such?

Avoidance of the monster as such occurs regularly in academic and popular efforts to understand the appeal of horror movies. Critic James B. Twitchell, for example, locates the psychological attraction of horror in the way that horror stories "carry the prescriptive codes of modern Western sexual behavior"[2]—again, not the monster as such, but something else. Like academics, the public at large is often inclined to think that horror movies are centrally about something other than the monster as such—most commonly, feeling scared, as if it were obvious that feeling scared were intrinsically appealing. No less a genre luminary than horror star Vincent Price once opined that the appeal of horror movies "is based, perhaps subconsciously, on an inherent need to be frightened."[3]

I wrote this book because it has long seemed to me that the central appeal of the horror film is nothing else than the monster as such. This was clear to me as a boy watching the Universal Pictures monsters on television—the Frankenstein monster, Dracula, the Wolf Man—assembling monster model kits, and reading *Famous Monsters of Filmland*. What I was most interested in was *precisely* the monsters. This has remained clear to me since in all the years of watching horror movies, despite many changes in the genre, from demonic possession films to slashers to torture porn. But it has also become clear to me why so many people find it difficult to grasp this point.

It is difficult because people today talk in the wrong vocabulary for the task—the vocabulary of the modern world rather than that of St. Thomas Aquinas, the medieval scholastic philosopher and theologian. Say what you will about the Middle Ages, but that era was probably better equipped to talk of horror than we are.

In Chapter 1, to explain why the monster as such is appealing, I draw on Aquinas and his predecessor, Aristotle, to define monsters as deformed and destructive beings whose deformity causes their destructiveness. For short, I call such creatures DDBs. This definition is important because a deformed being, in the Thomistic vocabulary, is, at least potentially, a new form of being, and a destructive being is a being that would, in real life, be too dangerous to be accessible to us. Thus, the horror movie, by presenting us with a DDB, makes us know a new form of being that would be virtually inaccessible if it really existed. This appeals to us because by nature we wish to know being, preferably new and difficult-to-access forms of being. The purpose of the horror film is to present a DDB to satisfy the audience's desire to know being, and thus to please the audience.

Because I am influenced not only by Aquinas but by the pragmatist philosopher Richard Rorty, I believe that the test of a new theory is how useful it is: how interesting and fruitful in illuminating different aspects of its subject. Therefore, the remaining chapters of the book apply DDB theory to various aspects of the horror film to show what can be done with the theory. In the first of the book's two parts, I analyze the horror film from a number of different angles: how the audience gets to know the DDB; the typical traits of a DDB; the structure and essential elements of a horror film; ethics within horror films; and determining the meaning and significance of a horror film and evaluating its aesthetic merit. In the book's second part, I discuss horror films in broader context: how they relate to other genres and have developed historically; their reputation and disreputability; the taxonomy of DDBs; the techniques by which DDBs are realized on film; directors and stars; and the relationship of DDB theory to aesthetics, biology, psychology, and society.

Most of the research for this book was done by watching and rewatching horror films and reading about them. For their efforts in promoting such research, I thank my fellow alumni of the Science Fiction Club at Archbishop Molloy High School, Briarwood, Queens, with whom I once snuck into R-rated horror movies and trolled through stills and lobby cards at one convention after another. I am grateful to Columbia University and the University of Chicago for educating me in literary studies. I thank the members of the Society of Christian Philosophers list serve, who discussed some of these ideas with me. Thanks also to my wife, Melinda Corey, and my daughter, Martha Corey-Ochoa, for reading and commenting on the manuscript. I owe a special debt of gratitude to Ms. Corey and her students in the Film History and Genre class at Mercy College, Dobbs Ferry, New York. They invited me to give them a talk about horror films, and when I realized I had more to say than could fit into one class, the result was this book. This confirmed what I have long suspected throughout more than two decades as a professional writer: I will write a book at the slightest provocation.

Throughout this book, plot twists and endings are freely disclosed. In common parlance, this book is full of SPOILERS. So if you would prefer not to read spoilers to movies you may not have seen, "Well," as they say in the 1931 version of *Frankenstein*, "we warned you!"

PART I: THE HORROR FILM ANALYZED

1
Purpose

Horror films, like the monsters that are their most prominent features, are widely misunderstood. In *Bride of Frankenstein* (1935), the Frankenstein monster offers himself innocently to his bride, and the bride screams. Horror films offer themselves innocently to audiences, and the audiences scream. Granted, the filmmakers intend the screams, and if the horror film is doing its job, the audiences scream with delight. But even ardent horror film fans may have difficulty understanding why their screams should bring them delight — what it is that attracts them to horror films; what is the primary purpose of these movies.

This puzzle is rooted in the name of the genre. The horror film is named for a subjective state, a feeling that its audience members characteristically experience and that is often assumed to be the reason they go to horror movies — they go to feel horror. The feeling of horror includes fear, but also something else — the reaction one has at seeing something ghastly, loathsome, repellent, or revolting, a reaction the dictionaries call "repugnance," or extreme dislike or aversion.[1,2] Horror is not a mild feeling but strong or intense, and it is unpleasant — in fact, the dictionaries call it "painful." But why would anyone deliberately seek out a painful state? Unless you are part of the relatively small population of masochists and self-cutters, pain is generally something to be avoided. But mass audiences have been watching horror movies almost continuously since the silent film era.[3] It makes no sense that so many people would pay good money for the purpose of experiencing pain. So what are horror films for?

The objection might be raised that this question is unanswerable, irrelevant or both. It might be considered unanswerable because of the supposed impossibility of determining a single point of view from which horror films have a purpose for existing — as Thomas Nagel might put it, a view of horror films from nowhere.[4] In fact, however, there is no mystery about whom horror films are for: just follow the money. Who pays to see them? Audiences. Who collects the money? Filmmakers and their financial backers. The horror film is a simple commercial relationship between people who want something (audiences) and people who deliver it to them (filmmakers). It is in this commercial relationship that the purpose of the horror film is to be found. The question of purpose might be rephrased, "What do audiences want horror films for (so much so that they are willing to pay for them)?" or, to put it another way, "What are horror filmmakers trying to deliver (to ensure that they are paid)?" In this cash nexus is to be found the purpose of horror films, their teleology. Teleology in this book is materialist, not idealist.

As to the objection that teleology is irrelevant to the understanding of horror films, this is highly unlikely. In finding out what anything is for, one is able to understand a great deal about it, more perhaps than in any other way. A device buried under the dirt could be any number of things, but if upon stepping on it one finds that it explodes, especially if this occurs in a war zone, one can conclude that it is a land mine with the purpose of harming the enemy, and this might lead to the understanding of such things as how it is constructed, how effective it is, who planted it, and where other mines might be. Finding out what a work of art is for can yield a similarly comprehensive understanding.

A further objection might be raised that teleology in this book is receiving an unnecessary privilege — that other approaches to understanding might have just as much right to be considered. And this may be so: they might have just as much right. But are they as useful? This can only be settled by showing what can be done with a teleologic approach. Adopting a Rortian pragmatic standpoint,[5] I intend in this book to show the usefulness in many areas of asking the question, "What are horror films for?"

In this chapter, I will begin by proposing an answer to that question. Drawing on Aristotle and St. Thomas Aquinas, I will argue that the horror film exists primarily to present deformed and destructive beings (i.e., monsters) so that audiences may satisfy their desire to see new beings otherwise inaccessible to them. Within this theoretical framework, later chapters will consider the horror film from a variety of angles, including epistemologic, narrative, ethical, critical, generic, historical, taxonomic, and technical, with a closing chapter suggesting avenues for further research. Throughout most of the book, the focus will be on horror films alone, not on other forms of horror entertainment, such as Stephen King novels or Goya paintings. Some of my arguments may have validity with these other artistic products, but I am not presently extending them in that direction. Horror films are complex enough to merit attention on their own without being confused with other sorts of works.

The Paradox of Horror

Many solutions have been suggested to what Noël Carroll calls the paradox of horror: "if horror necessarily has something repulsive about it, how can audiences be attracted to it?"[6] None has been entirely satisfactory. One popular answer is that, despite the apparent painfulness of horror, there is a kind of physical enjoyment that comes from having adrenaline pump through the bloodstream in a safe environment,[7] and a pleasurable relief at finding oneself alive when the experience is over. Such a sensation is analogous to the pleasure one feels when riding a roller coaster or watching an action movie.

However, if this were all there was to it, you could satisfy a horror movie audience by substituting a roller coaster ride or an action movie for the horror movie at the last minute. Some audience members might be sated by this, but many would demand their money back. When audiences come to see a horror film, a horror film is what they want, not just a generic feeling of fear or thrill. Further, horror fans can often enjoy a horror movie they have seen many times before and that is no longer as fearful or thrilling, because, evidently, there is something they want from it beyond the mere subjective feelings.

Another possibility is that horror films offer some other kind of psychological satisfaction besides an adrenaline rush. Perhaps they take our minds off our everyday problems, or perhaps they are a form of therapy. Depending on which critic you consult, horror films help us cope with our fear of death[8] or with real horrors,[9] serve as sexual wish-fulfillments (as Ernest Jones claims nightmares do),[10] illuminate "conflicts of aspiration and doom,"[11] or enable "the return of the repressed."[12] One might also claim that horror films provide a way to cognize difficult truths that are depicted through symbolism. The truths may be contemporary social, political, and economic concerns,[13] or something more mystical, such as "Dionysian truths."[14] Or the films may serve both therapeutic and cognitive functions, combining "instructional messages" with "psychosocial therapy."[15]

Although such analyses of thematic content can be interesting, they have little likelihood of explaining the primary purpose of horror films, because, like the adrenaline rush theory, they are pulling a bait and switch. If horror movie audiences wanted therapy or cognition of difficult truths, you could satisfy them just as well by substituting a therapist or lecturer at the theater. Or suppose you gratified whatever sexual fantasy they were expected to get through horror. Carol J. Clover proposes that "the first and central aim of horror cinema is to play to masochistic fears and desires in its audiences."[16] If in lieu of a horror movie, you supplied each audience member with a dominatrix (or dominator) who whipped and humiliated the individual, some audience members might be pleasantly surprised by the experience, but most would probably want their money back. If it were objected that the audience members could only be gratified by the particular masochism experience embodied in the horror film, then the question would become, "Why that one and no other? What is the specific appeal of the horror film as opposed to other supposedly similar pleasures?" And then we are right back to trying to define the specific

Grace Stewart (Nicole Kidman) embraces her children, Anne (Alakina Mann) and Nicholas (James Bentley), in *The Others* (2001, Dimension Films).

attraction of horror films. That task is only evaded by all such bait-and-switch explanations, not accomplished.

When horror film audiences go to see a horror film, it is specifically a horror film they want — and such a film is not reducible to the psychological effects or symbolic content it is frequently alleged to have. In addition, human beings have wildly varying psychologies, and society and politics have changed considerably since the first horror films were made. Yet horror movies can attract mass audiences of very different psychological makeups, and audiences today can enjoy horror films that were made decades ago, under quite different social and political circumstances. This also suggests that therapeutic and symbolic issues are not the core of the appeal of horror movies.

What, then, are horror movies for? I propose that what an audience is looking for in a horror movie is exactly the thing that is most prominent in the movie: the monster. Most horror movies clearly have a monster, and even when there is no clear monster some sort of center of monstrousness, such as the haunted hotel in *The Shining* (1980), is necessary to do what gives the horror movie its name — generate horror. Whether it is a supernatural creature, such as a vampire or demon, or a natural but disorderly entity, such as a mad killer or berserk shark, the monster is a horror generator. Sometimes, the identity of the monster may be obscure at first but becomes clear by the end, as with Nicole Kidman's stalwart mother who turns out to be a ghost in *The Others*. As Rick Worland writes, the monster is the "star" of the horror film, that which the audience "comes to see": "the creature, the thing, the supernatural menace in whatever near-human or non–human form it assumes."[17] To understand the monster's appeal it is necessary to look with some care at what it means to be a monster.

The monster of horror movies is first of all a being — a fictional or imaginary being, but within the horror narrative a real being, something that exists and can affect and be detected by other characters. Incidentally, no claim is made in this book as to the nature of being: only that it seems to people as if there is being, and as if the characters in films are beings within the film. This approach is not so much ontologic as hetero-ontologic — ontology as it seems to people; ontology mixed with seeming.

So within a horror film the monster is a being, like other characters in the narrative. It is unlike the non–monsterly beings in the narrative in that they are normal while the monster is abnormal. It is abnormal not just in any way, but in two key respects: it is deformed and destructive. Further, its deformity is the cause of its destructiveness.

Deformity and Destructiveness

Consider deformity first. The concept of deformity presupposes form — a natural pattern or type that is also the essence of each thing, according to Aristotle and Aquinas.[18] We recognize deformity in a creature because we know (or think we know) what a creature of that type should be like. People should have one head; if a person has two heads, as in *The Thing with Two Heads* (1972), that is deformity. In horror movies, the monster's deformity is often physical, as with disfigured people like the skull-faced Phantom in *The Phantom of the Opera* (1925) or bizarre, unearthly creatures like the title character in *Alien* (1979). (This alien may be normal for his planet, but aboard a spaceship from Earth he is not of the expected form for a living thing, and in that sense is deformed.) Deformity may also be psychological, as in the handsome but deranged Norman Bates in *Psycho* (1960), or spiritual: vampires and demons are both supernatural rebels against God, and in that sense have deformed wills or spiritual attitudes.

Deformity may be of yet another type. The form that is violated may be positional, with respect to the place that a thing ought to occupy in the order of being, the culture's basic understanding of the hierarchy of existent things. The ancient and medieval version of this order was explored most famously

The Frankenstein monster (Boris Karloff) disastrously attempts to make friends with little Maria (Marilyn Harris) in *Frankenstein* (1931, Universal).

by Arthur O. Lovejoy in *The Great Chain of Being*.[19] To be in the wrong place in the order of being is related to what Noël Carroll calls categorical interstitiality, crossing the boundaries of a culture's deep conceptual categories.[20] For example, most of us feel intuitively that the living ought to live and the dead ought to be dead; therefore, when the dead live, as ghosts and zombies do, the categorical walls have been deformed; the order of being has been violated. Similarly, most of us expect to be at the top of the food chain. When the shark in *Jaws* (1975) makes a practice of dining on bathers, the order of eating and being eaten has been violated. An especially bizarre positional deformity ensues when a monster mixes two species, such as in werewolf movies and the two versions of *The Fly* (1958, 1986).

A particular monster can be deformed in more than one way. In *The Mystery of the Wax Museum* (1933), the physically disfigured sculptor is also psychologically disturbed, to the point that he kills people and encases them in wax. The Frankenstein monster in *Frankenstein* (1931) is physically deformed, has an abnormal criminal brain, and, as an assemblage of dead body parts brought to life, is a member of the living dead; additionally, he is the result of his creator's blasphemous effort to usurp God's power over life and death. The Frankenstein monster in this 1931 version — the Universal production that is the most famous of several adaptations of Mary Shelley's novel — is thus physically, psychologically, spiritually, and positionally deformed: a quadruple achievement that perhaps accounts for his high status among monsters.

Deformity is not sufficient for a monster. The young naval veteran who is missing his hands in the post–World War II drama *The Best Years of Our Lives* (1946) is physically deformed, but he is not destructive, and is therefore not a monster. Even though the veteran may have killed people in war, he did so as he ought to have done (at least according to the ethics of war movies) — in the legitimate defense of his country. Destructiveness is essential for a monster, and this destructiveness must be of something that ought not to be destroyed in the way shown under the circumstances presented.

Human life is most often the object of the monster's destructiveness: vampires, werewolves, zombies, serial killers, and other monsters endlessly bite, stab, strangle, and otherwise dispatch people. Such taking of life must be wrongful, cruel, or both. When a police officer in an action movie shoots a bad guy in the line of duty, a life is taken but the audience does not consider the cop a monster. When Dracula feeds an infant to his brides in *Bram Stoker's Dracula* (1992), the infant is clearly innocent — not a bad guy at all — and the implied death by biting is cruel. Even when the victims are not innocent, as is often the case in horror movies, the killings are made horrible by their cruelty and by the unappointed nature of the agents of vengeance. The zombies in *Day of the Dead* (1985) kill a military commander, who was obviously a bad guy, by tearing him to pieces while alive and eating the pieces. The manner of this killing is monstrous and lacking in due process, even if the bad guy had it coming.

The destructiveness of monsters is not limited to taking lives. They can also take limbs and otherwise physically harm, disable, or mutilate their victims; in some horror films, the attack may include sexual assault or rape. In the course of harming their victims, monsters usually cause pain, both physical and psychological. In the remake of *The Fly* (1986), the hybrid scientist-fly does not kill anyone, but he does use his fly vomit to melt away, painfully, a victim's hand and foot.

Sometimes the destructiveness of monsters is most visibly to property, as when Gojira destroys Tokyo in *Gojira* (*Godzilla, King of the Monsters*; 1954). Sometimes the destructiveness is subtle. In *The Sixth Sense* (1999), the ghosts are not trying to kill or cause physical harm, yet they are not exactly benign. By terrorizing the one boy who can see them, they destroy his peace of mind until he finds a way to live with them. And there are fates worse than death, mutilation, pain, property damage, and terror. Vampires destroy the eternal salvation of their victims by turning them into vampires, a state of unholy living death. In a secular version of the same phenomenon, zombies turn their victims into zombies, destroying their humanity and making them undead.

Just as deformity without destructiveness is not sufficient for a monster, neither is destructiveness without deformity. There are plenty of destructive characters in movies, such as the villains in action movies and westerns, but unless they are significantly deformed, they have no claim to being monsters. The villainous Hans Gruber in the action movie *Die Hard* (1988) is a good-looking, generally sane man who has a reasonable, if ruthless, plan for stealing a lot of money. He is destructive, but not a monster.

The final requirement for monster status is that the deformity must be the cause of the destructiveness. If the deformity and destructiveness are unrelated, or the deformity is solely the effect of the destructiveness rather than the cause, there is no monster. For example, the villainous Ernst Stavros Blofeld, as played by Donald Pleasence in the James Bond thriller *You Only Live Twice* (1967), has a disfigured face, but the disfigurement appears to have no direct relation to his villainy. In fact, in later films in the series, the character of Blofeld reappears, played by different actors with no disfigurement. The deformity is not essential to this character's destructiveness, just accidental; therefore Blofeld, however vile, is not a monster. Similarly, the Nazi interrogator in the action film *Raiders of the Lost Ark* (1981) who burns his hand with the imprint of an ancient artifact he has been trying to steal has caused himself some deformity through his destructiveness, but this is the wrong causal direction. Real monsters destroy because of their deformity; if their deformity happens to increase as a result of their destructiveness, that is secondary. Vampires are primarily deformed in that they need to drink the blood of living people; this deformity directly causes their destructiveness. After being hunted down for their destructiveness, vampires are often burned up by sunlight, with the effect of deforming them physically. But the prior and more important deformity was in their being vampires, the cause of the destructiveness that led to their secondary deformity by burning.

Monsters, then are deformed and destructive beings—DDBs, we might call them — whose deformity is the cause of their destructiveness. (In this book, DDB and monster are generally used interchangeably.) Monsters are the most prominent feature of horror movies, and I suggest that people who see horror movies are primarily there for the monsters. But why would anyone want to see a monster? It is easy to see how a DDB would be fearful and repugnant — the core definition of horror — but why would it be appealing?

The Appeal of Being

The reason people want to see a deformed and destructive being is, first, because they want to see beings; beings, as such, are attractive to them. As Aquinas says, "Goodness and being are really the same."[21] Goodness, in Thomistic terms, is desirability, and being is desirable because it is the perfection of a thing; a thing that is not actual lacks the perfection of an actual thing. We desire to know what seem to us to be actual things, whatever they are, because we are built that way. This is why scientists study the intricacies of the natural world, children hunt bugs in their yards, and zoos and museums are steady attractions. People so want to know actual things that they will even extend their knowledge of being through fictional beings, things that do not really exist but can be presented to us as if existent in movies, plays, novels, and television shows. By meeting fictional beings, we can have the illusion of meeting actual beings, an illusion that satisfies, to some degree, our desire to know being.

Nowadays, we are likely to attribute the desire to know being to natural selection: individuals who were interested in knowing as much as they could about their environment, including its living things, were more likely to use that knowledge to their advantage and survive to reproduce than individuals with a lack of curiosity. Aquinas found a supernatural element in the human desire to know being—God, the supreme being whose essence is existence, is known through the being of his creatures.[22] Aristotle took the human interest in being as a historical fact: "And indeed the question which, both now and of old, has always been raised ... [is] what being is."[23] But whatever the reason, it does seem that people want to know beings.

Being, in the tradition of Aristotle and Aquinas, is related to form, a thing's natural pattern or type, or essence. To *be* in any intelligible sense, a thing has to have a form that can, in principle, be identified—the form of a tiger, for example. Even dust has the form "dust," a fine assemblage of minute particles. For people to fulfill their desire to know beings, they need to know forms. But there are two problems: in the real world, there is a limited quantity of forms sufficiently distinctive to arouse general interest; and if encountered directly, some forms would be hazardous to know. A tiger is a being any knower would find interesting, but if encountered in the street, the tiger would probably eat the knower. Although magnificent, the tiger's nature—its form—is essentially destructive of things valuable to the knower, such as life and limb. The action of the tiger's form causes the privation, or loss, of its prey's form, as Aquinas says of fire: "as the more perfect the fire is in strength, so much the more perfectly does it impress its own form, so also the more perfectly does it corrupt the contrary."[24] The tiger in action as destructive being is virtually inaccessible to us because of its destructiveness.

DDBs solve both these problems. In virtue of being deformed, the DDB establishes a new form—a new kind of being to know.[25] In one sense, a monster is lacking in form, exhibiting privation of the form[26] it ought to have, an imperfection we experience as ugly or repugnant. But in another sense, it is a new form—a Frankenstein monster, a vampire, a zombie, the giant mutant dinosaur Godzilla—a type with characteristics different from those found in normal experience (e.g., a flat head in the Frankenstein monster; fire-starting radioactive breath in Godzilla). That makes the DDB attractive, even beautiful, because the beautiful, according to Aquinas, is that which is "pleasant to apprehend,"[27] and our desire to apprehend being makes the apprehension of new forms pleasant. By extending the quantity of forms we can know, monsters are beautiful as new types of being, even if ugly as specimens of deformity. Thus the apprehension of monsters in horror films gives us pleasure.

Not every movie monster is an entirely new type of being. Some are new examples of old types—vampires, for example, have been depicted many times in movies. In Aristotelian terms, the form of the vampire (the principle of actuality) is the same from one movie to the next, but the matter (the principle of potentiality, the stuff from which the vampire is made, such as the distinct performances of the actors Bela Lugosi and Christopher Lee) is different. Each composite of form and matter is a new individual vampire. But a new individual is still a new being, even if not a new form, and that is attractive in itself. Further, some of the new individuals represent new subtypes. For example, the shape-shifting Dracula in *Bram Stoker's Dracula*, with his abilities to transform from old man to young man to wolflike and batlike monstrosities, is an innovative subtype of the vampire, and is therefore appealing as a new kind of being.

Even when essentially the same individual monster is encountered in sequels and remakes, it can satisfy because it allows us more chances to see an appealing creature, sometimes under different aspects; for example, the Frankenstein monster in *Bride of Frankenstein* acquires speech, an attribute lacking in *Frankenstein*. Sometimes the same horror movie can be watched over and over to pleasing effect, because we have forgotten some aspects of the monster or want to deepen or relive our knowledge of it.

Like the tiger, the form that a DDB represents is essentially destructive of things valuable to us. The very deformity that constitutes the DDB—the deformity that is equivalent to a new form—is the cause of its destructiveness. Vampires, zombies, slashers, by their nature as these types of beings, kill, hurt, terrorize, and do worse. If we were to encounter them in real life, we would not be pleased, because they would threaten our own existence and that of things we hold dear. But when we encounter them in a horror movie, we are completely safe. Movie monsters are fictional and therefore unable to harm us. Even if some kinds of monsters really exist, such as serial killers, the ones we encounter on screen are not really there. Yet we have the illusion of the monster's presence, and this satisfies our desire to know not only new forms but precisely those kinds of forms that would be hazardous for us to know in reality.

Perhaps the reason the desire to know DDBs runs so deep is that the generation of DDBs is essentially the process by which living beings evolve. As a population of one species evolves into another species, it becomes deformed with respect to the parent species, and may therefore be destructive both to the parent species (which may be a rival) and to other food species and rival species threatened by its superior fitness. In that sense, we living things are all DDBs, and the horror movie is our family home video. That is why, to some extent, we identify with DDBs. However, because we are also an established species who would feel threatened by invaders of a new species, we also identify with the normal characters in a horror movie, and feel horror at the sight of DDBs.

The Horror in Horror Films

The horror film is an engine for presenting monsters—DDBs who are appealing because they constitute new kinds of entities that would be antithetical to our existence if they were actual. The appeal is essentially cognitive and objective: what we seek from horror movies are objects of knowledge that represent new forms that would not even be accessible if they were real. However, to provide these objects of knowledge, horror movies must act on our subjective emotions, because they must convince us the monsters are real (at least to the degree that any audience enjoying a fictional story is temporarily persuaded to accept the reality of the characters, i.e., their fictional reality, in a kind of analog to true belief). To create this illusion, a horror movie must vividly present the deformity and destructiveness of the monster. For this presentation to be vivid, the monster must be depicted in action, and viewers must feel something like the emotion that they would feel if they were really presented with a being that was this deformed and was destroying them. That feeling would likely be an intense, painful feeling of fear and repugnance—in a word, horror. The fear would come primarily from the monster's destructiveness, perhaps secondarily from fear that we might "catch" its deformity. The repugnance would come primarily from the deformity, secondarily from the sight of the gory mess that often results from its destructiveness.

To make the monster more convincing, it helps if the audience also sees things partly from the monster's point of view, by feeling pity for the DDB or at least occupying his subjectivity. The title monster in *King Kong* (1933) is a classic example of a creature for whom one feels pity as well as fear (two of the attributes of tragedy, according to Aristotle).[28] Michael Myers in *Halloween* (1978) may not be especially pitiable, but a number of subjective-camera shots force the viewer to take his point of view, an effect that increases the horror and makes him seem more real.

Although intense and painful, the horror experienced in a horror movie is unlikely to be as intense and painful as the horror one might feel if one were being cut to pieces by a real insane killer. That is because in a horror movie, one can always say "This is only a movie" and feel safe, whereas in a real horrific event one could not. The emotional distance afforded by the safety of fiction allows the viewer to feel not only horror but an even more fundamental pleasure at the encounter with a new and otherwise inaccessible being. This double effect is why the audience at a well-made horror film screams with delight.

The horror felt at a horror movie requires the presentation of the monster, but that presentation need not always involve direct showing. Much of the horror in horror movies is indirect, often intended to build up fear and tension as the monster is gradually unveiled. This serves the ultimate purpose of presenting the monster as vividly as possible, by making the audience start to feel the horror even before the monster is clearly visible, and increasing the likelihood that the monster will be plausible when (or if) it finally is shown clearly.

Since the primary purpose of horror films is to present DDBs, horror movies can be readily distinguished from other movies that happen to have DDBs but are not primarily designed to present them. *Twilight* (2008) has some DDBs—a pack of evil vampires who hunt humans—yet the main purpose of this movie is not to present them but to showcase the love story between a human girl and a good male vampire, a creature who is not destructive and only deformed in the sense that he is undead and has supernatural powers. Therefore *Twilight* is a romance, not a horror movie.

Horror movies generate horror, and for this reason many people have thought that the purpose of the films is to horrify audiences. However, the primary purpose of horror films is to present deformed and destructive beings vividly, and not for any ulterior motive, such as to convey social and political ideas or provide therapy, but only because the audience wants to see monsters for their own sake as beings. The horror felt by the audience is a secondary effect that indicates the primary purpose is being met. Social, political, and psychological content is often present in horror films as part of the matter from which monsters are created and as part of the meaning and significance of the film, but it is subordinate to the monster. For example, racial conflict is central to the origin of the title character in *Candyman* (1992), and race is an important part of most readings of the film. But what primarily draws audiences to *Candyman* and satisfies them is not the theme of race as such but the monster Candyman.

This theory of horror films is heterogeneous in its origins: it is a materialist-teleologic-hetero-ontologic-Rortian-pragmatist-Aristotelian-Thomist theory of horror films, or to put it more simply, a teleologic-ontologic theory, or more simply still, DDB theory. By the Rortian test, however, what matters is not its origins but its usefulness. DDB theory is a useful way of talking about horror films. For example, DDB theory not only explains the purpose of horror films but provides a criterion for critically evaluating them. The best horror movies are those that most effectively present a monster in its deformity and destructiveness, convincing the audience of the creature's existence and clearly distinguishing it from other beings. In this way, horror movies, which by their nature show ugly things, can be beautiful. As Aquinas writes, "an image is said to be beautiful, if it perfectly represents even an ugly thing."[29]

DDB theory clarifies much else that is otherwise obscure about horror movies, such as epistemology; characteristics of DDBs; narrative structure; essential elements; ethics; meaning and significance; relation to other genres; history; reputation; taxonomy of DDBs; cinematic techniques; and more general issues of aesthetics, biology, psychology, and society. The rest of this book will support the theory of deformed and destructive beings by showing how it illuminates these areas.

2
Knowing

The primary purpose of horror films is to present DDBs to satisfy the audience's desire to know being, and thus to please the audience. But what precisely does it mean to know being? Why does the audience have to sit through the running time of a horror film to accomplish the task? Why, for example, cannot the filmmaker just show one still image of the DDB and let everyone go home?

For example, in the movie *Blood Feast* (1963), there are repeated images in which a mad killer, with wild eyes and blue-gray hair, stabs and mutilates women. It seems that any of these shots would get the point across. But people who have seen *Blood Feast*— a movie that is laughably bad in places but overall effective and original — know that a single image from the film could not substitute for the experience of watching the entire thing.

To understand why horror films have the shape they do, it is necessary to investigate the epistemology of these movies: what it means to know the DDB and how the audience gets that knowledge.

The Nature of Knowing

Just as no claim is made in this book as to the nature of being, no formal claim is made as to the nature of knowing. However, for convenience, and because of the Thomistic roots of DDB theory, I will talk about the nature of knowing more or less as Aquinas does. His view is, "The thing understood is in the intellect by its own likeness."[1] That is, if you understand Dracula, Dracula is in your intellect — not just an idea of Dracula, but Dracula himself is there *through* your idea of him. Your intellect, in fact, takes the form of Dracula; Dracula *is* your intellect while you are understanding him. For Aquinas, this is on the assumption that Dracula is a universal, a real nature of a genuine natural kind.[2] In reality, of course, Dracula is fictional, but, according to DDB theory, the horror movie viewer acts as if Dracula and other DDBs are real natures that are only just discovered when their horror movies are seen. The intellect of the horror movie viewer treats Dracula as a universal — a sort of species of the genus vampire — even though Dracula is also an individual.

From the Thomistic standpoint then, to know a DDB is to get the DDB inside you — to have your mind become the DDB. This language is useful because it expresses the intimacy of knowledge, the extent of the union between the knower and the known. If you knew nothing about Dracula but only drove past him while he was out for an evening walk, you would not have effected the necessary union of knower and known. You would have seen a man walking along, perhaps in a cape, but you would have missed knowing Dracula; you would have missed the intimacy that comes from knowing being.

In addition, the theory that the mind becomes Dracula when Dracula is known means, at least in principle, that we can know Dracula objectively. Dracula is not just something external to us about whom we have only subjective impressions in our minds. Different audience members can talk about Dracula and all be talking about the same thing. In practice, this can be difficult, because there have been many versions of Dracula — Lugosi, Lee, etc. — and unless we clarify which one or ones we mean, we may talk past each other. But even so, if we speak with sufficient clarity about the same versions of Dracula, we can speak of Dracula as if he were one entity in our minds.

To get to know Dracula in this way — with your mind becoming the DDB — you need more than one glimpse of him walking down a street; you need also, for example, to see him bite a victim's neck, stare hypnotically, speak menacingly, show blood on his lips, flash his fangs, or turn into a bat. Such sensory impressions are the beginning of all knowledge; as Aquinas says, "intellectual knowledge is caused by the senses."[3] In addition, such sensory impressions must be connected in some kind of explanatory narrative, a story that makes them meaningful, so that you can understand how the distinct impressions fit together. (Aquinas does not specify this step, but it seems implicit in this context.) Through such a narrative, you can abstract the form of Dracula from your mental images of him (your phantasms, as Aquinas would have called them)[4] and thereby know him.

The horror movie is a machine for dispensing knowledge of DDBs. It supplies to its audiences both the sensory impressions and the explanatory narrative needed for them to know the DDB at the core of each horror film — to know the DDB with the intimacy and union necessary for genuine knowledge.

Consider the mad killer in *Blood Feast*. Yes, he has wild eyes and blue-gray hair and stabs and mutilates women. But to know him, it is also necessary to know that his name is Fuad Ramses, and that he is carving up women to prepare a cannibal feast as a central part of his worship of the ancient Egyptian goddess Ishtar. To appreciate what this means, it is necessary to linger over the sight of the women's body parts and mutilated bodies, thus to experience both the loving attention Ramses gives to his work and the horror of the work from the point of view of the victims. It is also necessary to see Ramses in his day job, as an eccentric caterer who keeps his charnel house and temple of Ishtar hidden in the back. One needs to hear his bizarre accent and impassioned tone. One needs to see the police desperately at work trying to capture the killer, and listen with potential victims to the radios warning women to stay indoors. With all these different sensory impressions and narrative pieces—climaxing in Ramses's grotesque death in a garbage truck—one gets to know Ramses as a distinct DDB, which is to say, Ramses gets inside one's head.

This is why the horror film is not just a horror still. The primary purpose of horror films is to present the DDB, which means to make the audience know the DDB, and this is better done not statically, as with a horrific painting or photograph, but dynamically, using the resources of cinema: moving images and sound that tell a story, a connected series of events that unfold in time. Such a cinematic narrative makes it possible for the audience to know the DDB.

Normals

Because all horror films are constructed for the purpose of presenting the DDB (that is, making the audience know the DDB), they share a certain narrative consistency. Every narrative of any kind has a conflict, and in the horror film narrative the chief conflict is generally between the DDB and one or more characters who are not DDBs: the normal people, or, for short, normals. The conflict between DDBs and normals is the mechanism by which we primarily know the DDB.

This is because the normals represent us, the audience; we are meant to identify with them (even as we also identify to some extent with the DDB) and see the DDB from their point of view. Normals are neither deformed nor destructive (at least not to the same degree as the DDB), and therefore provide a point of contrast to the DDB. They look more or less normal, bringing into relief the deformity of the DDB. They react to the DDB as we would, with horror. At least some of the normals are attacked by the DDB, allowing us to see the DDB in action as a destroyer. Normals may also attack the DDB, permitting us, in some cases, to feel sympathy for the monster, and so to see him as a more complete individual. Thus, the normals in the horror movie allow the monster to be known as a DDB: as deformed, destructive, and a being. Robin Wood goes so far as to propose as a basic formula for the horror film, "Normality is threatened by the Monster."[5]

Necessary though they are, the normals are never the point of the horror film: the DDB is. Therefore, many of the normals in horror movies are not three-dimensional characters; one or two dimensions will usually do. A

2. Knowing

gravedigger killed by the title monster in *The Wolf Man* (1941) is known almost entirely by one characteristic: he is a gravedigger. Still, our identification with normals (and therefore the vividness of the DDB that menaces them) can be greater when the normals are more fully fleshed out. Some horror films therefore take more pains to add detail to their normals: for example, families, jobs, hometowns, personalities, love lives. Details such as these make the normals more like us, and hence better foils for the DDB.

There are two major ways that normals and the DDB come into contact: either the normals discover the DDB or they create it. In both cases, the epistemic processes of the normals are essential to the story: contact with the DDB is made when the normals get to know the DDB. Often, this is also when the audience gets to know the DDB, although the audience may get glimpses of the DDB even before the normals do. As befits a genre constructed to make the audience know the DDB, the story itself is typically about normals getting to know the DDB.

If the normals discover the DDB, they may do so unintentionally; their act of discovery may be as simple as driving to the place where the DDBs happen to live (e.g., *The Hills Have Eyes* [1977]) or coming across the DDB once he has driven to where they happen to live (e.g., *Halloween*). The normals may also discover the DDB intentionally, through an act of prolonged search based on hints such as a strange map or the remains of a partially eaten carcass (in, respectively, *King Kong* and *Jaws*). Creation, too, can occur with or without intention. The normals may create a DDB unintentionally, as through the careless fusion of a fly and a human in both versions of *The Fly*, or intentionally, as accomplished by Henry Frankenstein and his assistant Fritz in *Frankenstein*.

The examples of *The Fly* and *Frankenstein* point out two unusual facts about normals. First, sometimes the same character can be both a normal and a DDB. The scientist in both versions of *The Fly* is a normal until the accident that fuses him with a fly. Afterward, he is a DDB who still has some normal human feelings, a fact that increases both horror and sympathy for him.

Second, as shown by the example of Frankenstein and Fritz in *Frankenstein*, normals in horror movies are often not very normal at all. A world that centers on DDBs is bound to be a strange world, and often it contains people less appetizing than one would like to have living next door. Normals, by definition, tend to live by the norms or rules, but they may not do so very well. Frankenstein is insane and blasphemous, which might count him as psychologically and spiritually deformed, and he desecrates graves and corpses, which is somewhat destructive. Nevertheless, he is overall a moral person who ends up taking responsibility for his disastrous creation: "I made him with these hands, and with these hands I will destroy him." Therefore he is not a DDB (at least not as played by Colin Clive in Universal's Frankenstein series; he is a DDB as more malevolently played by Peter Cushing in Hammer's later

Police Chief Brody (Roy Scheider) comes face to face with the great white shark in *Jaws* (1975, Universal).

series). Fritz, a hunchback, is physically deformed and sadistic, with a taste for tormenting the Frankenstein monster by waving fire at him. But Fritz's levels of deformity and destructiveness are both low enough that he does not quite rate DDBness. Thus, Frankenstein and Fritz are both normals, not in the sense that they lack any abnormalities, but in the strict horror movie sense that they are not DDBs.

Once the DDB is discovered or created, its nature as a destructive being ensures that it will attack the normals one or more times. Each attack is another opportunity for knowing the DDB, seeing it from another angle, increasing the extent to which the audience member's intellect is becoming the monster. This attack, or series of attacks, builds up to a climactic confrontation, or final battle, in which, usually, the normals try to destroy, escape, banish, or subdue the DDB and either succeed or fail. In some movies, with multiple DDBs (for example, *Frankenstein Meets the Wolf Man* [1943]), the climactic confrontation may be between two or more monsters. Even then, normals figure in the climax, because the outcome of the battle has implications for the normals, who are usually hoping the monsters will destroy each other.

In some films, the roles of DDBs and normals are reversed by the final battle. In *I Spit on Your Grave* (1978), an example of the rape-revenge subgenre in which a woman is raped and takes revenge on her attackers, the DDBs are initially the four rapists, and the woman, Jennifer (Camille Keaton), is a helpless normal. But by the end of the film, the rapists appear less as DDBs and more as normal victims, whereas Jennifer is a sadistic killing machine, systematically hanging, castrating, axe-murdering, and causing death by motorboat. The DDB interest in this final battle is all in what Jennifer will do, not the rapists.

States of Knowing

Because the horror film exists to make audiences know the DDB, and because the horror film narrative is usually about normals getting to know the DDB, the horror film tends to be epistemically rich. There are many different states of knowing in the typical horror film, different shadings and grades both for the audience and the characters. The general movement is from a condition of less knowledge to more knowledge, with each step in the movement punctuated by deformity, destruction, or both. Yet the audience and the normals are rarely in synch in this movement; ordinarily, the audience knows more than the normals do.

The first step in the movement is *ignorance*. The normals—and perhaps the audience, if they have never seen the film—live in epistemic darkness, unaware of the existence of the DDB. However, even if the audience is new to the film, they are usually not new to the genre, and have usually seen some advertising or may have read a review or received word of mouth telling them this is a horror movie. With this knowledge, they are ahead of the normals. The audience knows to be on the look-out for a DDB, and the normals do not.

Throughout the film, the audience often has a *privileged view* of the DDB. For example, *Jaws* begins with a subjective-camera shot, from the shark's point of view, of the predator swimming underwater, with menacing John Williams music suggesting that the animal is looking for prey. No one but the audience and the shark can have this point of view; that is why it is privileged. Up on the beach, some normals are having a party in blissful ignorance of the predator that has just been implied to the audience (only implied; the audience has not seen it yet).

Such a combination of normals' ignorance and audience privileged view is essential for what Alfred Hitchcock called a *"suspense* situation."[6] The audience knows trouble is coming and may even want to warn the normals, but the normals just keep on about their business, leaving the audience in a state of excited anticipation and possibly fear (though Hitchcock pointed out that fear was not necessary to suspense). Suspense can also arise from wanting to know what happens next in a story, just from tagging along with the normals without a privileged view, though this is usually milder. In either case, suspense is a state of wanting to know, an emotion that must be engaged if the horror film is to make the audience know the DDB.

For the normals, the next step after ignorance is *discovery* or *creation*, the moment in which they first come into cognitive contact with the DDB. This moment may take the form of a DDB attack, or it may be more innocent (yet still creepy), as when Henry Frankenstein in *Frankenstein* detects the movement of his creature's hand and declares "It's alive!" Typically, this grade of knowledge is still low: the normals have a lot to learn about the DDB. All they have received so far is a slim clue.

Many horror films now introduce an element of *mystery* as the normals *search* for more information about the DDB. They try to understand what it is, where it came from, where it is hiding, how to stop it. As the audience follows along with this mystery, their own curiosity is engaged in the puzzle, another stage in their wanting to know, a desire that helps propel the DDB into their heads.

Along the way, the DDB usually *attacks* one or more times, or is *observed* one or more times. These attacks and observations are epistemically important because they provide the empirical information from which knowledge is built for both normals and the audience. The attacks are especially important because they present the DDB under the aspect of its destructiveness as well as its deformity, whereas the observations may only present its deformity. Its destructiveness is the point at which we see how its form is antithetical to the form of its victims (us, the normals), and is therefore essential to understanding it as a creature that would be too dangerous for us to know if it were real.

Often one or more characters are skeptics in a state of *disbelief* about the existence of the DDB; the attacks and observations, in time, bring about *conviction* in the DDB's existence. This process of convincing happens within the story for the skeptics and, analogously, it happens for the audience as they come to be persuaded about the fictional reality of the DDB.

Although some horror movies show the monster early and often (as in *The Creature from the Black Lagoon* [1954]), the more common approach is to show little or nothing of the monster early in the film and gradually provide

In *The Exorcist* (1973, Warner Bros.), Regan (Linda Blair) conjures up a statue of the demon possessing her.

more glimpses until at last, by the time of the final battle, the monster is seen clearly and vividly. This *gradual unveiling*, which includes the various attacks and observations, keeps the audience interested, builds a more complete knowledge of the DDB than would be possible otherwise, and tends to hide any defects in the special effects used to produce the creature until the audience is already invested in the DDB and willing to overlook such defects. Even when special effects are not used to create the monster, gradual unveiling can be an effective technique. In the shower murder in *Psycho*, we clearly see Marion Crane being stabbed but cannot make out the face of the killer, Norman Bates, at all. The identity of the attacker only becomes clear in the final battle, when Norman tries to kill Marion's sister, Lila.

Gradual unveiling is abetted by various cinematic techniques such as dark cinematography (shadows, night scenes), which makes it difficult to see the DDB, and off-screen noises (creaks, growls), which suggest the DDB without revealing it. (See also Chapter Fifteen.) Frequently, horror movie normals will come upon a closed door, locked box, draped thing, or other obstruction to their vision. The audience's fear is often at its peak as the normal considers penetrating the barrier, holds back, then opens the door, unlocks the box, pulls back the drape. Sometimes a DDB or evidence of a DDB emerges; sometimes it is just a fake-out, with nothing behind the barrier. Either way, the audience is kept on edge by its epistemic insufficiency, its inability to know all at once, even as it is making some progress in knowing the DDB, or at least learning where the DDB is not to be found.

The final battle of a horror movie is not only the climax of the conflict between DDB and normals; it is also the *epiphany*, the climax of the epistemic process, the stage at which the DDB is most completely revealed. The DDB's deformity and destructiveness are plainly apparent, and if the creature has had any surprises in store, the surprises come out now. In the final battle of *The Fly* (1986), for example, the creature, which has gradually been acquiring flyish characteristics, becomes suddenly and spectacularly flylike, giving the human characters and the audience a fly epiphany.

In *Night of the Living Dead* (1968), individual zombies are seen throughout the film, and dispatched fairly easily. But in the climax, a mass of zombies breaks into the house and swarms inside, overpowering the inhabitants—for the first time exhibiting the full force of these DDBs. In the climactic exorcism sequence of *The Exorcist* (1973), the demon reveals a number of abilities previously hidden: the ability to make the possessed girl, Regan, float above her bed; to appear as the mother of Father Karras, one of the priests; to summon up an ancient statue of a demon. Finally the demon reveals that it can switch bodies, jumping from Regan's body into Karras's, before exiting to points unknown.

Here is how the various states of knowing—fictional (those of the characters) and real (those of the audience)—are organically connected in a typical horror film, *The Abominable Dr. Phibes* (1971). First the audience gets a *privileged view* of the DDB, Dr. Phibes, playing organ music and dancing with his assistant, Vulnavia, in their secret lair, out of sight of normals. Then we see them *attack* a victim. The police, led by Inspector Trout, come out of *ignorance* to *discover* that a series of murders is going on in which a group of surgeons appears to be targeted. As they *search* for clues and make more *observations*, and as more *attacks* take place, they discern that the murderer is using the plagues of ancient Egypt as a pattern. Phibes's name comes under suspicion, because he may hold a grudge against the surgeons who were present when his wife died, but Phibes is presumed dead and therefore regarded as an unlikely suspect. Another character, Dr. Vesalius, who is considered to be one of Phibes's targets, joins the manhunt. The film cross-cuts briskly from Trout and Vesalius to Phibes, deepening the *mystery* and building *suspense*—mystery because of the puzzle; suspense because our privileged view allows us to see that Phibes is always a step ahead of the police, getting ready for his next murder while they are trying to solve the last. At various times events seem so unbelievable that characters react with *disbelief*, but, for Trout and Vesalius, *conviction* grows with the *gradual unveiling* of the clues. In the final battle,

Phibes is tracked to his lair where the *epiphany* takes place: Phibes removes his false face to reveal his true visage: a hideous skull-like face that resulted from the accident that had been thought to have killed him. Vesalius saves his son, who had been in jeopardy, but the fate of Phibes is left uncertain.

The various states of knowing in a horror film play out organically, so that the audience is typically unaware of how it is getting to know the DDB. This is fitting; although the purpose of this chapter is reflection on the epistemology of the horror film, that is not the primary purpose of the horror film itself. That primary purpose is to make the audience know the DDB, and it is through a certain epistemic process, noticed or not, that the audience does know the DDB.

3
DDB Profile

By definition, DDBs are deformed, destructive beings, but that is not all that can be said about them. By surveying the various examples of them in horror films and identifying the traits they most often have in common, a profile of the typical DDB can be drawn, a profile that is instructive about what sort of being the horror film audience seeks to know. Such traits are not absolutely universal — there are exceptions to all of them — and therefore the resulting profile is only typical, not true of every individual. Nevertheless, just as a profile of a serial killer can be helpful in capturing the murderer, a profile of a DDB can be helpful in specifying what audiences are trying to get at when they watch a horror movie.

As it turns out, there are nine typical traits that are commonly shared by most (but not all) DDBs. The traits are: animate, ugly, violent, male, sexually aggressive, invasive, strong, healthy, and immortal.

Animate

By animate, I mean that most DDBs possess some form of life such that they can move themselves, or move whatever body they inhabit. It may or may not be life as we possess it. Many DDBs are undead — ghosts, vampires, zombies, the Frankenstein monster. Who knows what it is really like to be undead, since most probably it is a fictional state of being? Nevertheless, in the movies, being undead looks a lot like being alive, because, as Aquinas says, "every animate thing, in some way, moves itself,"[1] and undead things move themselves just as living things do. When the demon possesses the little girl in *The Exorcist*, he moves her just as we move ourselves, so he is animate. Even the killer plants in horror movies, such as the vines in the "Creeping Vine" segment of *Dr. Terror's House of Horrors* (1965), possess a malevolent motion that is uncharacteristic of most ordinary plants.

DDBs, then, are generally not inanimate beings such as rocks, lakes, and clouds, but animate beings such as humans, vampires, demons, and mobile

This poster for *The Blob* (1958, Paramount) indicates its animate, engulfing nature.

plants—not to mention giant lizards, serial-killer-possessed dolls, and most of the other monsters of the horror film. Because these beings are animate, they also, in Thomistic terms, possess appetite and locomotion[2]—there is something they want, that is, something they intend to get, and they have some means of moving toward and acquiring the thing they want. To put it in more modern terms, they have intentionality and biomechanics. This is true of monsters as sophisticated as the title character in *Dracula* (1931), who wants the blood of young women and can use his charm and mesmeric abilities to get it, and as primitive as the title character in *The Blob* (1958), which wants anything it can engulf.

There is the occasional exception to the rule of animateness for DDBs. The impersonal force of Death seems to be responsible for the murders in *Final Destination* (2000). But even Death, in this movie, seems to be able to move things around at its will for a purpose, and thus to possess appetite and locomotion. Therefore it is almost (if not quite) an absolute rule that the DDB must be animate. Apparently, the horror movie audiences who seek after being are primarily interested in being of their own kind: the kind that is living and has intentionality and biomechanics. This may be because this type of being is the type most comprehensible to them. Inanimate being is more remote and obscure; animate being is what an animate being most easily knows. DDBs would be inaccessible in real life because of the existential threat they would pose, but when watching movies, the horror audience wants the DDB to be made accessible.

Ugly

The ugliness of the DDB may seem to follow from its deformity, but there is a fine distinction: a DDB can be deformed in some respect while not being physically ugly. As noted in Chapter One, Norman Bates in *Psycho* is handsome physically although deformed mentally; Nicole Kidman in *The Others* looks good physically; and so on. However, in this chapter we are seeking not the universal aspects of all DDBs but the common traits exhibited by most DDBs. Most DDBs are physically ugly, in addition to whatever other deformities they may have. In fact, most DDBs look terrible. The Phantom of the Opera has a hideous skull-face; Frankenstein's monster has a Neanderthal brow; and so on down the ages of cinematic monsters.

The physical ugliness of most horror movie monsters is the archetypal DDB deformity (to put it another way, it is the type of DDB deformity). Physical ugliness is how, in most horror movies, you can tell you are looking at a DDB. It is the outward sign of inward awfulness, the expression of the psychological or spiritual deformity that you cannot see. In *Psycho*, Norman Bates may appear outwardly handsome, but you achieve a better glimpse into the state of his mind when you see the taxidermy job he did on his mother. Just as horror fans prefer, it seems, to get their being in the most accessible form — the animate form — they generally prefer to get their deformity in the most accessible form, the visible form.

Violent

A similar distinction between violence and destructiveness operates as between ugliness and deformity. Destructiveness is the more abstract and universal term; all DDBs are destructive, if only spiritually or psychologically. But not all DDBs are violent in the sense of doing physical harm to a victim. Bruce Willis in *The Sixth Sense* is a DDB who unnerves his charge psychologically (in the sense that all ghosts unnerve this boy) but does no harm to him physically. However, most DDBs are violent — killing, smashing, maiming, abducting — and this violence is the type of all DDB destructiveness, whether it is Godzilla destroying Tokyo or the torturers in *Hostel* (2006) tormenting their captives.

The pattern of the first two traits holds for the trait of violence as well. Horror film audiences want their DDBs to made as accessible as possible. Therefore, they generally prefer the beings to be animate, the deformity to be ugly, and the destructiveness to be violent. They want the full power of moving pictures put to the work of presenting DDBs; they want to see pictures of creatures that move and are visibly violent and ugly.

Male

Most of the DDBs in horror movies are male, or are coded as male when sex or gender is uncertain. The Frankenstein monster, for example, is always played by a male, dressed like a male, and referred to as a "he." The genitalia of the shark in *Jaws* are not presented for our examination, but the animal has a large phallic head that is thrust erect out of the water, and the police chief refers to the creature as a "son of a bitch" when taking aim at him. Thus, we may conclude that the shark in *Jaws* is male.

There are many exceptions to the rule of DDB maleness. The title characters in *Bride of Frankenstein*, *Dracula's Daughter* (1936), *The Bad Seed* (1956), and *Lemora, A Child's Tale of the Supernatural* (1973) are a few of them; others include a werewolf in *Ginger Snaps* (2000), a ghost girl in *Honogurai mizu no soko kara* (*Dark Water;* 2002), and a torturer in *Hostel: Part II* (2007). Nevertheless, the vast majority of DDBs are male or male-coded: Dracula, the Mummy, Godzilla, King Kong, Norman Bates, the Creature from the Black Lagoon, Dr. Caligari and Cesare, Leatherface, Michael Myers, Jason Voorhees, Freddy Krueger, the Wolf Man, Hannibal Lecter, the Phantom of the Opera, the other torturers in the *Hostel* movies, Jigsaw, the Fly, and on and on. Even in *The Exorcist*, when the DDB appears to be a possessed little girl, the actual DDB is the demon possessing her, and that demon is coded as male: its statue looks male, and it is referred to in the film as a "he." It is not that there are no female DDBs, just that the males greatly outnumber them.

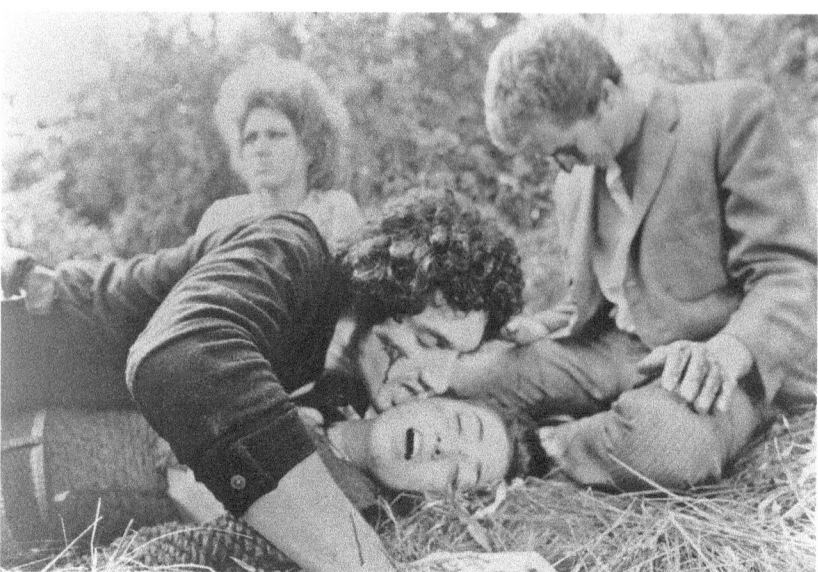

Escaped convict Krug Stillo (David A. Hess) rapes Mari Collingwood (Sandra Cassell) while accomplices Sadie (Jeramie Rain) and Weasel (Fred Lincoln) watch in *The Last House on the Left* (1972, Hallmark Releasing Corp.).

Male DDBs may sometimes exhibit touches of female gender — Norman Bates wearing his mother's dress, for example. They may also be maimed in such a way as to suggest sexual dysfunction, for instance, the Phantom of the Opera missing his nose. Such deviations from a basically male form contribute to the deformity of these DDBs, yet their general framework remains recognizably male.

There is no clear reason why the DDB should usually be male, but DDB theory allows a speculation. Violence is committed more often by males than females; roughly 88 percent of U.S. murders, for example, are committed by males.[3] Therefore, since violence usually (and destructiveness always) is a principal characteristic of the DDB, it is usually appropriate to cast a male in the role. Maleness makes it easier to believe, and therefore to know, the DDB's destructiveness. On the other hand, because in actuality some females on occasion do commit violence or are otherwise destructive, a more complete picture of possible DDBs is permitted if on occasion the DDB is female. This may be the main reason why femaleness is sometimes attributed to the DDB.

There are other possible reasons why monsters are usually male. It may be that horror movie fans are predominantly male[4] and identify more easily with a DDB of their own sex — an important consideration to the extent that some identification with the DDB is needed to get to know him. And there may be a primitive sort of sexual reasoning going on. Each new DDB is, in a sense, a new species, and ever since the story of Adam and Eve there has been a notion that the first of a species must be male. It may be a backward patriarchal notion, but there it is. Hence, the first movie vampire is Dracula, and only later, through one means or another, do we get Dracula's daughter. DDBs are an image of popular notions of a biological species originating and developing, and therefore they tend to be more male than female, but they still include some females to keep the species going.

Sexually Aggressive

Sexual aggression by DDBs is commonplace. The Frankenstein monster demands a bride; Dracula converts women into a harem of brides; King Kong peels the clothes off Fay Wray. Sometimes the sexual aggression becomes a blatant rape scene: the human rapists in *The Last House on the Left* (1972) and *I Spit on Your Grave*; the Devil in *Rosemary's Baby* (1968). Sexual aggression is usually male on female, although it can be female on male, as with Megan Fox in *Jennifer's Body* (2009).

Even more common than overt sexual aggression in horror films is symbolic sexual aggression. The alien in *Alien* has a phallic inner set of jaws that he thrusts into his victims. The numberless knives, drills, and other long sharp murder weapons of the slasher films are evident stand-ins for the erect penis. Most of this symbolic sex is male on female, but the female on male variety occurs— witness *Cat People* (1942), which uses transformation into a deadly black panther to symbolize female sexuality. The Blob, with its power to engulf, might be considered an amorphous female not only enveloping the male organ but enveloping the male and assimilating it. And symbols of homosexual sex are also to be found. The monster in *Jeepers Creepers* (2001) commits a sort of homosexual rape/castration on Justin Long, removing his eyes, ancient symbols for the testicles.

The connection of sexual aggression to the DDB is similar to that of maleness to the DDB. The horror movie audience is looking to know a new type of being, specifically an animate one, and such beings must resemble in some way biological organisms as we know them. All biological organisms seek to reproduce; therefore the DDB must too. Not only does this make biological sense, it makes destructive sense. The DDB must be destructive, and there is great destructiveness in the spread of an organism we do not want to see spread. As it expands its range or multiplies it obliterates the world we know, like an invasive species of fish taking over a lake. All the worse if the way it spreads is not like a fish — which only mates with other fish — but like a DDB, which frequently seeks to mate (actually or symbolically) with humans.

It is possible that DDB sex is, in part, a wish-fulfillment fantasy, in which the horror movie fan (usually male) identifies with a DDB (usually male) who grabs and has sex with a female, and is punished for it — thus getting his cake and upholding society's ban on cake too. And it is possible that the fear of sex with DDBs goes back much further than the horror movie fan, to prehistoric concerns about rivals from other tribes taking away a tribe's mates. Although this is only speculation, one can begin to see that the interest in DDBs may have originated in the primitive interest in knowing one's enemy — not just animal enemies, but human ones. The human ones might have looked different, with different features and decorations that would have made them seem ugly. They would have been violent, they would often have been male, and they would have wanted mates. The horror movie might be a reenactment of an ancient ritual to get to know the real DDBs in the environment of early humans. Research in evolutionary psychology would be needed to provide evidence for such speculations. For now, the most that can be said securely is that horror movie audiences want to know DDBs that are not only animate, ugly, and violent, but also male and sexually aggressive.

Invasive

As suggested above by the mention of "invasive species," the DDB is, in most cases, invasive: it comes in from outside the world of normals. Often this is literally the case: Dracula moves to England to prey on the English; the Devil's spawn moves into the household of Robert Thorn in *The Omen* (1976); the zombies in *Night of the Living Dead* invade the boarded-up house. Sometimes the geographical movement is reversed, to the same effect: Marion Crane drives away from home and off the beaten track to reach the Bates Motel, the world of the DDB. But once there, taking a shower in what she thinks is a safe room, the DDB invades, killing her.

Because it comes from outside, the DDB may be thought of as an outsider, and in several senses. It does not usually dwell in this world of normals; it does not abide by their norms; it is not one of their expected biota; it is not one of their community. The shark in *Jaws*, having swum to the waters of Amity Island, is, in all these senses, an outsider, as is the alien in *Alien*.

Sometimes the DDB is an insider. The evil child in *The Bad Seed* is part of a normal family who somehow (perhaps because of bad genetics) turns evil. But in most cases the DDB comes from outside, and in most cases it is unwelcome and tries to kill or otherwise harm members of the community, and is in those further senses invasive.

The invasiveness of the DDB is consistent with all that has been said about it thus far. It is an animate being, violent, ugly, coded as male, sexually aggressive, and it is invasive, coming into the community, harming it, seeking to spread itself. All of these characteristics suggest a sort of biological or military nightmare. It is what we would expect of a new, destructive form of being.

Strong

Most DDBs are physically strong. The Frankenstein monster has the strength of "ten men"; King Kong can kill a *Tyrannosaurus rex* and tear an airplane out of the sky; the Devil in *The Omen* can spear a priest with a lightning rod; and almost any garden-variety monster has at least enough strength to strangle or knife someone or carry a heroine to his lair. A few DDBs — some ghosts, for example — seem physically weak. But the typical DDB is powerful.

This is another aspect by which the DDB's being is established. Animate beings have to be somewhat powerful to feed their appetites and achieve locomotion. If, in addition, the beings are to be violent, they must have the strength necessary for violence. If their being is to be clearly presented so that we can know it, that strength should usually be exaggerated, depicted as if superhuman, as though we were hard of hearing and the filmmakers were shouting at us to get their point across. Thus, the often superhuman strength of the DDB is consistent with its presentation to us as a destructive and animate being.

Healthy

The exceptional health of the DDB is rarely noted. Nevertheless, most DDBs are healthy. The DDB almost never contracts a disease; even when it is itself a disease, such as the plague in *Cabin Fever* (2003), it is not plagued with any disease, the way bacteria are sometimes infected with bacteriophages. Dracula never catches cold, no matter how many women he gets close to. Monsters may look hideous as the result of past injuries, such as Freddy Krueger with his burn scars, but their vitality and function seem to have completely recovered: Freddy has no trouble chasing teenagers in the *Nightmare on Elm Street* movies. You can hurt some monsters, as the Frankenstein monster gets wounded by a gunshot in *Bride of Frankenstein*, but they handle their injuries admirably well, and the gunshot wounds never seem to get infected. After lightning temporarily renders the Frankenstein monster comatose in *Son of Frankenstein* (1939), he is still healthy enough that Wolf von Frankenstein, upon examining him, declares, "He's completely superhuman." Even a creature with obvious disabilities, such as the mummy Kharis (in *The Mummy's Hand* [1940] and sequels) with his limping gait and paralyzed arm, seems to do better than most men without disabilities, easily catching and killing enemies and scooping up women.

The health of monsters is of a piece with their strength. If they are going to be clear examples of animate beings, they have to endure and function well, and that means they must be in good health as well as strong. Health is needed also for their acts of violence. There are scenes in *The Fly* (1986) where the

DDB seems to be growing sick and weak as if from some cancer, but it turns out these are just stages in his transformation into a hybrid human-fly. By the time he gets to his final stages, his apparent ill health is forgotten; he is strong and well enough to abduct a woman, maim a man, and crawl around the ceilings of his domicile.

Immortal

If you did a survey of all individual horror movies, you might find that usually the DDB dies at the end of the film. But even if this were true, death does not stick for the most successful DDBs— the ones, by definition, that are most popular, therefore most commercially viable, most likely to come back for sequels and remakes, and most likely to represent DDBs enduringly in the popular imagination.

These DDBs only apparently die. In the next film, it turns out the monster was not destroyed — he was only sleeping. He is found buried in ice and brought back to life, as in *Frankenstein Meets the Wolf Man*, or blood drips on his ashes and restores them, as in *Dracula — Prince of Darkness* (1966). In some films, the miraculous resurrection happens at the end of the movie, as in *Halloween* when Michael Myers survives multiple gunshots and a fall out an upper-story window to disappear from the ground where he was last seeing lying. (He is back again, unharmed, in *Halloween II* [1981], and in many films after that.) These monsters have to suffer a kind of death, but only a temporary kind. They are only temporarily mortal; they are transmortal, and, in the long run, immortal.

If sequels and twist endings do not resurrect a DDB, a remake can simply restore him to life, no questions asked. There is no need to explain how it is that the same character is here once again, enacting more or less the same story as before. Once it was Lugosi playing Dracula; now, in much the same narrative, Lee plays him in *Horror of Dracula* (1958). This too, is a type of immortality.

Then there is corporate immortality. The individual zombies in the *Night of the Living Dead* series can be killed, but because there are so many, there is no way to kill them all. Ditto the birds in *The Birds* (1963). The Elite Hunting company in the *Hostel* series lives on even if a vengeful victim manages to kill one hunter or another. These DDBs are immortal because there is always more of them.

Finally, there is a kind of pure immortality not dependent on resurrections from the dead, remakes, or membership in a corporation. This is the immortality of the Devil in films like *Rosemary's Baby* and *The Omen*. You cannot kill the Devil, not even temporarily.

Thus, the most popular DDBs are immortal, and in that sense it can be said that immortality is a typical DDB trait. This is the clearest way in which DDBs possess being: their animate existence cannot be permanently dissolved, ended, or taken away. Shoot them, burn them, blow them up, and they just keep coming. Just as ugliness makes their deformity evident and violence their destructiveness, immortality makes it clear that they *are*, to a greater extent, perhaps, than we are.

The profile of DDBs that emerges from this study is a highly suggestive one. DDBs are animate because they are like the self-moving living beings we encounter in our environment. They are ugly and violent because a new form of being in competition with ours would appear to us ugly and violent. They are male because males tend to be more violent and because the male seems to us (from a primitive point of view) the original sex, sexually aggressive and invasive because they are trying to spread, strong and healthy because they can spread. And they are immortal, as if they keep coming, no matter what we do. In short, the DDB is something like an environmental catastrophe or invading army.

It may be that the DDB, as suggested earlier, hearkens back to a time when humans had to be constantly on the alert for just such things—new infestations, new predators, new rival warriors. The humans who were best adapted to survive among such dangers were those who were most interested in them, who took pleasure in knowing them and learning how to defeat them. This pleasure may also have been adaptive because sometimes the knowers would use the knowledge to invade other communities. This doubly adaptive pleasure, a taste for which may have been transmitted in our genes, may be the origin of the widespread interest in knowing deformed and destructive beings, which in our time is commonly satisfied by watching horror movies.

This speculation awaits corroboration from evolutionary psychology and related fields. In the meantime, it can be said fairly safely that, for whatever reason, the DDBs in horror movies are like nightmare images of invading organisms. And many of us like them, if only for the reason that they allow us to know beings that would otherwise be inaccessible.

4

Structure

The horror film narrative is designed to make the audience know the DDB, through a succession of fictional and real states of knowing tied to the attacks of the DDB. Although horror films vary in how they accomplish this, there is a basic plot structure common to all horror films. This can be difficult to discern, however, because one has to look to a sufficiently high level of generality. In this chapter, I propose both a basic narrative structure for horror films and certain elaborations visible at levels of finer detail.

The Basic Plot Structure of Horror Films

Accounts of horror film structure vary greatly, and for good reason. Analyses of film structure are never theory-neutral; they are always, at least in part, determined by the theoretical uses to which the analyst wants to put the films. Once the analyst determines which of the many events in a film are the most salient in the light of his theory, he builds a structure that supports his theory. Thus, *Jaws* is often viewed as having a three-act structure.[1] This structure fits the theory of, among others, Syd Field, screenwriting teacher, who holds that contemporary film characteristically has a three-act structure, in which plot points that turn the action in a new direction occur at the end of Act One (about thirty minutes into a two-hour film) and Act Two (about ninety minutes in).[2] The three-act structure is attractive because it provides a single, simple, portable guide to screenwriting. Disciples of Field who want to learn screenwriting, or screenwriting teachers following in this tradition, naturally would like to think that *Jaws* also has a three-act structure and often go looking for the plot points, although without reaching much agreement. Roughly, however, the three acts of *Jaws*, broken up according to what is happening at thirty and ninety minutes, would look something like this:

1. Ends with arrival of shark scientist Hooper on Amity Island.
2. Ends with shark hunter Quint's story about surviving a shark attack in World War II.
3. Ends with destruction of shark.

4. Structure

Noël Carroll, a philosopher whose aim is not to learn or teach screenwriting but to reason about horror, emphasizes the pleasures of ratiocination in the horror story rather than the monster as such. He suggests that *Jaws* is an example of his four-act complex discovery plot:[3]

1. *Onset:* Initial attack of shark.
2. *Discovery:* Police Chief Brody discovers evidence of shark attack.
3. *Confirmation:* Brody convinces mayor to hire Quint to fight shark.
4. *Confrontation:* Hunting and destruction of shark.

Carroll is clearly more interested in the rational processes of characters in a horror story than he is in helping writers write screenplays, leading him to develop a different structure from that which would be acceptable to Field or his followers. In both cases, theory defines or at least influences structure.

I am no different. DDB theory seems useful to me as a way of studying horror films, and its core is the idea that the monster as such is what audiences want to see, so that they can extend their knowledge of being. The horror film is primarily a showcase for the DDB. When *Jaws* is examined in the light of this theory, the approaches of both Field and Carroll are too elaborate. Only two things really happen in *Jaws*:

1. The shark attacks.
2. The shark is defeated.

Other things happen too, but they are details, not large-scale structure. Appropriately generalized, these two acts can be considered the basic structure of all horror movies:

1. *Attack of the DDB*: The DDB attacks one or more normals, often repeatedly.
2. *Final battle*: A climactic confrontation occurs that involves both DDB and one or more normals. It is usually a head-on DDB-normal clash, though it may involve a clash of two or more DDBs.

As it happens, Carl Gottlieb, co-screenwriter of *Jaws*, regards his film as having just such a two-act structure.[4] According to him, the first act is all the island-based action in which the shark repeatedly attacks islanders; the second act, beginning a little more than midway into the film (an hour and twelve minutes into the running time of two hours and four minutes), is when Brody, Hooper, and Quint are out on Quint's boat confronting the shark at sea.

Every horror movie can be reduced to this two-act structure — attack/final battle — and with good reason. The attacks of the DDB are the principal incidents in which the audience and the normals get to know the DDB, and the final battle is the epiphany, the episode in which the DDB is most clearly known. Since knowing the DDB is the primary purpose of the horror film, these two acts are the basic components of horror film structure. But even though all horror films can be reduced to this structure, some of the details that are then overlooked are rather interesting, revealing common alternatives for how to present the DDB through its conflict with normals—the central narrative idea of the horror film. Therefore, it is worth pointing out some elaborations of the two-act structure.

One common elaboration is to add another act at the outset, the entrance of the DDB. In this act, the DDB enters the action, becoming apparent at least to the audience, and sometimes to the normals. He begins to display his deformity, which may be further revealed in later acts. If the DDB is sympathetic, DDB sympathy may begin to develop in this act. An example of this three-act structure is *The Abominable Dr. Phibes*:

1. *Entrance of the DDB*: A hooded Dr. Phibes plays his organ and dances with his assistant Vulnavia, then puts his face together in preparation for going out to a murder.
2. *Attack of the DDB*: Phibes kills his first onscreen victim, then kills more.
3. *Final battle*: Dr. Vesalius saves his son from Phibes's wrath, although Phibes eludes capture.

Of course, if one wanted to maintain a more general view of the structure, the entrance of the DDB could be regarded as just a component of the attack of the DDB. That way the two-act structure could be preserved. The same is true with all of the elaborations on the two-act structure to be presented in this chapter.

Still another act can be added at the outset of the horror film: the setup, in which the normals are established as characters (for example, their settings, occupations, and love lives may be defined) while at least one or more normals, through a process of discovery or creation, prepare to come into contact with the DDB. An example of this four-act structure is the 1986 remake of *The Fly*:

1. *Setup*: Scientist Seth Brundle meets and falls in love with reporter Ronnie Quaife. He goes through his teleportation device, accidentally fusing himself with a fly.
2. *Entrance of the DDB*: The new creation, Brundlefly, emerges from the telepod. At first he looks and acts human, but he gradually grows stronger, looks uglier, and exhibits more aggressive behavior.
3. *Attack of the DDB*: Brundlefly maims a man in a bar. Brundlefly becomes hideously deformed, abducts Ronnie, and amputates the hand and foot of her old boyfriend, Stathis Borans.
4. *Final battle*: Brundlefly tries to fuse himself with Ronnie and their unborn

4. Structure   41

child, but Borans stops them. Fused with the telepod, Brundlefly motions to Ronnie to kill him, and she does.

A common variation of this structure is to forgo a separate "entrance of the DDB" act, going straight from setup to attack. In this variation, the monster attacks as it enters. An example is *Alien*:

1. *Setup:* A spaceship crew arrives on a strange planet, where they discover alien eggs.
2. *Attack of the DDB:* A small alien leaps from an egg onto the face of a crewman. The alien gestates inside him and explodes from his stomach. Full-grown, it kills the other crew members one by one, leaving only Ripley, who escapes in a pod.
3. *Final battle:* Ripley discovers that the alien is on board the pod with her. She eliminates the creature by forcing it into space.

Once one begins slicing up acts, it may not always be clear just how to slice up a particular horror film. For example, is this the structure of *The Silence of the Lambs* (1991)?

1. *Setup*: Clarice Starling gets her assignment to interview Hannibal Lecter.
2. *Entrance of the DDB*: Clarice interviews Lecter, the primary of the film's two DDBs.
3. *Attack of the DDB*: Buffalo Bill and Lecter commit violent attacks.
4. *Final battle*: Clarice defeats Buffalo Bill.

Or is this the structure of *The Silence of the Lambs*?

1. *Setup*: Clarice Starling gets her assignment to interview Hannibal Lecter.
2. *Attack of the DDB*: Lecter attacks Clarice psychologically during her first interview. More attacks, psychological and physical, follow from him, and physical attacks from Buffalo Bill.
3. *Final battle*: Clarice defeats Buffalo Bill.

The difference between these two proposed structures rests on whether a psychological attack counts as an attack of the DDB. I think it does, and therefore consider the second structure more appropriate than the first. But if one regarded only physical attacks as attacks, or did not regard Lecter as sufficiently on the attack in the first interview, then the first structure would make more sense. In any case, both structures should add the frisson at the end, in which Lecter calls Clarice on the phone (see "Teasers and Frissons" below).

More acts can probably be added, depending on how finely one wants to examine the horror film's structure. But these are some of the most common horror film plots.

Teasers and Frissons

However many acts a horror film has, the story can be expanded by including a teaser, a frisson, or both. The teaser is a short scene (a connected series of shots in a single setting) or sequence (a connected series of scenes) at the very start of the film that raises audience interest with a brief opening reference to or premonition of the DDB. The frisson is a coda at the end of the film that leaves the audience with a shudder of fear at the reality or the mere possibility that the DDB survived the final battle. The advantage of adding the teaser or frisson is to maximize the quantity of DDB presentation, creating a sense of wall-to-wall horror. The disadvantages of the teaser are that it delays the commencement of the story proper, and can spoil the later, carefully prepared-for entrance of the DDB by presenting him too early.

The frisson has a complicated history. It was rare in the days of the Production Code Administration (1934 to 1968), through which Hollywood studios censored themselves. At that time, it was required that the monster be destroyed by the end of the film, lest any young audience members think that you could be a monster and get away with it. The monster could be resurrected in a sequel, but you could not show the monster surviving at the film's conclusion. Often, these climactic monster demises were spectacular. The monster in *Frankenstein* was destroyed in a windmill fire; *The Invisible Man* (1933) was shot when he was identified by his footprints in the snow, and became visible as he died; *King Kong* fell from the top of the Empire State Building.

Since then, with the institution of the ratings system, it is permissible to have the monster live at the end, and many films have done so. Often, as in *A Nightmare on Elm Street* (1984), this is achieved by pretending to show the monster's destruction in the final battle, then indicating that he is still alive in the last moments after the battle. The advantage is to leave the audience with a final, horrific impression of the DDB; the disadvantage is that at this point in film history, the frisson has been done so frequently that it is often merely predictable, not horrifying.

The teaser can be constructed in several ways. One of the simplest examples appears at the beginning of *Frankenstein*. It consists of a single scene in which Edward Van Sloan, the actor who plays Dr. Waldman in the movie, steps out from behind a curtain and warns the audience of the shocking nature of the material to follow. The effect is to build anticipation for the ensuing DDB presentation.

A more complex teaser may take the form of an entire sequence. In *The Exorcist*, the teaser is set in and around archaeological sites in northern Iraq, far from the main action of the story, which will turn out to be in the Georgetown section of Washington, D.C. In Iraq, Fr. Merrin, who will not turn up again until late in the film, has intimations of the demon he will be called upon to exorcise. A small sculpture of the demon found in a dig leads him to visit a large statue of the demon, where he sees a white dog fighting with a black dog, an image of the coming battle. All of these are hints that set the atmosphere for the rest of the film, rather than an overt display or description of the DDB.

The frisson similarly varies in construction. Again, *The Exorcist* provides an example, this time a simple one. The final battle in which Merrin and another priest, Fr. Karras, confronted a demon

In *The Abominable Dr. Phibes* (1971, American International Pictures), Dr. Phibes (Vincent Price) wears his human mask, under which is a deformed face.

possessing a little girl is over; both priests died in the exorcism, but the demon appears to be banished. However, just at the end of the film, another priest, Fr. Dyer, still mourning the loss of his friend, Karras, in the exorcism, looks down the outdoor flight of steps where Karras met his death. The creepy, tinkly music of "Tubular Bells," previously associated with the demon, comes up. The final credits roll. This frisson is ambiguous; it does not entail that the demon lives or will come back, but it suggests that he might; further, it emphasizes the sacrifices made in defeating him and the mystery of his ever having come at all. It is a brief, suggestive frisson, not an elaborate one.

Another simple frisson comes at the end of *The Silence of the Lambs*, when the fugitive Hannibal Lecter calls Clarice on the phone and explains that he is "having an old friend for dinner"—Dr. Chilton, his former jailer, whom he intends to eat. The frisson establishes that Lecter, the primary DDB of the movie, is still at large and that he preserves his strangely intimate connection with Clarice.

A more elaborate frisson is found at the end of *Carrie* (1976). After a final battle in which Carrie, the teenage psychokinetic DDB who committed mass murder at her prom, has been buried under her collapsing house, the following sequence ensues: Carrie's normal friend Sue arrives at the spot where Carrie is presumably buried under the rubble of the house. Sue leaves flowers at the gravesite. Carrie's hand bursts up from the rubble and grabs Sue's wrist. Sue screams and struggles, and it is revealed that she is in her bedroom and this is a nightmare. As her mother tries to comfort her, Sue continues to scream.

At the prom in *Carrie* (1976, United Artists), Carrie (Sissy Spacek) gets covered in pig's blood, prompting her to commit mass murder.

Like the frisson in *The Exorcist*, *Carrie*'s frisson does not definitively state that the monster survived, but suggests it as a possibility. More important, the frissons of both films leave the audience still haunted by the idea of the DDB, and therefore intensify the DDB presentation.

At this point, four sequences of acts have been described (two act, four act, three act without setup, three act with setup), each of which can be further varied in one of four ways (teaser, frisson, both, neither), making a total of sixteen plot variations. What they all have in common are at least two acts: attack of the DDB and final battle. These two acts are the core of every horror movie, and, from a sufficiently general viewpoint, may be considered the entire horror movie.

Complications

There are further ways of complicating a horror film structure—for example, by introducing more than one monster. When done well, this can have the effect of multiplying and intensifying the DDB presentation, though when done poorly, it can be distracting and can weaken the DDB presentation. An example in which it was done well is *Bride of Frankenstein*, the first sequel to *Frankenstein*. In its simplest form, the structure of *Bride of Frankenstein* is a teaser plus the following three acts:

4. Structure

Teaser: Mary Shelley, author of the novel *Frankenstein*, and her companions recapitulate the first film and introduce the second.
1. *Setup:* Villagers crowd around the burning wreckage of the windmill, believed to contain the Frankenstein monster's dead body.
2. *Attack of the DDB:* The monster is revealed to be still alive, and immediately starts killing people; more murders and mayhem follow.
3. *Final battle:* The monster destroys himself and his enemies by blowing up the castle that contains them.

Although this structure is accurate as a broad outline, it fails to do justice to the complexity of the plot. Indeed, it leaves out the central distinguishing feature of the plot: the creation of a bride for the monster. It also leaves out the chief instigator of that creation, Dr. Pretorius. Both Pretorius and the bride may be considered to be new DDBs, rivaling the Frankenstein monster himself in the damage they cause. Pretorius, like Frankenstein, is a mad scientist, but unlike Frankenstein, he is crazier (for example, he likes spending time in tombs for sheer pleasure) and his demented desire to create a bride for the monster leads him to be more destructive than Frankenstein: he kidnaps Frankenstein's beloved Elizabeth and orders a girl to be killed merely for her heart. The bride of the monster is deformed in appearance and destructive in hating and rejecting the monster rather than becoming what she was created to be, his bride. This is a destructive rejection because it leads the monster to destroy the castle. In that destruction, the monster kills himself, Pretorius, and the bride—the three DDBs. He deliberately spares the lives of Frankenstein and Elizabeth, two normals whom he declares worthy of life, whereas the DDBs "belong dead."

A more detailed analysis of this plot should note the attack of all the DDBs. The plot structure then has the following sections:

Teaser: Shelley.
1. *Setup:* Villagers at windmill.
2. *Attack of the DDBs:*
   a. The Frankenstein monster (the first DDB) attacks.
   b. Pretorius (the second DDB) proposes to Frankenstein his scheme to collaborate in creating a bride, and forces him to comply.
   c. The bride (the newly created third DDB) rejects the Frankenstein monster.
3. *Final battle:* The monster blows up the castle and all three DDBs.

Horror film structure can also be complicated by adding more normals, settings, or conflicts. For example, in *Night of the Living Dead*, the zombies launch one long attack of the DDBs that begins in a graveyard in daylight and continues to a house at night. But this long attack can be subdivided into the

Zombies congregate outside a house of normals in *Night of the Living Dead* (1968, Walter Reade Organization).

attack in the graveyard and the attack on the house, because the two have different casts (united principally by one normal, Barbara, and one zombie), settings, and dramatic qualities. The attack on the house can be further divided by the appearance of successively more normals who join Barbara—first Ben, then a group that has been hiding in the basement, then the normals who are broadcasting over the television. It is further complicated by the conflicts that arise among the normals, most notably between Ben and Mr. Cooper over whether to hide in the basement or stay upstairs.

Due to such structural complexities, horror films may seem quite diverse and difficult to analyze. Yet their core narrative structure is universal and simple: presentation of the DDB through DDB-normal conflict, which is depicted in two basic acts: attack of the DDB and final battle. All the other acts, teasers, frissons, and complications are elaborations on this core.

5
Essential Elements

Horror movies vary greatly, but even their variations point to their essential similarities. Consider, for example, two very different horror films separated by forty-five years—*The Invisible Ray* (1936) and *The Funhouse* (1981). The DDB in *Ray* is articulate; the DDB in *Funhouse* is inarticulate. The DDB in *Ray* becomes a monster through scientific experiment; the DDB in *Funhouse* is born that way. The normals who are victims of the DDB in *Ray* are adults, while most of those victimized by the DDB in *Funhouse* are teenagers. The lead female in *Ray* keeps her clothes on, whereas her counterpart in *Funhouse* does not. On the other hand, there are essential similarities, most strikingly that both movies have DDBs and normals. The similarities between *Ray* and *Funhouse* are even more specific: for example, a total of six killings occur in each film, as if six were a good working number for total corpses in a horror movie.

Movie genres always embody a dance between similarities and differences. The similarities are what make a genre—the people breaking into song and dance in musicals; the nineteenth-century American frontier in westerns. But the differences are what make for individual films sufficiently distinct that audiences are satisfied they have seen a new film.

In addition to sharing a more or less common plot structure, all horror films contain five essential elements, all of which are related to the primary purpose of presenting a DDB. Absence of any of these elements disqualifies the film as a horror film. The elements may be handled in various ways, which is what gives diversity to horror films. The horror film may be of lesser or greater quality depending, in part, on how effectively any of these elements is executed. Unlike the plot structures described in the last chapter, the five essential elements do not occur in any particular chronological order; they may be relevant to the entire plot or just to one or more stages of it. The elements are:

1. Subordination in principle of all story components to the presentation of the DDB
2. Deformity display by the DDB

3. Destructiveness display by the DDB
4. Account of the DDB indicating that the deformity causes the destructiveness
5. One or more normals for whom audience sympathy is possible in principle and who are attacked by the DDB

This chapter discusses these essential elements in detail. The examples of *The Invisible Ray* and *The Funhouse* are raised repeatedly not because they are major films (even to many horror fans they may seem obscure) but just to show that the essential elements apply to all horror films, regardless of their status within the genre.

1. *Subordination in principle of all story components to the presentation of the DDB.* This is the most important element of a horror film. The story components include everything that the audience perceives on screen (and through the sound system) that the filmmakers created as part of the narrative, such as acting, editing, cinematography, special effects, makeup, production design, costumes, dialogue, sound effects, and music. (These components and the techniques they encompass are discussed in detail in Chapter Fifteen.) Also included are structural components such as plot, subplots, sequences, scenes, shots, motifs, and themes. Not included are phenomena that the filmmakers did not create, such as scratches on the print or whispering by audience members. Even though some horror movie audiences, particularly in crowded theaters, shout and scream at predictable parts of the movie, their vocalizations are not components of the movie, but reactions to it; the same movie can be viewed by a lone watcher on DVD without these vocalizations.

In principle, all the story components in a horror film are subordinate to the DDB presentation in the sense that their primary purpose is to enact or support that presentation. In practice, the subordination may be more or less adequate. In an adequate subordination, no story component outshines the DDB, and all story components contribute their expected part to making the DDB effective. An example of outshining the DDB is Oliver Reed's enthusiastic performance as a menacing island thug in *The Shuttered Room* (1967). His acting is good, but he is not the DDB, and when the real DDB appears she is a weak shadow of him.

An example of not contributing sufficiently to the DDB presentation is the confusing setting of *The Invisible Ray*, which uses a variety of locations, globe-trotting from Europe to Africa and back to Europe. Monster attacks are usually more frightening if they occur in a restricted space from which the victim cannot escape. The setting in *The Funhouse* is more effective in supporting DDB presentation because the DDB attacks people trapped with him in the claustrophobic carnival funhouse. This occurs after a foreshadowing scene in the teaser, in which the heroine is mock-attacked in the restricted

5. Essential Elements   49

In *The Invisible Ray* (1936, Universal), Dr. Janos Rukh (Boris Karloff), left, is the DDB. Here he is pictured with Dr. Felix Benet (Bela Lugosi) and Rukh's wife Diana (Frances Drake).

space of a shower by her little brother, who is playing at *Psycho* with a fake knife. The play claustrophobia in the teaser prepares for the real thing later.

Adequate subordination generally results in a good horror film, distinguishable in part by the audience's feelings of horror, but also by other aspects. As stated in Chapter One, the audience seeks DDB presentation primarily for objective, cognitive reasons: to take in a being that represents a new form that would not even be accessible if it were real. However, when this presentation seems real, the act of cognition is associated with subjective feelings, and three in particular should be recalled, three types of interest in the DDB: horror, delight, and sympathy. In all good horror movies — movies in which all story components are effectively subordinated to DDB presentation — horror and delight are present. Horror is generated largely by the deformity and destructiveness displays of the DDB (see below). Delight is a pleasure in the DDB itself — its being as such — and is connected to a sense that the monster is the thing with the most energy and reality in the film, the ontological center of the story, the force that excites. With a well-made horror film, the audience perks up whenever the monster appears or seems about to appear. Quite apart from any sympathy that might exist for the monster's plight, the audience

Amy (Elizabeth Berridge) is mock-attacked in the shower by her little brother Joey (Shawn Carson) in *The Funhouse* (1981, Universal).

experiences ambivalence when the monster is destroyed or if it is resurrected in the frisson. Such ambivalence results from a mingling of horror, which desires to see the monster go, and delight, which enjoys the monster's powerful presence and would like to see it stay. For example, when little Damien, the son of Satan, turns and smiles sweetly at the audience at the end of *The Omen*, it is horrifying to realize that the boy survived the final battle with his adoptive father, Robert Thorn, and has been adopted by the president of the United States. But it is also pleasing, because Damien — in company with his true father, the invisible but ever-present Satan — is a well-realized DDB.

This feat of DDB presentation is accomplished by subordination of many story components, but one in particular stands out: the performance of Gregory Peck as Damien's adoptive father Thorn. At the time, Peck was a bona fide movie star, somewhat past his prime but still well known and associated with heroic roles, most notably that of anti–racist lawyer Atticus Finch in *To Kill a Mockingbird* (1962). In *The Omen*, Peck does his usual heroic thing: with square jaw and steely determination, he uncovers the truth that his adopted son is really the Antichrist, and bravely tries to kill him before the child can bring about the Apocalypse. In the final battle, the police kill Peck before he can accomplish his goal, and Damien survives. What is notable here is that *Gregory Peck is beaten by a little boy!* Atticus Finch, who once stood in the

5. Essential Elements

Damien Thorn (Harvey Stephens), the son of Satan, stands amid crosses in this publicity still from *The Omen* (1976, 20th Century–Fox).

street and killed a rabid dog with one shot, is unable to wipe the smile off the son of Satan. In the Hollywood star system, the leading man almost never dies unless it is in an act of self-sacrifice that restores peace and justice to the community — yet here Peck dies for nothing, in a futile attempt to thwart Satan. The effect, at the end of *The Omen*, is to transfer all of Peck's star power to Damien — to present this little boy as a threat so serious that not even Gregory Peck can stop him. This is a shining example of what can be achieved when all story components — even the star — are subordinated to the presentation of the DDB.

Lest it be thought that just anyone could have played Thorn and achieved the same result, a control to this experiment was arranged thirty years later in a remake, *The Omen 666* (2006). Although very similar, the remake was not as successful as the original either commercially or critically, and one of the few major differences was that Thorn was played by Liev Schreiber, a good actor who was not then a movie star and was not associated with playing heroes. The result was that Thorn's defeat by the little boy was neither exceptional nor horrifying, just forgettable.

Sympathy is often, but not always, felt for monsters in horror movies. Sympathy includes pity and fellow-feeling, a sense that the monster is, in a way, one of us, which can have the effect of making the DDB seem more complete and vivid, and therefore real. A common way to create sympathy for the monster is to give him a love interest; this can be effective as long as it does not undermine his monstrousness. A proper subordination of components is maintained in *The Wolf Man*, in which the subplot of romance between Larry Talbot (the DDB, the Wolf Man) and Gwen Conliffe increases our sympathy for the DDB as he struggles to protect Conliffe from his werewolfian side; it also provides a climactic, sympathetic victim for him once his werewolf side takes over. The same concept — animal-man hybrid who loves a woman — was handled more poorly in *The Alligator People* (1959), in which a man struggles to protect his wife from seeing how he is turning into an alligator man. Although this DDB had a love interest and was therefore somewhat sympathetic, the filmmakers almost entirely neglected to make him destructive, seriously unbalancing the story components and contributing to an inept DDB presentation.

There are good horror movies without any noticeable sympathy for the monster. Few, if any, viewers have expressed pity for the pods in *Invasion of the Body Snatchers* (1956), or the alien in *Alien*, or the germ causing the infection in *Cabin Fever*. Generally, the less humanoid a monster is, the less likely we are to pity it or feel it is like us. Nevertheless, the viewer can be made to identify even with an unsympathetic creature, such as the shark in *Jaws*, through techniques such as subjective-camera shots.

If some story components are inadequately subordinated to DDB presentation, the result is usually a less effective horror movie, even a laughable one. The very bad, although inadvertently funny, *Frankenstein Meets the Space Monster* (1965) features unconvincing creature makeup, an overuse of stock footage, and a bad case of musical incongruity: the film's fluffy folk-rock tunes undercut the supposedly horrific plot about a modern Frankenstein monster vying with invaders from space. *The Alligator People* is similarly funny, particularly with its climactic depiction of the alligator man as someone who more closely resembles a duck. Such humor, because based on poor cinematic design, is a sign of aesthetic failure (which can itself be entertaining, although at the filmmakers' expense), whereas good horror movies may have humor that is aesthetically successful as long as it remains subordinate to the presentation of the DDB.

Indeed, humor is a common element in horror movies; some viewers respond even to good horror movies by laughing at the most savage DDB attacks while other audience members are screaming. When the film is working, this is a way for those viewers to let off tension and relieve fear, rather than a sign of artistic error. In other cases, horror filmmakers deliberately introduce comic relief to make the DDB more bearable. In small quantities, this can work well: for example, when Bela Lugosi as the title character in *Dracula* says "I never drink — wine," and the pregnant pause before "wine" draws laughter, the line both relieves tension and contributes to the characterization of this urbane, blood-drinking vampire. But if the entire movie becomes overloaded with comic relief, it may lose all claim to being a horror movie and become a comedy with horror elements, such as *The Return of the Living Dead* (1985), a pleasure to those who like their monsters silly but a burden to those who prefer them real.

2. *Deformity display by the DDB.* Whether the DDB deformity is physical, psychological, spiritual, or positional, it must be displayed at some point in the horror film. Otherwise, the DDB is not presented, and the purpose of the horror film is unachieved. Often the display is delayed until relatively late in the running time, and it may occur gradually, in slow stages. As suggested in Chapter Two, this type of gradual unveiling may enhance suspense, build a more complete knowledge of the DDB, and hide the unreality of the DDB until the audience is already invested in the monster and more prone to overlook defects in the special effects used to realize it.

The Invisible Ray and *The Funhouse* provide examples. In *Ray*, the physical deformity is that the mad scientist Dr. Rukh, after experiments with a new element called radium X, glows in the dark. This effect might seem tepid or even risible except that the script has prepared for it through an increasing sense that Rukh's work is driving him closer to dangerous consequences. Further, the scene connects the deformity to a newly developed destructive power: the ability to kill by touch.

In *The Funhouse,* the DDB is grotesquely deformed, but this is hidden from view until late in the film because the character, the son of the funhouse keeper, wears a mask of the Universal Frankenstein monster. By the time this appropriate mask is ripped off and he reveals his deformity, he has established himself as a mute, pitiful murderer who does not want to show his real face. The effect is to build interest in seeing the face and to prepare the viewer to accept the makeup effects used to create it.

Purely psychological deformity, as in the case of Norman Bates in *Psycho* and Hannibal Lecter in *The Silence of the Lambs,* can usually be displayed through nothing but good writing and acting, although the other cinematic arts can help. The creepy lighting on Lecter in his Baltimore cell, and the stuffed corpse of Bates's mother in his basement, contribute to the sense that these are two extremely disturbed men.

Indeed, deformity display does not require the direct showing of the monster at all. In *Paranormal Activity* (2009), the demon possessing the house of the normal couple is never shown directly, but only through its effects — the opening and closing of a door in the middle of the night; strangely shaped footprints; the possessed face of the young woman.

Because some horror movies do not show the monster, or show it very little, there have developed two camps as to which is preferable — showing the monster or not showing it. The perennial popularity of visible movie monsters argues for the pleasures of this type of display; on the other hand, William K. Everson opined that "the best horror films have always been those that relied more on suggestion than on outright statement."[1] In particular, the films of producer Val Lewton, such as *Cat People*, are sometimes praised for their use of suggestiveness rather than overt shocks, as if there were something wrong with overt shocks.[2] DDB theory settles this question: either showing or not showing the monster is fine as long as the DDB is fully presented, that is, made real to the audience. This tends to be easier to do if there is at least some direct visual display of the DDB, which is why such display is generally preferred. However, under certain circumstances, completely indirect display can also work. Most often, as in *Curse of the Demon* (1957) — which blends monster shots with intense suggestiveness — a combination of indirect and direct display is used.

Deformity displays can be done well or badly. The makeup of the monster in *Frankenstein* is exceptionally good: its flat head, Neanderthal brow, and bolts in the neck suggest a never-before-seen mixture of the mechanical and prehistoric appropriate to the creature's origin, while the face of the actor, Boris Karloff, is admirably chilling, fits well within the makeup design, and is fully capable of mute expression. The makeup artistry is convincing and the whole is exceptionally memorable, a design widely known even to people who have never seen the movie. This Frankenstein monster's face is plausible, original, memorable, coherent, and horrifying, a package of horror-film aesthetic virtues relevant to the representation of a new form of being initiated through the deformation of other beings. Plausibility corresponds to the sense that this organism is really alive; originality to the organism's distinctiveness from previous beings; memorableness to the power of the organism to self-replicate (since memory is the replication of a thing in the mind); coherence to the organization that characterizes a living thing; and horrifyingness to the deformity that marks a being malformed with respect to previous beings, and to the destructiveness that marks any being that must consume or produce food from the environment.

By comparison, the makeup of the monster played by Robert DeNiro in

Mary Shelley's Frankenstein (1994) is a mass of scars that is hard to remember except that it looks a lot like other unimpressive Frankenstein monster incarnations. Worse, it has a circular scar around the left eye that makes the creature resemble Petey the dog in the *Little Rascals* comedies—an association that jars with the idea of the monster as horrific. This deformity display is competently executed—it is plausible—but it is neither original, memorable, coherent, nor horrifying, and therefore fails to support the presentation of the DDB.

    3. *Destructiveness display by the DDB*. Like deformity display, destructiveness display can be done more or less suggestively (the unnerving hints of ghosts in *The Others*) or graphically (the surgical removal of a face in *Les Yeux sans visage*, also known as *Eyes without a Face* or *The Horror Chamber of Dr. Faustus* [1960]). The graphic "blood and gore" approach is more frequently the target of moral objections. Horror movies in general are often reviled for their supposedly disgusting and dangerous content, and have been since their early days (see Chapter Thirteen), but their destructiveness displays are particularly subject to disapprobation, and the gorier, the worse. The 2004 edition of *Leonard Maltin's Movie & Video Guide* condemns the explicitly violent *The Last House on the Left* as not only a BOMB but "really sick," a phrase suggesting that it was pathological of the filmmakers to create the film, and of audiences to enjoy it.[3] (By the 2011 edition, the phrase "really sick" has been toned down to "repellent," and the rating has climbed to 1½ stars, suggesting that even a sick horror movie can be at least partially redeemed if it survives long enough.)[4] David Edelstein coined the disparaging term "torture porn" about gory films such as *Saw* (2004) and *Hostel*.[5] This sort of moralizing sometimes includes an empirical argument that media violence, including horror movie violence, may cause audiences to go out and imitate the aggression they have seen, or be deadened to real violence when it occurs. Though some evidence has been offered for this viewpoint,[6,7] the issue remains unsettled, with social scientists such as Jonathan L. Freedman arguing that scientific evidence does not support the view that media violence "causes aggression" or "makes people less sensitive to real world violence."[8] Pending conclusive empirical evidence for the supposed ill effects of horror movies, the distaste for horror movie gore remains essentially emotional rather than a product of moral reasoning. It cannot be a matter of our mistreating the characters in the films, because they are not real people, just characters. Perhaps the distaste for horror movie gore is related to a personal feeling of insuperable disgust that leads the critic to make a categorical error that it is morally wrong to feel differently. Aesthetically, neither the suggestive nor the graphic destructiveness display is intrinsically superior to the other as long as they remain subordinate to the primary purpose of presenting the DDB. In many horror films both approaches are used.

    The best destructiveness displays exhibit the package of horror-film aesthetic virtues identified in the deformity display in *Frankenstein*: plausible, original, memorable, coherent, and horrifying. The scene in *Psycho* in which Marion Crane is stabbed to death in the shower had all these virtues. The plotting and staging of the scene were believable. Shower murders of the main character midway through a film had not been done before, and in this case the main character was played by a movie star, Janet Leigh, producing a similar transfer of star power to her murderer as Gregory Peck achieved with Damien in *The Omen*. All of this made the scene original and memorable. Director Alfred Hitchcock's expert presentation of the scene, in a series of quick editing cuts that mirrored the cutting of the knife and captured many angles of the murder weapon, the obscured murderer, and the victim's reactions, ended with a palpable sense of Marion's body lying lifeless while her blood drains away. The result was a clear, coherent story about what had happened in the shower, reinforced by the screeching violins of Bernard Herrmann's score that reflected the stabbing of the knife. The entire effect was horrifying, because viewers could identify with the vulnerability of being in a shower and suddenly coming under attack. Plausible, original, memorable, coherent, and horrifying: all signs of a good destructiveness display, as of a good deformity display.

For a bad destructiveness display, one does not need to search far in the long list of bad horror movies. Does anyone remember the first murder in *Halloween II*? Probably not. A teenage girl named Ellen hears an intruder in the house and looks for him. Michael Myers, who got in through a door left mysteriously unlocked, springs up and kills her. We know he kills her because we hear a chord of indiscriminate horror movie music and the sound of a knife, and see blood splatter on her face. That's it. The scene is almost invisible because the character is a nobody without personality or connection to the story, the style of murder is overly familiar, the specifics are not very credible and make little sense, and nothing creative is added to make the scene stand out. Implausible, derivative, forgettable, incoherent, and not horrifying: all signs of a bad destructiveness display.

The Invisible Ray and *The Funhouse* offer two other examples of the variety of destructiveness displays. Dr. Rukh's ability to kill by touch is first displayed when he has just started glowing in the dark and sits down with his dog. As soon as Rukh's glowing hand touches the dog, the animal dies, with a skeletal handprint glowing on its body. The scene is moving and effective, in part because of the sympathy audiences normally have for dogs, in part because Rukh's power of death is so vivid and swift.

In *The Funhouse*, the monster uses more conventional means to kill: strangling, hanging, shooting, and stabbing. But the energy with which he goes about his work, as if he had superhuman strength (a common trait of monsters, as noted in Chapter Three), and his ferocious animal noises as he kills, make his destructiveness displays interesting and intense.

Although the *Funhouse* monster's murders are graphic, the most graphic stroke in the film occurs when a teenage boy, thinking the monster is approaching, swings an axe and accidentally buries it in the head of an already dead friend. This type of destructiveness display by a character who is not the DDB against another normal occurs with some frequency in horror films, memorably by the normal who shoots the survivor Ben at the end of *Night of the Living Dead* (1968). Such episodes contribute to the violent milieu in which the DDB lives, making the entire onscreen world a sort of extension of the DDB and thus enhancing its presentation. Similarly, deformity displays by non–DDB characters, such as the hunchback Fritz in *Frankenstein*, intensify the deformed milieu of the DDB.

Extreme destructiveness: splatter films. The term "splatter films" is sometimes used for horror films that are particularly gory in their destructiveness displays. The splattering is generally produced by the destructiveness displays of DDBs as they tear up and root around in human bodies, although when normals fight back they may also splatter the DDBs. In either case, splatter cinema is widely regarded as focusing on the visual exhibition, through makeup and special effects, of destroyed bodies: blood, tissue, organs, and all.

However, the concept of splatter films is somewhat confused. It is sometimes used synonymously with slasher films, which concern a psychopathic killer stalking a series of victims.[9] Sometimes splatter films are regarded as dating back to the blood-soaked cinema of B-movie auteur Herschell Gordon Lewis, whose cannibalistic *Blood Feast*, with its close-ups of bloody body parts, has been heralded as the first splatter film.[10] George Romero, maker of *Night of the Living Dead* and its sequels, is credited as coining the term in relation to his *Dawn of the Dead* (1978).[11] And certain films of the 1980s, such as *Dead and Buried* (1981), *The Burning* (1981), and *Scalps* (1983), have been cited as the first splatter films.[12]

In fact, the increasing gore of horror films dating from at least the Hammer productions of the 1950s make it difficult to identify a line that was crossed such that this or that film on this side of the line should be regarded as the first splatter film. In addition, complex films sometimes identified as splatter films, such as *Re-Animator* (1985), may suffer over-simplification from the tag, as if the only thing they had going on in their heads was goriness.

It is an aesthetic confusion to think that the primary focus of any horror film is the depiction of gore. The primary focus of all horror films is the presentation of the DDB. Terms such as "splatter film" and "splatterfest" may sometimes be used informally, but it is a mistake to give them too much weight. Whether more or less gore is used in the destructiveness displays is incidental, not consistently evaluable, and insufficient for the delineation of a separate construct such as splatter films.

4. *Account of the DDB indicating that the deformity causes the destructiveness.* The account of the deformity-destructiveness causal chain need not be

long or detailed, but it is essential to make clear that the monster counts as a DDB, rather than something else. Every horror movie has it somewhere. The account need not be spoken; the filmmakers can use any or all of their cinematic resources to make the account, including visuals, dialogue, music, and sound effects. What matters is that the audience be clear that the deformity causes the destructiveness.

Often, though not always, the account of the DDB will include an origin story. In cases where the monster is created during the film, we see the origin story. This occurs in *Invisible Ray*: we follow Rukh as he discovers radium X, which turns him into a monster. In the scene where he kills his dog, we observe directly how his glowing deformity leads to his destructive ability to kill by touch; we later learn in dialogue from Rukh's colleague, Dr. Benet, that the deformity will affect Rukh's brain, making him mad, and we soon see evidence that Rukh is mad, his paranoia leading him to destructiveness (murder). Thus, this account of the DDB includes both a clear origin story and a clear deformity-destructiveness causal chain.

In *The Funhouse*, where the monster is discovered rather than created, the origin story is much slighter. The DDB's father briefly explains that the monster was born that way, as a result of a trick of nature's. The deformity-destructiveness causal chain is established through a scene in which the monster prematurely ejaculates in an encounter with Madame Zena, a fortune-telling prostitute, and becomes so upset he kills her. An implicit line is thus drawn from his poor performance (sexual deformity) to his irrational rage (psychological deformity) to his great strength (physical deformity) to his violence (destructiveness). The monster's father later confirms that the monster has done this sort of thing before, establishing that this is a pattern for him, not an isolated instance.

In other horror movies, the origin story is virtually nonexistent. In *Cloverfield* (2008), there is some speculation about the origin of the giant beast that attacks New York, but no clear explanation. Nevertheless, with or without an origin story, the deformity-destructiveness causal chain is clear: only a beast of deformedly large size could knock the head off the Statue of Liberty, and only a beast of a deformed level of aggression would want to.

The account of the DDB is done best when it does not overwhelm the story with unnecessary details but still tells the audience what it needs to know. *Exorcist II: The Heretic* (1977) fails on both fronts, giving the audience more theological information about the demon Pazuzu than it needs while remaining amazingly unclear about what is going on.

5. *One or more normals for whom audience sympathy is possible in principle and who are attacked by the DDB*. Normals are necessary to the horror film, whether as the DDB's victims, antagonists, or even allies, like the boy who befriends the vampire girl in *Låt den rätte komma in* (*Let the Right One In*;

2008). Audience sympathy must be possible in principle for at least some of these normals, or else the DDB will seem insufficiently destructive to be a DDB. In practice, audience sympathy can be more or less adequate. Even in good horror films, only a few, or one, of the normals may be strongly sympathetic.

The problem is that the DDB usually kills so many normals there is not time to develop fully sympathetic characterizations for all of them. If too much time is spent developing the normals as characters, the DDB may be all but forgotten, leading to weak DDBs such as the shuttered girl in *The Shuttered Room*, outshone by Oliver Reed's character (as previously mentioned). Therefore, audience sympathy is almost always focused on the normal who is expected to enter the final battle and, usually, to survive. In some cases, as in *Psycho*, *Night of the Living Dead*, and *The Omen*, this expected survivor does not survive, which can be as effective as the opposite outcome. However, in most cases, the expected survivor prevails as expected.

In horror films of the 1930s and 1940s, as Wood noted, a heterosexual couple usually survived[13] and was designed to command the most audience sympathy. Such a couple offered the promise of marriage and regeneration without DDBs extending life in unorthodox directions. *Frankenstein*, for example, ends with Henry Frankenstein and his beloved Elizabeth, amid the hopes of "a son to the House of Frankenstein." *The Invisible Ray* features its own heterosexual couple, Rukh's wife Diana and her beloved Ronald Drake, who marry after Rukh is presumed dead. Neither character is exciting, although they have gained some sympathy because of the moral struggle they had over whether to have an affair while Rukh was still presumed alive.

From the 1970s on, in Clover's phrase, the "final girl" has dominated the normals of the horror movie, a lone young woman who survives the deaths of other victims.[14] Although best associated with slasher films such as *Halloween*, the final girl can be found in films as disparate as *Alien* and *The Silence of the Lambs*. She is usually pretty, plucky, resourceful, smart, good-hearted, virginal, and otherwise sympathetic. She can be found in *The Funhouse* in the person of Amy, who survives the monster's murders of her friends to be the only one to stagger away. Amy runs somewhat counter to the stereotype of the final girl in that she begins as a virgin but appears to have sex during her night in the funhouse. This makes her slightly more idiosyncratic and paradoxically provides her a gain in sympathy.

Sympathetic normals cannot rescue a horror movie from the weakness of a DDB, but they can contribute to presenting a strong one to best effect. *The Abominable Dr. Phibes* features a wickedly fine performance by the horror star Vincent Price, supported by tense scripting, hideous skull makeup, and an interesting collection of normal victims. The most sympathetic of these victims confronts Phibes in the final battle: Dr. Vesalius, a cultured surgeon who races against time to save his son from one of Phibes's deathtraps. As played by the distinguished actor Joseph Cotten, this normal made for a memorable match-up with Price's Phibes.

By contrast, horror movies without sympathetic normals can be among the most ponderous of films. *Phibes*' sequel, *Dr. Phibes Rises Again!* (1972) featured another collection of normal victims subjected to Phibes's depredations, but the normals were less interesting and none was as sympathetic as Cotten's Dr. Vesalius. Despite Price's reprise of his performance as the evil Phibes, the result is boring and unpleasant.

Besides identifying basic constituents of horror films, the five essential elements provide criteria for evaluating whether a particular horror film works aesthetically. Other issues are also important in that evaluation, including the significance of the movie and the overall impression of the DDB. Before considering those issues, I will discuss another topic of importance to understanding horror films: the ethics within those films.

6
Ethics

This chapter is not about the ethics of making or viewing horror films. As explained in the previous chapter, conclusive empirical evidence of the impact of horror films on society would be required to reach informed opinions about such matters, and that evidence is lacking. However, within horror films there is a considerable amount of ethical thinking, and this should be analyzed, in part because of its contribution to the presentation of the DDB, and in part because of the light it throws on society, whose ethics is reflected in horror movie ethics.

The ethics within horror movies, like every other story component, is subordinated to the purpose of presenting the DDB. For example, the ethical injunctions against such major offenses as murder, rape, assault, and torture exist within the horror film largely so that the DDB can violate them. They happen to be injunctions with which most audience members agree, and that is precisely their value within the horror film: audience members come to the film with the presumption that these destructive acts are morally abhorrent, and are therefore ready to abhor them when the DDB commits them. (In this chapter, the terms morality and ethics are used interchangeably.)

Because audience members really believe that these offenses are unethical, they expect to see the DDB punished for the offenses, thus restoring ethical order. Hence the horror film punishes the DDB in one of two ways. The DDB may receive the death penalty by being destroyed at the end, although sequels may bring him back. Or the DDB may live at the end, but only as the DDB, with all his deformities and without humanity, frequently banished to some other place until the next sequel. This is a sort of life in the prison of his DDB-ness. Only rarely is the DDB redeemed at the end and allowed to become human; when this does happen, as in *The Invisible Man Returns* (1940), the destructiveness of the DDB is usually fairly limited or excusable.

Although the ethical curve of the horror movie swings from code to infraction to restoration of code, the main interest of the audience is in seeing the infraction. It is in the infraction that the DDB becomes fully realized as a destructive being, and the presentation of the DDB is most fully achieved. In addition, there may be an element of suppressed wish-fulfillment in the DDB's flouting of the ethical code. I say "suppressed" rather than "repressed" because Freud's theory of repression (the automatic driving into unconsciousness of an unwanted memory, thought, or wish), though frequently cited in criticism,[1] has not been empirically corroborated and has been undermined from several quarters, scientific and philosophical.[2] For my purposes, no commitment to Freud is necessary to suggest that people have wishes they know they cannot act upon, including some related to aggression and sexuality, and they suppress these more or less consciously, all the while appreciating a chance to vent them imaginatively in situations such as movie-viewing.

Thus, despite their commitment to their own ethics, most audience members may harbor a suppressed wish to have the power and unrestrained energy that underlie the violent and sexual transgressions of the DDB. The horror film allows audiences to enjoy these transgressions vicariously, while providing the safety and satisfaction of having the ethical code restored at the end. In this respect, horror films provide a similar service to action, crime, and comedy films, which also allow audiences to transgress vicariously but walk away ethically pure.

So far, I have talked about the DDB's relation to the ethical code as largely negative—the DDB does whatever it wants, regardless of the code. For the normals in the horror film, life is more complicated. Normals, like audience members, have to navigate the ethics of their world, remembering what their codes say, trying to discern the right thing to do in a particular situation, attempting to act virtuously, and resisting—or succumbing to—temptation.

When normals take the wrong step, it often happens that the agent of their punishment is the DDB. An example occurs in *The Wolfman*, the 2010 remake of *The Wolf Man*. In the remake, a psychiatrist who treats his patients with methods that amount to torture and teaches incorrectly that werewolves are a delusion is punished with death on a spiked fence by the Wolfman. Such a role for a DDB may seem peculiar: the DDB is the biggest moral transgressor in the horror film, and is also the agent of punishment for the moral transgression of others. But the concept is as old as Satan, a fallen angel whose immoral behavior somehow suits him perfectly for the punishment of immoral people in hell. The connection between the two is rarely made explicit in horror films, but implicitly the connection is this: the DDB, by his very destructiveness, shows what not to do and is therefore a teacher of ethics; as a teacher of ethics, he is also qualified to teach by punishing others when they do what they should not. In this double sense, DDBs, and the horror films that present them, educate audiences ethically.

All the big ethical rules apply to normals: they must not murder, rape, assault, or torture without provocation, although they are given some latitude in these areas when exacting just revenge or defending self or others, particularly against the DDB. In addition, normals are often punished severely for smaller ethical infractions. The rule against having sex without benefit of marriage, an important rule in the slasher genre, is constantly being violated by normals and punished by DDBs.

Allusion to the small ethical rules of horror movies was jokingly made in the *Scream* series of self-referential slasher movies. In the first movie, *Scream* (1996), the first rule was, "You can never have sex," but, despite *Scream*, this is only true for sex outside of marriage; married people have sex routinely in horror movies but are not necessarily killed by DDBs. For example, Wolf von Frankenstein and his wife in *Son of Frankenstein* had to have sex to produce their son, yet all three make it to the film's conclusion alive. *Scream* adds, "You can never drink or do drugs," and it is true that this is risky behavior in a horror film, particularly when done by underage people, but again, the fully grown Wolf von Frankenstein drinks and he makes it through. *Scream's* third rule is, "Never, ever, ever, under any circumstances, say 'I'll be right back,' 'cause you won't be back." In reality, this falls under a more general rule of being careful about what you say and do, which in turn is a corollary of a more general rule of being conservative.

The ethical rules for horror movies are not fixed; they change over time, reflecting the changing mores of society. But certain rules have been particularly long-lasting, and are especially likely to incur punishment from the DDB if violated.

1. Be conservative. The most important ethical rule in horror films, the injunction to be conservative has stayed in force in the genre from early days to the present. All the other rules listed below under separate headings are, in a way, corollaries of this rule. In a horror film, to be conservative does not necessarily refer to political conservatism, although that can be an aspect of it: the old baron Frankenstein in *Frankenstein* believes in maintaining the established order of the village, and he survives the film safely. Gwen Conliffe in the original *Wolf Man* loves above her class (she is a shopgirl, Larry Talbot a lord's heir), and she is nearly killed for it. Nevertheless, what conservatism means more broadly in horror films is that things should be done the way they have always been done, and change is to be viewed with suspicion. In a horror movie, change is bad.

An example of the conservatism rule is the gas station owner's warning to a family of vacationers to "Stay on the main road!" in *The Hills Have Eyes*. They disobey, and end up besieged by cannibals living in the wilderness. The main road is, symbolically, the mainstream, the road most traveled, the well-lit places, the way of life that keeps people safe by insulating them from the dangers that lurk in less traveled, darker, potentially more anarchic areas. The rule to stay on the main road is often literally violated in horror films, from Renfield traveling past the Borgo Pass in *Dracula* to *Psycho*, *Two Thousand Maniacs!* (1964), *Jeepers Creepers*, *Wrong Turn* (2003), *Wolf Creek* (2005), and many others. Because this type of violation often takes travelers from the normal city to the monstrous country, it has been suggested that the city/country split is significant in horror films,[3] and in some cases it is. But what is more important is to stay where you and your kind have always been. This rule is figuratively violated every time a normal rejects tradition and does something rebellious, whether it is as complex as switching genders in *Dr. Jekyll and Sister Hyde* (1972; "Stay in your own gender" is a proviso of conservatism sometimes violated in horror films) or as simple as running away from home, as the young girl Lila does in *Lemora, A Child's Tale of the Supernatural*, only to fall into the hands of the vampire Lemora.

One aspect of the conservatism rule is that tradition should be respected. If the villagers say garlic and crosses should be used to ward off vampires, use them. If local lore says werewolves exist, they do. Do not scoff or attempt to institute modern innovations. Another aspect of conservatism is to distrust strangers, especially foreigners: the foreigner might be the kindly Van Helsing, but it might be the dangerous Dracula. Still another aspect is to be careful. Lack of caution is what makes it dangerous to say, without knowledge of the future, "I'll be right back." Lack of caution is what allowed a fly into the telepod in both versions of *The Fly*. A cautious person does not overdo drinking and does not use illicit drugs (as *Scream* pointed out), and definitely does not drive under the influence or alcohol and drugs. People who do drive that way might end up like Brandi in *Stuck* (2007), crashing into a homeless person who gets stuck in her windshield.

Some horror films appear to take a liberal or even radical point of view, yet a deep conservatism is often underneath. In *Day of the Dead*, the soldiers running the zombie-surrounded installation are, in a sense, conservatives, concerned with law and order and military control; the scientists studying the zombies are concerned with traditional liberal values such as knowledge and democratic discussion. In this film, the more dangerous position appears to be the conservative one, and it is the conservatives who suffer the worst punishment from the DDBs. But the soldiers are only superficially conservative. Because this film is post–apocalyptic, all the safe traditions have already been destroyed; there is no main road. The choices are among options all of which are radical, because no society has ever before been in this position.

Of all the characters in *Day of the Dead*, the heroine, Sarah, who prevails to the end, has the best claim to being conservative in the horror movie sense, because she is chiefly concerned with traditional human values (her boyfriend's life, the group's survival; see Number Six, "Be charitable," below) rather than with the trendier military and scientific quarrels going on around her.

2. Do not commit sacrilege. Sacrilege, disrespect toward a sacred being or desecration of a sacred thing, has consistently been an ethical infraction in horror films from the beginnings to the present, although the characteristics of sacrilege have changed over time. The injunction against sacrilege is closely related to the injunction to be conservative: God, or the gods, have been around a long time; therefore they should be respected.

Scientists in horror movies often commit sacrilege by probing too far into God's domain of nature. Frankenstein did so in *Frankenstein*; so did the title character of *The Invisible Man*, who admitted on his deathbed, "I meddled in things that man must leave alone." Nowadays, in our secular society, horror films are less likely to talk explicitly about God in characterizing the scientific crime of probing too far into nature. Nevertheless, in films such as *Isolation* (2005) and the television movie *Organizm* (2008), the idea persists, as a ghost of the injunction against sacrilege, that manipulation of nature is an infraction punishable by DDB attack. Perhaps because horror films are conservative, they tend to keep expressing ethical injunctions once they are developed, even if the reason for the injunctions has become obscure.

Sacrificed by Satanic cultists, high school girl Jennifer (Megan Fox) comes back to life as a demon in *Jennifer's Body* (2009, 20th Century–Fox).

Another example of the conservatism of the sacrilege injunction is the Satan worship film. There had always been horror films in which Satan worship was the cause of the trouble, such as *The Black Cat* (1934), but these were fairly rare until the late 1960s and 1970s. Then, as society became more secular and God talk became more difficult to do overtly, horror films increasingly turned to Satan worship as a substitute way of showing sacrilegious people working their own doom. The screen abounded with Satanists, in films such as *Rosemary's Baby*, *Dracula A.D. 1972* (1972), *The Omen*, and *The Devil's Rain* (1975); the tradition has continued to the 21st century with *The House of the Devil* (2009) and *Jennifer's Body*.

It is just as important to avoid sacrilege toward the gods and spirits of non–Christian cultures as toward those of Christianity. In the mummy films, beginning with *The Mummy* (1932), trespassers on sacred Egyptian sites incurred the wrath of Egyptian gods. In other films, trespassers on American Indian burial grounds, as in *Poltergeist* (1982) and *Pet Sematary* (1989), suffered severe fates.

Occasionally the horror film suggests that atheism itself is a sort of giving

In *Rosemary's Baby* (1968, Paramount), Rosemary (Mia Farrow) inspects the son of Satan to whom she has given birth.

in to the DDB. This occurs in *From Dusk till Dawn* (1996) and *Signs* (2002), in both of which a character (played, respectively, by Harvey Keitel and Mel Gibson) is a Christian-minister-turned-atheist who recovers his faith in the course of fighting monsters (respectively, vampires and aliens). This is part of an old tradition in movies that requires a hero who is an atheist to convert by the end of the film (e.g., Clark Gable in *San Francisco* [1936]).

3. Do not have unmarried sex. This rule has already been mentioned, and it too, is connected to conservatism: sex is permitted only within the bonds of the traditional institution of matrimony. In the old days of the Production Code, sex before marriage could not even be implied easily, so this issue rarely came up. By 1960, the censorship rules were loosening, and Marion Crane had sex out of wedlock in *Psycho* and came to a bad end. Beginning in the 1970s, when the sexual revolution was in full swing and sexual depictions were freely permitted onscreen, horror film characters—particularly teenagers—had a great deal of premarital sex. It was as bad an idea for them as it had been for Marion Crane: the DDBs in slasher films beginning with *Halloween* seemed to target their attacks selectively on the teenagers who were having the most sex. The survivors were usually virginal, although there were exceptions, such as Amy in *The Funhouse*. Even mere nakedness without sexual intercourse may bring on a DDB attack, as is the case with the nude women cavorting at spring break in *Piranha 3D* (2010).

Both for this ethical rule and all the others, it is important to note that horror films do not guarantee security for anybody, even those who follow the rules. For example, even married people who appear to be restricting sex to their spouses can get into trouble in horror movies, such as the married heroines in *Rosemary's Baby* and *The Astronaut's Wife* (1999), each of whom has to bear nonhuman offspring as a result of unexpected sexual episodes. Even virginity is no guarantee of survival. The policeman who investigates the pagan cultists in *The Wicker Man* (1973) dies a virgin at their hands.

4. Do not get contaminated. Again, this is a conservative rule: stay clean, avoid foreign matter, steer clear of people who look sick or dirty. As Noël Carroll writes, "horrific beings are often associated with contamination."[4] A monster's impurity, he explains, is what makes it disgusting (i.e., repulsive) rather than merely fearful. Nevertheless, in horror films, victims have been violating the rule against contamination since the origins of the genre, but in fairness, they are often unable to help it. If a vampire, werewolf, or zombie jumps on you and bites you, and you live, you are going to become one of them, however clean you try to stay. Their oral fluids mix with your blood, and that is all there is to it. But if you can, avoid contamination.

If you do get contaminated, there may be help. In *The Brides of Dracula* (1960), Van Helsing gets bitten by a vampire and saves himself by burning the bitten area with a crucifix. In *Day of the Dead*, an attempt is made to save a man who is bitten by a zombie by amputating the bitten arm. If there is no help, the best thing may be to destroy yourself to avoid propagating the species of DDB that attacked you.

Biting is only one of many methods of contamination in horror films. In *Invasion of the Body Snatchers*, falling asleep is enough to allow the aliens to take over the victim's body. In *The Crazies* (1973) and *Cabin Fever*, drinking water transmits lethal germs. In *28 Days Later* (2002), blood spreads the infection. In *They Came from Within* (1975; also known as *Shivers*) and *Rabid* (1977), sexual contact is the means for transmitting, respectively, parasites and rabies. Even electronic media can contaminate: in *Ringu* (*Ring*; 1998) and its remake *The Ring* (2002), watching a certain videotape brings on death unless you copy the tape and pass it to someone who sees it for the first time — thus contaminating that person.

5. Beware of youth. The horror-film ethical rule about being wary of young people only came into existence when there were a great deal of young people around: during and after the baby boom of about 1946–1964, a period that saw a great rise in the birth rate. Evidently, anxiety about all these rambunc-

Becky Driscoll (Dana Wynter) and Dr. Miles Bennell (Kevin McCarthy) are chased by the alien-possessed townspeople of Santa Mira, California, in *Invasion of the Body Snatchers* (1956, Allied Artists).

tious children, and the countercultural, decidedly non–conservative young adults they grew into, sparked the horror genre to create a rule that was new but still consistent with its overall conservatism. Young people were rebellious, and therefore potentially dangerous.

In horror films, they were very dangerous. The evil child subgenre, in which the DDB was a child whose innocent look concealed monstrous intentions, began with the 1956 film *The Bad Seed* and included *Village of the Damned* (1960), *Rosemary's Baby*, *The Other* (1972), *The Exorcist*, *The Omen*, and, more recently, *Orphan* (2009). Even worse were children who did not even look innocent, like the mutant youngsters in *It's Alive!* (1974) and *The Brood* (1979) or the spooky dybbuk child in *The Unborn* (2009). Once children grew into teens and young adults, they were still dangerous. *I Drink Your Blood* (1970) featured young hippies who worshipped Satan and ate meat pies contaminated with rabies—breaking in a triple-threat the rules against youth, sacrilege, and contamination. Even the music of young people was dangerous. In *The Last House on the Left*, a rock concert attracts two young women who end up in a nightmare of torture, rape, and murder.

In the slasher subgenre, teenagers were mainly dangerous to themselves, what with all their unmarried sex, as well as their binge drinking and illicit drugs. But in horror films more broadly, young people could be dangerous to older adults as well. In *Cabin Fever*, the visit of college kids to a secluded wooded area helps to spread a deadly germ to the entire community.

6. Be charitable. This rule is conservative in that it encompasses all the traditional ways in which people are supposed to show love for their neighbor. Be kind; respect their property; if they need a hand, help them; follow the laws. This rule enjoins charity not just in the sense of giving money to the needy, but in the broader Christian sense of unselfish love. Because the rule is conservative, it does not require commitment to socialism or government welfare programs, just a neighborly good-heartedness.

As simple as this rule may seem, horror movie victims are always violating it. Even the smallest violations of charity may doom them to attack from the DDB. In *Drag Me to Hell* (2009), a bank loan officer, Christine, refuses a home loan extension to an old Gypsy woman because Christine is angling for a promotion and needs to prove her fiscal toughness. The old woman puts a curse on her that condemns her to hell.

In *I Know What You Did Last Summer* (1997), young people in a car run over a pedestrian (remember: young people are dangerous), and fail to follow the basic charitable rule of reporting the accident. A DDB comes to take vengeance on them. In *The Funhouse*, one of the young people trapped in the funhouse steals some money belonging to the funhouse keeper, raising an alarm that results in attack by the DDB.

Ethical Case Studies

Horror movie ethics presents the opportunity for ethical case studies, in which the audience may consider the right and wrong of various extreme situations that could only happen with DDBs. Such a quandary occurs in *Bram Stoker's Dracula*—namely, What is the duty of a woman who is married to one man but is the reincarnated wife of another?

Winona Ryder, as Mina Murray, is first engaged to and then marries Keanu Reeves, as Jonathan Harker. Mina appears to be following all the rules: no sex before marriage; sex, presumably, within marriage. But it turns out that she is the reincarnation of Elisabeta, the one-time wife of Gary Oldman's Dracula. It was Elisabeta's death that drove Dracula into vampirism as a revolt against God, and he has been searching for her spirit ever since. Now he has found her. What should Mina do? Stay with Jonathan or go with Dracula?

Mina, it appears, is willing to go with Dracula, even to the point of letting him make her a vampire. In a climactic fit of nobility, he lets her go and has her kill him, lest she too be condemned to vampirism. The effect is to rescue the normal heterosexual couple (Mina and Jonathan) from the DDB, a traditional horror movie ending. But Mina's devotion to Dracula has laid bare something more deeply ethical: the rightness of an undying love, even when it is with a monster. The love between Mina and Dracula is the final emotion expressed in the film, and is, in that sense, endorsed. Mina's devotion has also illustrated an important horror movie principle: no one is safe from the monster, even the woman who tries for a normal marriage.

Here is a second ethical case study: if you are a child, should you obey your father even if he tells you to kill someone? According to *Frailty* (2002), the answer, under certain conditions, is yes.

In *Frailty*, Meiks (Bill Paxton) is a serial killer who believes God is telling him whom to kill, and that all the people he kills are demons who deserve to die for their evil deeds. One of his two sons, Adam, supports him in his cause, but the other, Fenton, is morally appalled and refuses to cooperate. Following the horror movie code of being charitable, Fenton believes Meiks's victims are innocent and that Meiks is insane.

But what if Meiks is not insane? What if God really is speaking to him, and the victims really are evil? Then helping Dad with his executions is a duty — not only to Dad, but to God. After all, Abraham was rewarded for being willing to sacrifice Isaac to God, and Aquinas says, "[T]hose who, at the Lord's command, slew their neighbors and friends, would seem not to have done this themselves; but rather He by whose authority they acted thus."[5]

As *Frailty* reveals, Meiks really is doing God's work, violent though it is, and the good son is Adam, who helps him. Other interpretations of the ending may be possible, but this seems the most likely. It is a horrific universe, one in which the DDB is the supreme being himself. But within that universe, it is ethically consistent to throw one's lot with one's father. It is also conservative, a wise thing to be in a horror movie.

Ethical Division

These are the basic ethical rules that normals must follow to increase their chances of surviving in a horror film, and that they often break, triggering

6. Ethics

punishment from the DDB. These rules reveal the horror genre as essentially a conservative genre, in which conservatism, piety, sexual purity, cleanliness, maturity, and charity are the most highly valued ethical attributes, and wrongdoing of all kinds, from the most heinous to the most trivial, is regarded as cause for punishment, often severe punishment.

At the same time, the horror film is divided in its core. It is conservative in its ethical attitudes, but also focuses primarily on the most rebellious, anarchic, amoral, violent, and unrestrainedly sexual of beings—the DDB. The purpose of the horror film is to present the DDB—the antithesis of all that is ethical. And yet in doing so, the horror film reinforces the very attitudes that the DDB flouts. There are rules; the DDB breaks them (or punishes infractions of them); the DDB is destroyed or banished, restoring the rules. The DDB itself, rebellious as it is, can be seen as an ethical educator. Yes, it is a wild thing, but it is, as it were, framed and contained by ethics. However, its wildness is primarily what viewers want to see, with the ethical frame only a device to help see it.

It is because of this ethical division that it is not clear what the ethical impact of the horror film on society might be. Assuming that impressionable audience members might learn from what they have seen on screen, it is not evident what they would learn. Would they start acting monstrously, in an effort to imitate the DDBs? Or would they act more conservatively, piously, maturely, and charitably, washing their hands more and abstaining from sex until marriage, in an effort to avoid destruction by DDBs? The empirical answer is not yet clear, but the ethical content of the horror film is. It is a mix of a strong, conservative ethical system and a powerful, radically subversive, amoral force that challenges it from one film to the next, now apparently confined by the system and now apparently bursting free of it, with the resolution never complete.

7
Meaning and Significance

Purpose and meaning are sometimes spoken of as the same thing. "What are you trying to say?" (what is your communicative purpose?) is much the same question as "What do you mean?" But whereas the primary purpose of any horror film can be summed up as the presentation of a DDB, the meaning of any horror film is more particular, grounded in the specific characters and situations in that film. Also particular is the significance of the film, which is not the same thing as meaning.

In distinguishing meaning from significance, I follow E.D. Hirsch, whose theory of objective interpretation defines verbal meaning as that aspect of a speaker's intention (or act of awareness) that, under the linguistic and cultural conventions of the time, may be shared with others.[1] Verbal meaning, in Hirsch's view, is objective, unchanging, and accessible through acts of interpretation. Significance, however, is the relation of meaning to something else (such as standards of value or present concerns); it is always changing and varies among subjectivities, and is the object of criticism.

Hirsch's position has been the subject of much criticism of its own; Terry Eagleton, for example, regards it as a "rearguard" and "authoritarian" attempt to safeguard the primacy of the author's intention from the ravages of ever-changing textual readings.[2] Yet Eagleton himself allows that there is some sense in which the distinction between meaning and significance is valid; his objection is that the distinction cannot be made absolutely. Hirsch, however, does not argue for an *absolute* distinction between the two, only for a construction of meaning that recovers the author's *probable* intention.

Recovering the author's probable intention is difficult enough when it comes to a literary text, but it becomes seriously complicated with regard to cinema, because films have no single author. Despite the claims of auteur theory, voiced by such critics as François Truffaut and Andrew Sarris,[3] that the director can often be considered the author of the film, a movie is normally the result of a collaboration of many people, particularly in the case of commercial films made for widespread distribution, such as horror films. Therefore, in discerning a film's meaning, it is better to speak not of the author's probable intention but of the probable intent of a collaboration, or, for short, the collaborative intent — what the film, as a product of collaboration, seems intended to show within the system of cinematic and verbal language and cultural references in which it was created, a system that might be called the immediate context. We know that this is how the collaborators intended the film to have meaning because we know that the collaborators wanted to make money, and they could only make money by having the film be readily interpretable within the immediate context.

This is a fairly limited kind of meaning — it amounts to what a viewer reports when he hurriedly recounts the plot to a friend who has stepped out for popcorn in the middle of a horror movie. A number of images have gone by, edited together in a sophisticated way, but the viewer is able to summarize them by saying, "The monster ate her" or "They had sex." That is film meaning, such as it is. It is limited, but it is the basis for the narrative enjoyment the audience gets from the film, and is also the basis for the film's significance: what the film has to say when the meaning is brought into relation by someone's critical sensibility with this or that aspect of the world. After the horror film, when the two friends argue about whether the monster's eating habits were a symbol of colonialism or rife with sexism or something else, that is significance. Meaning is usually agreed upon by most people who see the film and share the same immediate context; significance, because it depends on relating meaning to matters outside the film, is more frequently varied and the subject of disagreement. Meaning is determinate, significance indeterminate. Meaning is what almost everyone thinks they are seeing when they see a movie; significance is what they argue about afterward.

Meaning often has more subtlety than may be apparent from this explanation. At the end of *The Shining*, after Jack Torrance, who has been turned into a killer under the influence of the ghosts of the Overlook Hotel, has gotten lost in the hedge maze and frozen to death, we see that one of the old photographs inside the hotel, dating from the 1920s, includes him in the midst of a party at the site. But we know that Jack only just arrived at the hotel circa 1980, when the film was made. Anyone who sees the film can tell that much — that is clearly part of the meaning. It is a little less clear, but still strongly implied, that the Overlook has taken Jack in as one of its ghosts. But how exactly did Jack get into the picture? Has he been in the picture since the 1920s, and is his present self a reincarnated form that has finally made its way to join the picture? Or did he only become part of the picture now, in 1980, after he died? Or is there a better explanation? The film does not say, and the clearest elucidation of the meaning is that the film is ambiguous with respect to the mechanism of Jack's appearance in the picture, and that the filmmakers intend to leave the audience unsettled on this point.

Meaning is not necessarily limited to plot mechanics. It can include symbolism, so long as the symbolism is clearly implied by the film's overt content.

When Jack is lost in the maze at the end, one can surmise that he is symbolically lost in his mind. This is supported by an earlier scene in which he looked down at a model of the maze and, through editing, it seemed as if he were looking down from a God's-eye view at the real maze, where his wife and child were walking. The entire maze seemed to exist in his mind; thus, when he is lost in the maze later, it is his own mind in which he is lost. This interpretation is a little more of a stretch than the earlier readings, but it seems grounded enough in the film that it probably belongs to meaning rather than significance.

Jack Torrance (Jack Nicholson), homicidal caretaker of the Overlook Hotel, stalks his prey in *The Shining* (1980, Warner Bros.).

There is no point checking with the filmmakers about all this. Stanley Kubrick, director of *The Shining*, is dead; those colleagues of his who are alive may not remember accurately what they were thinking at the time, and even if they do, the meaning of the film is found in what is shown on screen, not in what one of the filmmakers says about it afterward. All the more so with significance. Kubrick has been quoted as saying he was attracted to the source material, the novel by Stephen King, because it dealt with "the evil side" of "the human personality."[4] While this is interesting, it does not demand that critics build their accounts of the movie *The Shining* around the idea of the evil side of the human personality.

An interpretation of meaning is judged by how accurate it is: how faithfully it represents what is in the film. When a construction of significance is being judged, the key issues are how interesting and fruitful the reading is, and whether it can be justified based on the film's meaning. The requirement to base a reading on a film's meaning is important not because it is owed to the filmmakers, but because one will seem like a sloppy critic if one does not, and one's claims will be undermined. And if one's reading is neither interesting nor fruitful, no one will care and it will be forgotten. Indeed, critics of criticism typically judge film readings in terms such as these: when Cynthia Freeland surveys and critiques feminist approaches to the horror film, and proposes her own framework for producing new feminist readings, she uses evaluative words such as "intriguing," "fruitful," "interestingly," "illuminating," and "useful."[5] With those caveats, the critic is free, in seeking a film's significance, to be what Rorty calls a strong textualist critic, who "asks neither the author nor the text about their intentions but simply beats the text into a shape which will serve his own purpose."[6]

Orphan (2009)

To be interesting and fruitful, significance should first of all be coherent and forceful. An incoherent and weak reading stands little chance of being interesting. If a film is able to generate coherent and forceful significance, that is a mark of aesthetic merit, because it suggests that the film connects to the world in ways both strong and subtle. It would be no surprise if *The Shining* managed to do as much, because it is a much studied classic film from a great director, based on the work of a great horror novelist. But forceful and coherent significance can be found even in lesser known films. Consider *Orphan*. A B movie and a modest hit, this horror film received mixed reviews and had no actors who were then major stars, although it did have a capable cast that included Vera Farmiga and Peter Sarsgaard (Kate and John Coleman) as the adoptive parents of the menacing Isabelle Fuhrman (Esther). *Orphan* had neither a literary pedigree nor much daring originality, being part of the old "evil child" subgenre of horror films dating back to *The Bad Seed*. Despite what might seem to be a lack of promise, *Orphan* provides a useful example of how interpretation and criticism work within DDB theory.

The plot of *Orphan*—the basic narrative component of its meaning—is straightforward. After a nightmare teaser revealing that Kate had a stillborn daughter (Jessica), the setup introduces Kate's surviving family: her husband John, her deaf daughter Max, and her son Daniel. They are an upper middle-class family with a few problems, gradually shown to include Kate's drinking (from which she is recovering) and John's infidelity (from which he is recov-

The original evil child, Rhoda Penmark (Patty McCormack), is innocent on the surface but vicious underneath in *The Bad Seed* (1956, Warner Bros.).

76 Part I: The Horror Film Analyzed

Esther (Isabelle Fuhrman), the adopted child in *Orphan* (2009, Warner Bros.), wields a bloody hammer.

ering). The family decides to adopt another child, whom they meet in an orphanage — nine year-old Esther. This DDB makes her entrance smiling innocently, though followers of the subgenre will discern almost instantly that there is something wrong with her, including her vaguely Russian accent, her high intelligence, her separation from the other children at the orphanage, and her excessively frilly, girlish appearance, down to the ribbons she refuses to remove from her neck and wrists. The DDB swiftly begins attacking, escalating from killing a bird to murdering and attempting to murder people. She is a liar, a manipulator, a bully, a sadomasochist, and an arsonist. As if this were not enough, in a surprise twist near the end, it is revealed that Esther is actually a psychopathic grown woman with a hormone condition that makes her look like a child. Aged thirty-three, she has been going around the world passing herself off as a little girl and butchering families along the way. She is also a sexual predator who tries to seduce John and drive him away from Kate. The ribbons on her neck and wrists are there to hide the scars where she used to fight against restraints in an insane asylum. Thus she is deformed physically (hormonally and through scars) and psychologically (through violence and sexual aggressiveness), and at least some of these deformities are causes of her destructiveness, making her a DDB, a deformed-destructive being. By the end of the film, she puts Daniel in the hospital, nearly kills Max and Kate, and kills both John and a nun from the orphanage. The final battle, between Kate and Esther, ends with Ester's death in a night struggle in a frozen pond.

So much for the meaning of *Orphan*. What does the film signify? To elucidate the significance of any horror film in DDB theory, a useful question to ask is what makes the DDB different from the normals. What normal expectations (i.e., expectations of normal members of the audience vicariously expressed in the film) is the DDB defying?

Esther in *Orphan* defies the following normal expectations:

1. Children are innocent, in a sense that includes both not being violent and not being sexual.
2. Children and adults are radically different.
3. Family should be preserved.
4. Children should be raised by their biological parents.
5. Foreigners should be avoided.
6. Children should be average.
7. Women should be subordinate to men.
8. The upper middle class should be preserved.

In contrast to all these expectations, Esther is:

1. a violent and sexual child
2. simultaneously an adult and a child
3. a threat to a family
4. an adopted child
5. a foreigner
6. a superchild (hyper-intelligent, musically and artistically accomplished, criminally cunning, etc.)
7. a powerful woman
8. an intruder in an upper middle-class home

It is doubtful that anyone who has seen *Orphan* will argue with the listed attributes of Esther, yet the listed normal expectations may seem controversial. Who in this modern age, when so many children are adopted, expects that children should be raised by their biological parents? Who has such strong antipathies against foreigners, above-average children, and women, and such a preference for the upper middle class? The only expectations that might seem like authentic expectations are the first three: the innocence of children, the radical difference between children and adults, and the importance of family.

In fact, part of the job of the horror film is to reveal to normal people what they really believe: to hold to them a warped mirror that shows, in the outlines of the DDB, what beliefs are so basic to us that we feel horror at seeing them threatened. These beliefs are a varied lot, but they include beliefs to which nearly everyone in the culture feels openly committed (universal beliefs) and others that at least some educated people acknowledge they would be better off not holding (controversial beliefs).

Consider the universal beliefs first: childhood innocence, adult/child difference, family. These beliefs are almost universally held in western culture, and it is naturally horrifying to find a DDB who threatens them all. Yet there is more to horror than blank rejection of what is wrong. When a teacher corrects a math sum on a student's paper — say, "2+2=5"— the teacher rarely feels horror. Rejection of real and obvious wrong is normally painless, without fear or repugnance — in a word, horror-free. The fear and repugnance enter the picture when there exists some subterranean doubt, which even to express exerts a threatening pressure on the prevailing view. For this to happen, it means that the prevailing view is weaker than it looks. It is built precariously on the suppression of its opposite. As noted in Chapter Six, the DDB often represents suppressed material, and the horror film is welcome, in part, because it allows the audience to connect with pieces of themselves that they generally keep at a distance.

Thus, Esther allows the audience to connect with their suspicions that children are not so innocent — that, for example, children are sexual, as is visible when Esther starts trying to seduce her adoptive father. Similarly, she allows them to connect with the violence of children, the indeterminate border between children and adults, and the notion that the family perhaps should not always be preserved. Esther is appealing because she expresses things we suspect but that are forbidden by our supposedly universal beliefs. She is also horrible and dangerous because she is violating those beliefs. Psychologically, the role of the DDB is to allow expression of forbidden thoughts, then to restore the proper order of thinking by punishing the DDB. In this respect, the horror film as carrier of significance embodies the same mix of conservatism and subversion that it does in ethics (see Chapter 6).

The same can be said for the controversial beliefs as for the universal ones. Esther calls to mind controversial views against adopted children, above-average children, foreigners, female equality, and the lower classes. These views— prejudices, really — are rejected by many people, particularly liberal intellectuals, and, sure enough, some adoption advocates protested against *Orphan* even before its release because of fear that it would cater to prejudices against adopted children.[7] They went so far as to persuade Warner Bros., the studio that released the film, to censor the following line of Esther's from the trailer: "It must be hard to love an adopted child as much as your own." This censorship was really unnecessary, because the horror film's treatment of controversial views is the same as its treatment of universal views: it subverts them as much as it conserves them.

Although many people may hold negative opinions of adopted children, smart children, foreigners, strong women, and the proletariat, in seeing *Orphan* these people were treated, in a sense, to the opposite: to the sight of an adopted, foreign, socially marginalized girl who is smart, strong, exciting, and drives the story. In fact, they must have been drawn to see this, because the ads and pre–publicity (notwithstanding the efforts of censors) made it clear that this is what they were going to see. People with such prejudices have, like everyone else, doubts about even their strongest beliefs, contrapuntal thoughts that leave them unsure, and their unsureness is embodied in the DDB. A DDB is constructed from subversive materials, the better to present the new form of being the audience craves. A DDB is the thing people think they do not want to see and for that reason want to see. It is the opposite of what we say we believe.

With this background, it is possible to construct a unified reading of *Orphan*. More than one reading is possible, depending on how and where the critic draws the lines of significance between the film and things outside the film. This reading takes as its starting point the rule that Esther breaks, "Family should be preserved," and the subversive contrary idea that she embodies, "It is not necessarily true that family should be preserved." Why should family not be preserved? *Orphan* makes it clear why: *in a family, everyone's interests are mortally opposed.* That is, family is a place where there is often good reason to kill the others. This proposition has some support from evolutionary science and animal and human physiology and behavior, fields that are increasingly useful to criticism from the perspective Joseph Carroll calls literary Darwinism.[8] For example, there is evidence that in placental animals, mother and fetus vie over nutrients during pregnancy[9]; that animal siblings kill each other over rights to parental care[10]; and that human stepparents are more dangerous to children than are parents.[11] Of course, there are genetic motives for family members to care for one another: each biological parent has 50 percent of its genes invested in a child; siblings share 50 percent of their genes. Yet, aside from identical twins, the only individual with 100 percent of its own genes is that individual, and therefore that individual has a motive to look out for itself at the expense of other family members, even if killing the others is necessary.

Orphan makes this point in several ways, most markedly by suggesting that having children — any children — is a bad idea. This theme is raised in the opening teaser, Kate's nightmare of the birth of Jessica, her stillborn baby. The first sign that something is wrong are the bloody streaks coming from between Kate's legs and smearing the floor under the wheelchair as Kate is wheeled to the delivery room. They are reminiscent of the bloody streaks the title character found in *Carrie* when she discovered calamitously that she was having her first period. *Orphan's* teaser continues with various absurd nightmare moments, such as John cheerfully encouraging Kate to smile for the camera even as the tragedy of the stillbirth is unfolding. The nightmare concludes when Jessica is born as a bloody, wailing zombie baby wrapped in mummy bandages.

This scene suggests that there is something wrong about the entire process by which children are born and raised. Menstruation, alluded to by the bloody streaks, is barbaric. Childbirth is barbaric. People like the deluded husband act as if the arrival of a baby is good news to be captured on camera, but it is really just welcoming another organism to its inevitable death — the wailing zombie baby. As the film continues, it becomes clear that there is something wrong with every child who is born. Max was born deaf. Daniel has budding signs of sexual and violent urges of a prohibited nature — he hides pornography in his treehouse and wounds a bird with his paint gun. Adoption makes things no better — perhaps even worse, because you cannot even vouch for where the sperm and egg came from, and because the essentially parasitic nature of children is clearer. You give to them; they take from you; repeat. Esther's foreignness and intellectual superiority only bring out further the problem with children: they are younger and therefore more powerful than you, and will supplant you. Still, you cannot help but be attached to your children, natural or adopted — you are genetically driven to behave that way — and this is the other problem: the children are vulnerable. They can be cut down at any time. Jessica is stillborn, Daniel and Max are menaced by Esther, and Esther is eventually destroyed.

To make things worse, an entire social and political system has been constructed to make sure that parents — especially mothers — devote their lives to these creatures, their children, and take the blame for whatever goes wrong. The upper middle-class world of the Colemans is largely child-centered, from its lavish school playground to the vast rooms of the children to the sculptured treehouse in the Colemans' yard. John and Kate are stuck in an unhappy marriage that they have kept going probably for the sake of the children. When a psychiatrist is consulted, Kate is blamed for the tensions she is having with Esther; no blame accrues to Esther, because children in this child-centric society are too innocent to be blamed. Parents are to blame, and mothers especially. Mothers have to look out for themselves, because no one else will. *In a family, everyone's interests are mortally opposed.*

The movie does not side only with Kate; Esther gets some sympathy. Yes, Esther is a sadistic killer, but she is psychologically confused, is a masochist who breaks her own arm to get pity from John, exhibits most of the energy in the movie, and is in danger for her own life when Kate comes after her. At one point, she is even outnumbered, when Max holds a gun while Esther and Kate wrestle. From her point of view, Esther is only trying to do the same thing as Kate and everyone else in the family: look after her own interests. She is trying to muscle her siblings out of the way so she gets all the parental care. She wants to mate with her adoptive father, perhaps to produce a child of her own. She kills anyone who threatens to expose her or stop her. It may seem extreme behavior, but it is just following the same principle as Kate and everyone else. *In a family, everyone's interests are mortally opposed.*

Kate and Esther finally clash in frank mortal opposition on the icy pond. Esther, about to drown in the frigid water, pleads for her life, and makes the mistake of calling Kate "Mommy." Kate responds, "I'm not your fucking mother" and kicks Esther back into the water, where she sinks out of sight. To give credit where it is due, a few years earlier in *The Ring Two* (2005), Rachel (Naomi Watts) used a similar line, with similar import, when dealing with a ghost child: "I'm not your fucking mommy!"

Two sets of images are working in that last scene of *Orphan*: freezing/thawing and birth/death. Set in winter, the entire movie has featured snowy, ice-encrusted landscapes, a symbol of the frozen state of a society in which the virtue of everything is measured by what good it does for the children. It is fitting that Kate and Esther, during the fight, break through the ice, symbolically breaking through the surface of their frozen society. Underground and underwater places are hidden places, where, symbolically, we put the thoughts we do not want to look at everyday, and it is in an underwater place that this symbolic final battle between a mother and child take place. This is what parents and children alike do not want to face—their own desire to kill each other. When Kate gets to the surface, she does face it with respect to Esther. By saying, "I'm not your fucking mother," she forsakes the child and implicitly forsakes the entire process of impregnation and child-rearing—both the fucking and the resulting motherhood.

At the end of the battle, Kate kicks Esther back into the hole in the ice, into the watery depths. In so doing, she symbolically reverses the birth process, sending this child back into a version of the birth canal, erasing what she did at the beginning of the movie—give birth to a stillborn baby—and also, by extension, erasing her other births, of Daniel and Max. She comes out of the fight an unencumbered woman, no longer a mother, a successful rebel against the system of having families.

But then there is Max. Max is waiting for her on the ice, and Daniel is back at the hospital. Naturally, Kate embraces Max, and it can be expected she will embrace Daniel. The police finally arrive, in one of those post–climactic police arrivals that happen in movies just after the hero has defeated the villain in single combat. Under the conservative rules of the horror movie, the subversion is stopped, the social system is restored, and Kate returns to being a model mother. But for a brief time—the space of the movie—the desire to kill one of her children, with her child's desire to kill her, was revealed. Even now it is not entirely suppressed. Over the closing credits images play of Esther and her macabre artworks, suggesting the continued presence of the DDB. The significance is that the family is still a dangerous place, despite the momentary resolution of conflict. *In a family, everyone's interests are mortally opposed.*

The Persistence of Significance

It has long been noticed that a director often exhibits similar themes from one movie to the next. Less often noticed is the ease with which even a production company can repeat its favorite significance.

The year after *Orphan's* release, its production company (Dark Castle Entertainment), studio (Warner Bros.), and executive producer (Joel Silver) released a film that was superficially very different: *Splice* (2010). Unlike *Orphan*, this horror film had a strong science fiction strain; it involved the genetic engineering of Dren, a female creature with elements of human, bird, and reptile, with disastrous results. The directors were also different: Jaume Collet-Serra for *Orphan*; Vincenzo Natali for *Splice*.

Even so, in many ways *Splice* was a repeat of *Orphan*; as one Web site declared, "It's like this year's *Orphan*, but with more slime!"[12] Like Esther in *Orphan*, Dren is "adopted" into a human family (a couple of co-habiting scientists, Elsa and Clive), where she proves dangerous and unpredictable, even to the point of seducing Clive, just as Esther tried to seduce John, and killing Clive, just as Esther killed John. In the end, Dren turns male, rapes Elsa, and leaves her pregnant — a bit of science fiction magic that would not have been possible for Esther. But in general, at least part of the significance of *Splice* is the same as that of *Orphan*: *In a family, everyone's interests are mortally opposed*.

The wonder of the horror movie is that it can take a subversive thought like this — *in a family, everyone's interests are mortally opposed*, a plausible, probably common but widely suppressed thought, a thought that would spell species suicide if it led everyone to stop having families — and bring it to the forefront. What makes it possible is the DDB. By embodying all the suppressed material that was earlier described (childhood sex and violence, adult-child ambiguity, family danger, adopted children, above-average children, foreigners, women, the lower classes), the DDB Esther in *Orphan* is both pleasing as a new subtype (evil child-woman) of an existing horror movie form (the evil child) and significant as the expression of an otherwise suppressed thought. The significance is coherent and forceful, and both bizarre enough and sufficiently connected to the real world to be interesting. Because it leads in several directions of inquiry (e.g., evolution, childhood sex, class structure), it is potentially fruitful, though whether it is actually fruitful will depend on whether it is followed up by later criticism.

8
Evaluation of a Good Horror Film

An important aspect of horror film criticism is evaluation, the judgment of a horror film's aesthetic or artistic worth. It is usually the first question a friend will ask when you disclose that you have seen a new movie: "How was it?" or "Did you like it?" or "Was it any good?"—all ways of saying, "What was its aesthetic worth?"

DDB theory is grounded in a teleologic view of art, in which the decisive fact about a work of art is its purpose. This holds in evaluating horror films. When evaluating any human-made thing, the first question to ask is: What is it for? A hammer, for example, is for pounding nails. The next question is: How well does it achieve its purpose? A hammer that pounds nails well is evaluated as good, one that does so poorly as bad. Similarly, when aesthetically evaluating a horror film, the first question to ask is: What is it for? DDB theory provides the answer: a horror film exists for presenting a DDB. The next question is: How well does this horror film present a DDB? To answer this, one must ask three subquestions:

1. Does the film's DDB make a strong overall impression?
2. Does the film do a good job handling the essential elements of horror films?
3. Does the film have a coherent and forceful significance?

If the answer to all these questions is yes, the film is a good horror film. If the answer to most or all of these questions is no, the film is probably bad. Such an approach differs from that of most movie reviews in its theoretical basis and systematic inquiry. Personal preferences and allegations regarding "scariness," the substance of much of what passes for aesthetic evaluation of horror films, are minimized.

To show how this type of DDB-based evaluation is done, I have selected two movies to judge critically: *Bride of Frankenstein* and *The Fly II* (1989). I have chosen these two not at random, but for their usefulness as illustrations

The bride (Elsa Lanchester) and the Frankenstein monster (Boris Karloff) touch hands in *Bride of Frankenstein* (1935, Universal).

of opposite ends of the aesthetic spectrum. In fact, I consider *Bride* the best horror movie ever made and *Fly II* the worst. I do not intend to defend these superlatives—with the large degree of subjectivity involved even in a DDB-based evaluation, proving a movie is best or worst is a hopeless endeavor. But I do intend to show why, according to DDB theory, *Bride* is a very good horror film, and *Fly II* a very bad one.

Even with these limited aims, there may be some objections. *Bride* may be regarded as not scary enough even to be considered as a very good horror movie. And it is true that there are scarier films. But DDB theory does not depend on scariness as the main measure of a horror film's worth: presentation of the DDB is primary. As for *Fly II*, some might object that it is not bad enough to merit discussion as a very bad film. Why not, for example, *Plan 9 from Outer Space* (1959)? Indeed, there are many horror films, such as *Plan 9*, that are much worse than *Fly II* in the sense of being ludicrously incompetent. But the problem is that many of these movies are so bad they're good: their very ludicrousness makes them comically entertaining. For that reason, *Plan 9* is a cult classic, and on Rotten Tomatoes' Tomatometer (a popular Web measure of film worth based on critics' reviews), it squeaks by into freshness (goodness) with a critical rating of 62 percent.[1] In contrast, *Fly II* gets a low 27 percent on the Tomatometer, less than half that of *Plan 9* and far lower than the perfect 100 percent of *Bride*. The key is that *Fly II* has just enough good qualities to put it in the running for mediocre, and just enough bad ones to make it not even that. It is bad enough to be a chore to watch, but not bad enough to be fun.

There is one other reason to examine these two films together: they are both sequels. Therefore, no one can say I am judging *Fly II* too harshly just because it is a sequel to the 1986 remake of *The Fly*, or giving *Bride* too much credit for topping its great predecessor *Frankenstein* (although it did). *Fly II* is bad in part because of how poorly it compares to its original, and *Bride* is good in part because of how well it compares to its, but both had the opportunity to measure up to their originals. In any case, they ultimately stand or fall as horror films in their own right.

In this chapter, I will evaluate *Bride of Frankenstein*; in the next, *The Fly II*.

Overall Impression of DDBs

To evaluate *Bride of Frankenstein* aesthetically (for a plot summary, see Chapter Two), the main question to ask is how well does it present a DDB. This issue is complicated because, as explained in Chapter Two, *Bride* has three DDBs: the Frankenstein monster, Pretorius, and the bride. All three must be well presented for the movie to work, and all have to be mutually reinforcing and united almost into one monster, or they will seem disconnected from each other and therefore weaker. This was a problem in later films of the Frankenstein series, such as *House of Frankenstein* (1944), in which Dracula almost seemed to inhabit a different movie from the Frankenstein monster and the Wolf Man.

Do the film's three DDBs make a strong overall impression? To specify what this means, it is well to apply the horror-film aesthetic virtues proposed in Chapter Three for the evaluation of deformity and destructiveness displays. Such displays, after all, are what most define a DDB, so the criteria used to evaluate them should also be useful for evaluating the DDB as a whole. By those criteria, a DDB makes a good impression if it seems plausible, original, memorable, coherent, and horrifying.

In Chapter 3, these criteria were applied to the face of the Frankenstein monster as presented in *Frankenstein*, and, by those standards, that face — the work of actor Boris Karloff, makeup artist Jack Pierce, and director James Whale — was shown to make a strong impression. With Karloff, Pierce, and Whale renewing their collaboration in *Bride*, it continues to make a strong impression, as do other characteristics carried over from the first film — the shambling gait, the long arms with scarred wrists, the proletarian suit ("labourer's clothes," as Wood described them),[2] the height and bulk, the superhuman strength, and the mutely expressed mix of wonder, rage, and loneliness. If *Bride* did nothing but repeat all this, it would have had a monster that was effective but not original. Instead *Bride* makes the monster original by developing him in plausible ways.

The monster is physically different, his face scorched and clothes tattered in the windmill fire, his hair burned short, revealing metal clamps at the top of his forehead we had not seen before. These increase the weird sense that he is part mechanical, and remind us of the way he was stitched together from dead parts. The monster's cheeks appeared sunken in the first film, but are more robust in the second film, making him look even stronger despite the efforts to destroy him.

Still more impressive are the monster's behavioral and personality changes, all motivated by what we know of him. He learns to talk — not well, but in character, in a gruff monster talk limited to a few words. We knew from *Frankenstein* that he could understand words — he sat when commanded to sit — and he does have human parts, so it follows he could learn to speak. He discovers that he wants friends. He already sort of knew it, when he played with little Maria in *Frankenstein*, but now it is a driving force. And he wants a bride — something he had only fleetingly snatched at in the first film, when he invaded Elizabeth's bedroom, but now is a live option.

And yet despite what might be considered humanizing tendencies, the Frankenstein monster has kept his destructiveness — in fact, he is worse, both more cold-blooded and more prone to rage. In his first scene in *Bride*, he kills Maria's parents, as if it were not enough for him to kill Maria in the first movie. He kills another child — a first communionite, no less — while rampaging through the streets, beats or kills various other villagers, murders one of Pretorius's henchmen, and abducts the long-suffering Elizabeth. He finally blows up the castle containing him and the other DDBs, an act of destruction that is significant for his development in two ways. Though driven by rage, the act requires cold premeditation, because the lever that blows up the castle is a mechanical device that must be grasped and pulled for anything to happen. And it involves selection, because the monster decides to spare Henry and Elizabeth while destroying the DDBs. The monster had never before been so technical and so charitable in his destructiveness.

Thus the Frankenstein monster in *Bride* is a fresh development of the character in the first film. He is plausible, because all the new developments seem like organic outgrowths of the monster as first presented in *Frankenstein*. He is original, because so much is new about him. He is memorable, a fact that can be established by the accessibility of this characterization to parody, from *Young Frankenstein* (1974) to the "Tonto, Tarzan, and Frankenstein" skits on *Saturday Night Live*. He is coherent, because the new developments all fit together with each other and with the character inherited from *Frankenstein*. And he is horrifying, because he is, in some respects, even more deformed and destructive than before.

The other DDBs in *Bride* are easier to evaluate because they are original to the movie. Dr. Pretorius is biologically an ordinary human being, and therefore makeup effects are not needed to render him plausible. The plausibility is all in how his part is written and how he performs it. Ernest Thesiger is believable in this part. Born to the British aristocracy, Thesiger carries an amused, tyrannical bearing that fits the character, and his face, manner, and action are suited to a mad scientist.

Pretorius is original, because although there had been mad scientists before him, there had never been one with quite his motivations. Whereas Frankenstein in *Frankenstein* had wanted to create life for the sake of expanding knowledge, Pretorius wants to create life for essentially aesthetic reasons— the creation of life is "enthralling"; the homunculi he creates and keeps in jars are evaluated for their aesthetic qualities (a tiny ballerina is "charming, but such a bore"). He likes death for the same aesthetic reasons— he sits laughing alone in a crypt with a skull for company, apparently out of sheer amusement. Pretorius transmits various signals that coded for gay at that time, such as effeminacy, the suggestion of various "weaknesses" (each of them, such as gin and cigars, characterized as his "only weakness"), and the disapproving looks he casts at Elizabeth for interfering with his scenes with Henry. Homosexuality, aestheticism, and aristocratic decadence all fit together nicely in the 1930s, but packaging all of that with being a mad scientist wanting to create life made for an original cocktail. Yet it all makes sense; the pieces reinforce each other psychologically. A gay man who could not father children directly might want to create life another way; aesthetes are interested in creation; aristocracy gets what it wants. Hence Dr. Pretorius acts as he does, a coherent personality.

Pretorius is not horrifying to look at, but his actions are horrifying, chiefly because of his lack of conscience. He uses Henry, Elizabeth, the Frankenstein monster, the bride, his homunculi — everyone for his own ends of aesthetic pleasure. When a fresh heart is needed to finish his bride, he orders the murder of a girl to procure one. Pretorius is a sociopath of art.

Pretorius has not been embraced by subsequent mass culture the way the Frankenstein monster has, but he is well known to the subculture of people who like old horror movies. An editorial comment accompanying Elizabeth Stein's article on Pretorius in *Horror-Wood Webzine* describes him as "one of the best-rendered 'mad scientists' in the classic horror film genre. We confess to a real fondness for him — it's our only weakness..."[3] The allusion to one of Pretorius's catchphrases suggests how memorable this character is.

The bride does not have much time to be memorable. She is onscreen for only a few minutes, at the climax. Yet she has had remarkable staying power in popular culture. With her Nefertiti cone of frizzy black hair, emblazoned

88   Part I: The Horror Film Analyzed

Inspiration for *Bride of Frankenstein* (1935, Universal): Inventor Rotwang (Rudolf Klein-Rogge) prepares to transform his robot into a copy of Maria (Brigitte Helm, on table) in *Metropolis* (1927, UFA).

on both sides with white lightning strikes, her attractive face, discreet scars, and white bridal gown, she is a perennial of parodies and costume parties. Without having uttered a line onscreen, she is even today widely recognized as the bride of Frankenstein. Due to Pierce's expert makeup and Elsa Lanchester's studied performance, the bride is plausible. To produce her screams at the sight of the monster, the actress said she was inspired by the sounds of swans hissing, which gave her an unearthly yet animalistically grounded sound that seemed believably monstrous.[4] She is original, too. No one had depicted a bride of the Frankenstein monster on film before; even in the novel *Frankenstein*, the source for the idea of the bride, the female monster is destroyed before being brought to life. The closest cinematic creature to her until that moment is the robotic woman in the science fiction film *Metropolis* (1927), who is variously metallic and human-looking; the bride bears some resemblance to her, but with her own scarred, Gothic look.[5] One of the most original touches is having the same actress, Lanchester, play both Mary Shelley and the bride. It deepens the significance of the bride, suggesting a kind of fantastic equivalence between author and creation.

The bride is horrifying, because although she is not hideous, she is scarred, has strange hair, and moves with an odd, jerky motion. And her rejection of the monster sets into motion the final destruction of the castle at the hands of the monster. Her aspect and action are coherent: newly created from human parts, it makes sense that she would do what most of the other humans do when confronted with the monster: scream.

So all three of the DDBs meet the aesthetic criteria for DDBs who make a strong overall impression. In addition, the three together fit into a tripartite whole, unified around the idea of the bride. Pretorius conceives of the bride and wants to create her; the Frankenstein monster wants the bride for himself and helps Pretorius create her; the bride, once created, does not want the Frankenstein monster, shattering the alliance between Pretorius and the Frankenstein monster. The dynamism of these three monsters creates an overall impression even stronger than that of the individuals.

The Five Essential Elements

The next question to ask is whether *Bride* does a good job handling the five essential elements of horror films. The answer is yes. Regarding "Subordination in principle of all story components to the presentation of the DDB" (element 1), *Bride* has long been admired for being a stellar example of studio crafts working in harmony to create an effective whole. "In terms of acting, direction, photography, set design, editing and overall presentation, the film is close to flawless," write the film historians Michael Brunas, John Brunas, and Tom Weaver.[6] The most important element, Karloff's reprise of his part as the Frankenstein monster, drew this comment from the *New York Times* critic: "Mr. Karloff is so splendid in the rôle that all one can say is 'he is the Monster.'"[7] Among the other elements to note are the plot that balances the three DDBs (see the discussion of *Bride's* plot in Chapter Two), giving each sufficient but not excessive screentime; Franz Waxman's magnificent score, which filled a gap left over from the scoreless *Frankenstein*; the clean and convincing special effects used to achieve Pretorius's homunculi; and the beautiful, mock-pastoral waterfall set where the monster saves a shepherd girl from drowning, only to be shot for his trouble.

This is not to say that the subordination of elements is perfect. *Bride* strives throughout to balance horror and humor, and sometimes the scale slips too far toward humor. Minnie the maid's comic antics can be irritating, and there may be a little too much of hysterical tone and frenzied pacing.

The deformity and destructiveness displays by the DDB (elements 2 and 3) have already been noted in the discussion of overall impression. Two specific examples will suggest how well these displays are accomplished. When the bride is unveiled, her face is viewed from several angles, in a series of quick cuts, increasing the drama of the deformity display. When the Frankenstein monster first appears, he emerges slowly from shadows under the wreckage of the windmill, intensifying the menace of the destructiveness display as he kills Maria's father. Yet again, there is room for criticism. Many of the destructiveness displays in *Bride* are not given quite enough time to horrify; they are rushed, without much building of suspense. This is one reason *Bride* is not as scary as it has the potential to be.

The account of the DDBs indicating that the deformity causes the destructiveness (element 4) is communicated almost effortlessly: through synopsis of the Frankenstein monster's history in the teaser, and through our observation of Pretorius and the bride in the subsequent action. There are normals who stir our sympathy and are attacked or menaced by the DDBs (element 5), including Maria's parents, the first communicant, and Elizabeth and Henry, although sympathy for at least some of the victims (such as the first communicant) could have been increased by allowing us to get to know them better.

Coherent and Forceful Significance

As discussed in Chapter 7, a film's significance is indeterminate, and yet one wants a good horror film to have some kind of significance, even if there will never be agreement about it. One wants to be able to think about the DDB presentation as well as witness it and feel about it. For the significance to have an impact, it must make sense — be coherent — and it must be forceful. And so, the ability of viewers to find coherent and forceful significance in a horror film is part of what makes it good.

Bride has been much studied over the years, and critics have discovered various kinds of significance in it. Elizabeth Young analyzed it in terms of gender and race,[8] Gary Morris as a sustained "homosexual joke" on "heterosexual communities."[9] Though the theory of objective interpretation does not require that just one reading of significance be correct, it is possible to conclude that one reading is more or less useful than another, because it provides a more fruitful range of significance while remaining closer to the film. By these criteria, *Bride* is best understood as signifying that DDBs are desirable. This claim may seem suspicious, as if I am reading into my proposed best horror film the essentials of DDB theory, but that is what significance does: connect the film to the world in novel ways. In any case, this is putting the situation backward. *Bride* was one of the sources from which DDB theory was developed, and one of the film's virtues is that it reflects so trenchantly on the nature of horror films even while being itself an exemplary horror film.

Throughout *Bride*, characters express their preference for deformity, destructiveness, or both. It begins in the teaser, when Lord Byron praises Mary Shelley's novel *Frankenstein* by saying, "I take great relish in savoring each separate horror." Mary follows up by volunteering to tell the story of what happened next—"I feel like telling it." The drive toward DDBs begins with the first people to tell and hear the story.

The normals around the burning windmill, gawking at the destructiveness, take obvious pleasure in it. Minnie the maid praises the fire in aesthetic terms, saying, "Well, I must say that's the best fire I ever saw in all me life." Maria's father, with his thirst for revenge, is all too eager to see the blackened bones of the monster. Henry is still thinking wishfully about creating life, and Elizabeth is seeing a horrible phantom that is not there. When the Frankenstein monster is briefly captured, the peasants gape at him through the jailhouse window.

Thus, nearly all the normals in the movie are obsessed with monsters, deformity, and destructiveness. And the monsters are no different in their obsessions. When the Frankenstein monster breaks free, he takes refuge in a blind hermit's house. Though the relationship between these two men has sometimes been suggested to be homosexual,[10] what is more important is that the blind man, too, is deformed. We may not normally think of blindness as a deformity, but in DDB theory it is, because it is a defect in the form the species essence ought to have. In a mole, it would not be a deformity; in a man, it is. Therefore, when the hermit and the monster meet, it is a meeting of two deformed people, and the match could not be better. Because of his blindness, the old man cannot see the monster's hideousness and react with horror as all the normals do. And because of his hideousness, the monster has been unable to make any friends, and desperately wants one. So does the blind man, who is lonely at least in part because of his blindness. The blind man points out that the monster cannot speak, and suggests that this deformity can bring them together. But what really does it is the combination of blindness on one side and hideousness on the other.

So the two become friends and live together a while, with the monster listening in rapture to the hermit's violin music and learning from him how to speak—two kinds of music, both marks of civilization, the music of instruments and of conversation. Each party has cause to love the other's deformity, because it is the mutually compatible deformity that makes them friends. Even destructiveness becomes a comfortable part of daily life. The hermit knows how to use fire to cook and smoke—he has harnessed destructiveness—and he begins to teach the monster not to fear fire, until now a form of destructiveness that has panicked him. The hermit and the monster, who restrains his own destructive power in the hermit's cottage, have formed a community of deformed and destructive beings, with their destructiveness peacefully contained.

The sojourn ends when two normals come along, a pair of lost hunters, and with their hatred of DDBs (masking, as we have seen, a perverse fascination with DDBs) unleash the dormant destructive forces and start a fire that separates the monster and the hermit. However, now that he has done it once, the monster seems to have found the knack of how to make friends: look for other deformed people. He finds one in the crypt where Pretorius sits alone, laughing about death. Pretorius's deformity is of the mind, and it is his warped mind that allows him to find just the right thing to say when the monster appears. Pretorius does not scream, run, or fight; he looks at the monster calmly and says, "I thought I was alone." The priceless phrase has a double meaning: Pretorius is politely acknowledging the arrival of company, and he is implicitly suggesting that until meeting the monster, he thought there was no one else like him in the world, no one with his taste for death. Pretorius and the monster agree that they both prefer the dead to the living, and they become friends. Their mutual goal is to piece together a woman to be the monster's mate. Once again, and more fatefully than in the hermit's cottage, DDBs have expressed the same interest in DDBs that drives normals as well.

Bride's interest in DDBs reaches to cosmic suggestions about why DDBs are important. Pretorius toasts Henry with the words, "To a new world of gods and monsters!" Why does he include gods? Is it because the scientists are going to act like God in creating life? Or is it that God, in creating life, acts like a scientist—like a maker of DDBs? According to evolutionary theory, as suggested in Chapter One, everything that lives owes its existence to deformation and destruction — one form evolves from another form that may have to be destroyed to make way, and still other forms—food sources and rivals— become threatened by the superior fitness of the newly evolved DDB. According to DDB theory, DDBs are desirable in part because they mimic this process, the natural method by which beings become existent. With regard to his homuncili and the bride's brain, Pretorius suggests that all he is doing is following the lead of nature, growing his creations from seeds, like cultures. *Bride* is not only showing the desirability of DDBs, but hinting at the DDB theory of why DDBs are desirable.

The theological strand continues in the much noted Christ imagery in the film. The Frankenstein monster is trussed up by the villagers in a pose similar to that of Christ crucified, and there are crucifixes large and small throughout the film. This has led many viewers to think that the monster is supposed to be Christ-like,[11] when what is more significant is that Christ is supposed to be monster-like. Christ, after all, is both God and man, making him a positionally deformed DDB, hybrid variety. Through Christ all things were created: he was the DDB through which all living things— all of them in a sense, DDBs—came to be. In his final battle Christ dies a horrible death, like other DDBs. But there is a frisson — the rising from the dead — and a promised destructive sequel: he will come back and judge the living and the dead, sending the damned to their fate in hell.

Why does God create DDBs? Could it be for the same aesthetic reasons that drive Pretorius— he likes how they look? But of course he likes how they

8. Evaluation of a Good Horror Film

look: he made them in his image. If they are DDBs, so is he. By the Christian account, God too is deformed — three beings in one, much like the tripartite monster of the Frankenstein monster, Pretorius, and the bride. No wonder Pretorius says he follows God's lead in his creative efforts, and Henry, too, compares himself to God as creator in seeking "the secret God is so jealous of." Even the hermit who prays to God, thanking him for sending him the Frankenstein monster as a companion, credits God as the source of DDBs.

Thus, in its quest to convey the desirability of DDBs, *Bride* reaches to the cosmic level, suggesting that the desiring and making of deformed, destructive beings runs as deep as nature itself, and perhaps deeper than that into the metaphysical foundations of the universe. But it also stays at the personal level, the level of the audience, which delights in the DDBs presented to it. This is also the level of the Frankenstein monster, who desires his own DDB, his bride, so that he can delight in her. In the supreme irony, it turns out he cannot have her, because even though she is a DDB, she thinks like a normal. She screams at him as all the normals do; she does not want him, and wants instead her handsome normal creator, Henry. Her destructiveness is precisely in her taste for the normal — the ultimate deformity for a DDB.

The Frankenstein monster realizes there is only one way to achieve his community of DDBs: they must all die. As he should have learned in the hermit's cottage, that is the fate of DDBs; they are too destructive to stay at peace with one another. When he urges Henry and Elizabeth to leave the castle and live, he is only in part being charitable. In larger part, he is rejecting them — excluding them. They have no business in the community of DDBs.

Once the Frankenstein monster destroys the castle, the film ends with Henry and Elizabeth. But there is no great satisfaction in being with them. They were not what brought us to see the film; we desired the DDBs. Henry, Elizabeth, and we, and all the other normals, are all grown from a heritage of DDBs, and we want to see more. But for that we will have to wait for the next horror film. That is the significance of *Bride*: that DDBs are desirable, and for that reason we see films like *Bride*.

Perhaps because of its enduring significance, *Bride of Frankenstein* has had a strong and lasting influence. A simple example of this is how it transformed the previously more or less innocent word "bride" into a horror term that, placed in the right context, suggests mayhem. The proof of this influence can be seen in the succession of horror films since *Bride of Frankenstein* that include *Bride* in their title. There was *Bride of the Gorilla* (1951), then *Bride of the Monster* (1955), *The Brides of Dracula*, *Bride of Re-Animator* (1990), and *Bride of Chucky* (1998). There was even a loose sequel to *Bride of Frankenstein* called *The Bride* (1985), with Sting as Frankenstein and Jennifer Beals as the Bride. In this version, both the bride and the monster survive the destruction of the laboratory in the opening sequence, and eventually end up together after the villainous Frankenstein dies.

In *Bride of Chucky* (1998, Universal), a film influenced by *Bride of Frankenstein* (1935, Universal), Tiffany (Jennifer Tilly) resurrects the psychopathic doll Chucky, whose bride she will become.

Sometimes these movies carried through the original conceit of giving a monster a bride, as when Chucky, the evil doll in the series that began with *Child's Play* (1988), gets a love interest doll of his own in *Bride of Chucky*, a film that even features a clip from *Bride of Frankenstein* and a quote of the line "We belong dead," to acknowledge the influence. Sometimes the plots are only loosely connected to their titles: *The Brides of Dracula* does feature young women transformed into vampires by a male vampire, but Count Dracula is nowhere to be seen; David Peel as Baron Meinster fills in for him. The films vary in quality, with *The Brides of Dracula* pretty good, *Bride of the Monster* so bad it's good, and *Bride of Re-Animator* just bad. But regardless of quality, horror films of the future are likely to retain "bride" in their vocabulary, because *Bride of Frankenstein* made it a horror term.

Summary of Evaluation

By every standard, *Bride of Frankenstein* is at least a very good horror film, and perhaps the best. Its overall presentation of the DDBs is excellent, its handling of the five essential elements is generally superb, and its significance is profound, delving into the nature of horror films, DDBs, God, and all living things. *Bride* has flaws—chiefly the overly comic and insufficiently horrific tone—but the film as a whole is so good it would be hazardous to wish such flaws corrected, since that might inadvertently spoil the exquisite overall presentation of the DDBs.

9

Evaluation of a Bad Horror Film

Having examined the artistic value of a very good horror film, I now consider a very bad one, perhaps the worst ever: *The Fly II*. Even though this film differs greatly in quality from *Bride of Frankenstein*, the same critical method used to assess the aesthetic worth of *Bride* is applied to this film, and rightly so. To be useful, a method of aesthetic evaluation should be applicable even before one knows the value of the film in question, and that means it has to be consistently applied regardless of what one might suspect in advance about the film. As with *Bride*, the basic question about *Fly II* is how well does it present a DDB. To answer that question, one needs to assess the overall impression of the DDB, how well the film handles the five essential elements, and whether the film has a coherent and forceful significance.

In the tradition of the original *Fly* (1958) and the remake (1986), the subject of *Fly II* is teleportation and the mishaps that can result. In *Fly II*, picking up shortly after the end of the 1986 *Fly* (whose plot was summarized in Chapter Four), Ronnie gives birth to Seth Brundle's son, Martin, who shares his father's fly genes. Ronnie dies in childbirth and Martin, who looks human and grows at an accelerated rate, is raised by Bartok Industries, the company that funded his father's teleportation experiments. Under the eye of company owner Bartok, the firm is continuing research into the telepods that transformed Martin's father into a monster. Martin makes friends with a laboratory dog that the telepods also turn into a monster; when Martin learns the unfortunate animal is being kept alive for study, he euthanizes it. Martin falls in love with Beth, a Bartok employee, and the two have sex. Shortly afterward, Martin's fly genes are activated and he is transformed into a homicidal flylike monster. Having discovered that he can become normal if he goes through the telepods with a normal human being, but that the normal person will then become a monster, Martin seizes Bartok and drags him into a telepod. With Beth's help, teleportation is successful, Martin becomes normal, and Bartok becomes a disabled monster who is kept alive for study as the dog was.

In the original version of *The Fly* (1958, 20th Century–Fox), Andre Delambre (Al Hedison) was the scientist studying teleportation, and Helene Delambre (Patricia Owens) his wife.

Overall Impression of the DDB

How is the overall impression of Martin, the DDB of *Fly II*? Is Martin plausible, original, memorable, coherent, and horrifying? Martin is presented in several stages, each of which has to be considered separately before considering them as a whole:

1. newborn
2. as played by child actors (Matthew Moore, Harley Cross)
3. as played by the teenage Eric Stoltz without creature makeup
4. creature in transformation makeup
5. fully-formed creature (commonly known as Martinfly)

The newborn is not original. Almost the same scene was played as a dream sequence in the 1986 *Fly*, with the main differences being the actress who played Ronnie (the more accomplished Geena Davis in the original; lookalike Saffron Henderson in the sequel) and the appearance of the newborn. In the original, the newborn looked like a larva, a white, wormlike thing that made biological sense as the offspring of a fly. In the sequel, the newborn makes no

Scientist Seth Brundle (Jeff Goldblum) studies his gradual transformation into Brundlefly in *The Fly* (1986, 20th Century–Fox).

sense. It has a monstrous exterior that cracks open to reveal a normal human-looking baby inside. This is neither plausible nor coherent: it is too good to be true, that deformity would be so neatly contained in an outer shell, apparent humanity in the inner core. One has the feeling that the film is trying to have it both ways: to represent Martin as superficially monstrous but inwardly human (this indeed is what the film later turns out to be seeking, to its own detriment). The creature is somewhat horrifying, but its monstrous appearance is too vague and jumbled to be memorable. So Martin's newborn phase makes only a weak overall impression.

During Martin's upbringing (as a child and teenager), he exhibits no DDB features other than accelerated growth and supposed high intelligence; he therefore has barely any DDBness to judge, and little in the way of personality traits to make him interesting. The accelerated growth itself, which makes him look like a teenager at the age of five, seems like a gimmick to avoid having to age the other actors with expensive aging makeup and to add changing fashions and décor while waiting for Martin to mature. With so many other implausible things going on, it is a bit much to ask the audience to swallow this too.

Once Martin starts transforming with the help of makeup effects, he begins to be visibly deformed, but he is not really destructive until his fully-formed Martinfly shape, which is achieved mainly through puppet effects. As he transforms he gets progressively uglier, as his father became in the 1986

Fly, but most of the stages in *Fly II* are not as memorable. The best bit of deformity display in *Fly II* is a night-time moment in a motel room where he is shot in blue light picking at cocoon threads and ranting in a deep voice about how he is getting "better" and "stronger." But even this scene suffers from an implausibility: Beth, to whom he is speaking, is shot in normal light, and one has to wonder what kind of motel supplies two different lighting schemes for people just a few feet away. Despite the potential for at least one good DDB impression, the effect is incoherence.

The fully-formed creature is Martin's last chance to make a strong DDB impression, and he blows it. A tall, skinny, lumpy thing the consistency of black oatmeal, the creature is hardly if ever seen in a full-body shot, probably to hide the weakness of the special effects, but what we see of it is an unoriginal successor to the fully-formed Brundlefly at the end of *Fly*. That creature successfully merged human characteristics (the eyes) with fly characteristics (the mandibles) to make a monster that could express emotion while being horrifying. The face of the creature in *Fly II* is such a molten mess that one can barely find the eyes or mouth, much less discern emotion in them. The monster is strong, fast, sprays acid vomit, and quickly accumulates a body count, but this DDB never rises to the level of horrifying, perhaps because its victims are so unlikable. Martinfly is vaguely plausible, but the lack of a clear pattern to its deformity makes it incoherent and unmemorable.

So Martin, the DDB in *Fly II*, fails at any stage to make a strong overall impression.

The Five Essential Elements

Of the five essential elements of horror films, element 5 (normals who stir our sympathy and are attacked or menaced by the DDB) is handled worst by *Fly II*. Most of the normals who are victims of the DDB in *Fly II* do not stir our sympathy, and the only two that do — the lab dog and Bartok — are instructive cases that will be dealt with presently. The other victims are all either unlikeable or have so few personality traits as to be unknown. Jainway and Shepard, two scientists who observe Martin growing up, are mean and snippy. Scorby, the security chief, is also mean, to the point of taunting Beth about having seen her have sex with Martin on a security tape. All three of these characters are killed by the DDB, and no tears are shed, because nobody likes them. A few other characters are killed in the mayhem, guards and a scientist, but these are unknowns, forgettable. One of these is a guard whose face is melted away by fly acid vomit, and although the gruesomeness of the death makes for a good destructiveness display, the lack of identifying characteristics for the guard — his facelessness *before* he lost his face — makes the incident seem more like a gratuitous stunt than like a motivated part of the story.

None of this is an accident. The makers of *Fly II* seem to have decided that Martin is a good monster who will only kill unlikeable or unknown people. During his rampage, Martinfly stops to pat a guard dog's head, and he never menaces Beth in any way. Like his newborn self, he is superficially monstrous but inwardly human. In keeping with horror movie ethics (Chapter Six), this allows him to be redeemed at the end and become human, a path available only to DDBs whose destructiveness is considered limited or excusable. The filmmakers want it both ways: Martin as a gore-producing DDB who nevertheless has a happy ending.

There are only two victims of Martin who might elicit any sympathy and get in the way of the happy ending: the lab dog and Bartok. When the lab dog is scrambled into dog mush and kept alive in monstrous agony and loneliness, Martin euthanizes him, and that is the DDB's first killing. But we excuse him for that, because we pity the dog. Thus, even when we are made to pity the victim, Martin is let off the hook, to make way for the happy ending.

Then there is Bartok, a megalomaniac corporate heel who thinks he answers only to God and lies freely to get his way. Despite Bartok's flaws, the actor who plays him, Lee Richardson, gives the best and most engaging performance in the cast, and Bartok is at least superficially nice to Martin. And, after all, he did not make Martin what he is: Martin's father did that. Bartok supervises the ill-fated teleportation of the dog, but Martin's father also teleported an animal (a baboon) and made baboon mush out of him, and no great fuss was raised about that. Nevertheless, Martin reserves for Bartok the most horrible fate of all his victims: he forces Bartok to go through the telepods with him and take on all of Martin's deformity, with none of his destructive power, and to spend the rest of his life alone with this deformity while Martin is normal.

Is this not overkill? Is not the punishment disproportionate to the crime? If so, then Martin does not deserve a happy ending, and the film's attempt to redeem him will collapse. The vehicle to try to avoid collapse is the torture of the dog. Audiences like and care more about dogs—especially a cute pet dog—than they do baboons, so we are expected to abhor whoever mistreated this dog. It was Bartok; therefore we are supposed to be glad when he suffers the dog's fate. But it does not work. For one thing, there is almost an iron law of movies that you never torture a cute pet dog. You can torture a man, you can kill a dog, but you cannot torture a friendly golden retriever to the point where its agony is apparent. *Fly II* loses its audience at the moment it does so. We do not blame Bartok, despite the film's efforts to assign blame there; we blame the film for defying movie ethics—not just horror movie ethics, but the ethics of movies in general.

During his transformation, Martin declares that it would be immoral to turn somebody else into a deformed hulk just to free himself of his bad genes. But once he has become Martinfly, he and Beth do exactly that with Bartok.

9. Evaluation of a Bad Horror Film 101

The fly-human hybrid Martinfly forces Bartok (Lee Richardson) to join him in a telepod in *The Fly II* (1989, 20th Century–Fox).

Because Bartok was mean to a dog, we are supposed to accept that this is morally permissible. But because we never fully accepted Bartok's blame for that — and because we know Martin is just looking for some way to get himself out of his curse — we do not accept Bartok's severe punishment or Martin's redemption. Just at the moment when we are supposed to feel happy for Martin, we are annoyed at him. He is worse than a DDB: he is a hypocrite, and the film is hypocritical too, trying to make us accept Martin and Beth as the happy-ending heterosexual couple when we just saw how ruthlessly they acted.

In the film's frisson, the misshapen remnant of Bartok looks at a fly on his supper dish, and we are supposed to conclude that a fly was the cause of all the trouble. But it was not the cause. The human characters of the *Fly* films were the cause. Seth Brundle in the 1986 *Fly* caused his own predicament, and the film acknowledged that. Martin turned Bartok into a hideous lump, but the film hypocritically forgets that and blames an insect. This is the most profound failure of *Fly II*, the thing that makes it a candidate for the worst horror film ever. It makes you feel too much sympathy for the wrong characters, and makes you regard the DDB not with horror but with contempt.

There is nothing wrong in principle with a horror film defying movie ethics. In *The Silence of the Lambs*, the pet dog of the serial killer Buffalo Bill is pulled into a shaft by a trapped victim of Buffalo Bill and, while it is held hostage, we are told its leg may be broken. In *Ringu* and *The Ring*, the heroine passes on the deadly curse of the videotape to innocent people to save her own child. But these atrocities are done with finesse. The broken leg of the dog and the horrible deaths of the cursed innocents are not shown; the desperate plight of the perpetrators is emphasized. Horror movie ethics can be bent and even broken, but if the bending and breaking are done ineptly, the result is *Fly II*.

Fly II handles most of the other essential elements of horror films as poorly as it does sympathy for normals. Element 1, subordination in principle of all story components to the DDB presentation, is routinely violated. The production values are good enough to pass for a major-studio-produced B film, but not good enough to support the presentation of the DDB. The music, for example, is generic, the lighting bland (except for the oddity of the blue monster, already noted), the production design cluttered and boringly corporate. As described, the script is a disaster in its efforts to figure out where the sympathy should go, and there are many dead spots where the story is just boring, such as most of Martin's childhood. Richardson's strong performance as Bartok helps to put the sympathy in the wrong place, while all the other actors range from mediocre (Stoltz) to bad (Daphne Zuniga as Beth, who is generally portrayed whimpering). Since director Chis Walas did the original creature effects for the 1986 *Fly* and does them again here, you would think at least the makeup and effects would be good. But with a few exceptions (blue monster), they are elaborate without being clear, convincing, or horrifying.

The deformity and destructiveness displays (elements 2 and 3) have already been shown to be wanting under the overall impression of the DDB. Even element 4, the account of the DDB indicating that deformity causes destructiveness, usually the easiest thing for a horror movie to get right, is handled badly in *Fly II*. Before Martin becomes the full-blown Martinfly, he spends a period incubating in a cocoon, during which time all of Bartok Industries waits for him to emerge in what they can expect to be a destructive form (to judge by his father). Nevertheless, they leave the cocoon in a room unattended except by a single scientist with her back to him and an open door leading unobstructed to the rest of the complex. Sure enough, Martinfly hatches from the cocoon, kills the scientist, and goes on his rampage. The deformity-destructiveness causal chain is clear, but it is undermined by the stupidity of Bartok's security precautions. And so needlessly. All the film would have needed to do is to isolate the cocoon under observation in a barred or shatterproof cage, and then show Martin emerge and rip apart the cage. His destructiveness would have been that much more effective.

Coherent and Forceful Significance

Fly II's last chance at horror movie redemption is if the viewer can at least generate from it significance that is coherent and forceful. But the film is too incoherent and weak for that.

The clearest message that can be drawn from the film is: *corporations are bad*. But this is a tired message that plays to a common prejudice without adding anything of interest. The message is particularly lame in view of the fact that *Fly II* was financed by a corporation, 20th Century–Fox (a subsidiary of Rupert Murdoch's mammoth News Corporation), for corporate financial gain. That is hypocrisy, not significance.

Less obvious, but perhaps more promising, is the significance: *sacrifice another person to save yourself.* That is what Martin does in sacrificing Bartok. It is not a moral message, but at least it is a suppressed thought that runs deep in a species built on self-preservation. In fact, if Martin had sacrificed a random person, or Beth, to save himself, as Brundlefly tried to do with Ronnie in the first movie, that would have been more interesting. But this message of naked self-interest is confused by the film's ludicrous justification that Bartok is sacrificed as payback for what he did to the dog. The message then becomes: *sacrifice a person to avenge a dog*. This is not even a suppressed thought — just a childish one. So the promise for a good dark significance to the film is lost in its vain efforts to make Martin look better than he is.

And so on with every other effort at generating significance from *Fly II*. For example, you could say that Martin and Beth represent sexual freedom, since they are the only people who have sex in the movie. Except that they have virtually no screen chemistry and they have a kind of maidenly horror at having a sex tape made of their exploits. Or you could say that Martin is an Oedipal figure, rebelling against a father figure, Bartok, whom he describes as "Dad." Except that Bartok is not his Dad; Seth Brundle was, and yet Martin looks adoringly at old tapes of Seth and seems not to blame him for anything. Martin is a low-rent Oedipus: idolizing the real father who got him into this jam, while rebelling against his fake father.

Fly II is just too confused to be significant, and this may account for the paucity of critical analysis it has inspired.

Summary of Evaluation

The Fly II is deeply bad because it presents a DDB very poorly. Its DDB makes a bad overall impression; the film makes hash of the five essential elements of horror films; and it is insignificant.

And yet it has fans. Scattered reviews on the Internet indicate that a few people are moved by the dog's plight and regard Bartok's fate as "poetic justice."[1] Some consider *Fly II* entertaining as a "cheesy monster flick."[2] There is no point trying to argue people out of their pleasures. I have pointed out certain bad aesthetic qualities in *Fly II*, based on measures that can be applied consistently across horror films and are grounded in a unifying theory of the genre, but if someone still likes the film, there is nothing more to say. It is possible that *Fly II* failed with me, and with many critics and audience members, because we were not the audience for it. The real audience were those who would experience it as cheesy fun (whereas I, for example, would look to *The Brain That Wouldn't Die* (1963) for cheesy fun) and would assign sympathy as the filmmakers intended. With this small group, *Fly II* found its audience.

Simplified Evaluation

The comprehensive analysis to which *Bride of Frankenstein* and *Fly II* have been subjected in this book may make it seem that the DDB method of aesthetic evaluation is too long and complex for everyday criticism. In fact, the method boils down to one question: How good is the monster? where "good" means aesthetically satisfying and the monster is understood as including not only the DDB itself but the extent to which it is supported by all the other story elements and generates significance. With this single criterion — "How good is the monster?" — horror movies can be quickly assessed, as will be seen in the following six capsule reviews:

- *The Brain That Wouldn't Die*: Woman's disembodied head in pan, allied with carrot-headed monster in closet, are funny, fake, and draw ludicrous support from normals, enough to make the film so bad it's good.
- *Dawn of the Dead*: Flesh-eating zombies plaguing small band of normals in shopping mall are scary, amusing, and sympathetic, with their attacks building to a great final battle and leaving a strong sense of social significance. A classic.
- *Frankenstein and the Monster from Hell* (1974): There is not enough of Peter Cushing's demonic Dr. Frankenstein and too much of his silly-looking, rotund furball of a monster. In this final entry of Hammer's Frankenstein series, the series peters out.
- *Hostel*: Torturers exhibit Gothic style and fiendish creativity, eastern Euro-

pean atmosphere is rich, and runaway victim Paxton (Jay Hernandez) is appropriately savage in his revenge. Worth seeing.
- *The Man with Nine Lives* (1940): Boris Karloff is typically good — both gentle and menacing — as mad scientist playing with cryogenics, but plodding pace and low intensity make this film mostly forgettable.
- *Dog Soldiers* (2002): Tall werewolves mostly kept in shadows are effective menaces as they surround and attack a houseful of soldiers, although the film is overly derivative of *Aliens* (1986) and *Night of the Living Dead*.

PART II: THE HORROR FILM IN CONTEXT

10
Genres

Until now, this book has focused on the analysis of horror films: their purpose, epistemology, profile, structure, elements, ethics, meaning and significance, and evaluation. They have been studied almost in a vacuum, as if the only thing that existed in the world were each individual horror film. Now a new part of the book begins, in which horror films are considered in a larger context, starting in this chapter with the position of horror films among other genres.

The system of film genres that we all know — westerns, musicals, comedies, horror films, and so on — is not an accident. It is a historical byproduct of a studio system that sought to maximize profits by repeating success.[1] Films are expensive to make and box-office revenues are uncertain, so if a certain film worked, studios tried to repeat that success by making a similar film. Thus, cycles of movies were born, and if a particular formula were sufficiently secure and long-lasting, it became a genre. Each genre worked because it somehow appealed to audiences: it gave them something they wanted. With horror films, it is apparent that what audiences want from the genre is the DDB. The genre is defined by its primary purpose, DDB presentation, the main thing filmmakers want to give and audience members want to take. Similarly, other film genres are classifiable teleologically, according to their primary purpose: each genre is defined by a principal thing filmmakers want to give and audience members want to take. As John Swales writes, "*The principal criterial feature that turns a collection of communicative events into a genre is some shared set of communicative purposes.*"[2]

The approach of distinguishing genres by their primary purpose offers a way of speaking about genres without becoming confused. Logically, a film cannot have more than one primary purpose; therefore, once you have ascertained what the primary purpose of the film is, you are able to define it solely in one genre, although it may have elements of other genres. Confusions born of speaking of multiple genres can be clarified. For example, if someone asks for a recommendation of a horror-comedy, you might suggest both *Ghostbusters* (1984) and *Re-Animator*. Yet the two hardly seem like members of the same class: the former is a funny romp peppered with wacky ghosts and demons; the latter is a gruesome splatterfest, laced with offbeat wit, about reanimating the dead. The difference is that *Ghostbusters* is a comedy with horror elements—a film whose primary purpose is to get laughs, and only secondarily to present DDBs—whereas *Re-Animator* is a horror film with comedy elements, a film whose primary purpose is to present a DDB and only secondarily to get laughs. The teleologic theory of genre that underlies this type of distinction is important in clarifying what belongs and does not belong in the horror genre, and understanding how horror characteristics in some films can be mixed with elements of other genres.

Almost any genre can be blended with horror. Occasionally, horror is mixed with history, as in *Tower of London* (1939), where Richard III and his executioner Mord are the DDBs; even more occasionally, it is mixed with the western, as in *Jesse James Meets Frankenstein's Daughter* (1966); most rarely of all, it is mixed with the musical, as in *The Rocky Horror Picture Show* (1975). But the genres that get the most intergeneric traffic with horror are science fiction, fantasy, crime, action, comedy, and romance. These will be considered in this chapter.

Not under consideration is the genre of thrillers, because it is not a real genre. Hanging conceptually on nothing but the idea of a movie that is thrilling, it can include any type of thrilling movie: *Jurassic Park* (1993), which is science fiction; the action movie *Goldfinger* (1964); the crime film *Pulp Fiction* (1994); and all horror films. Similarly, the suspense category, which can include any suspenseful movie of any genre but is usually associated with the work of Alfred Hitchcock, is not a genre. In this book, an effort is made to define genres by objective criteria that can be found on screen (e.g., the DDB in horror films) rather than by subjective criteria (thrills, suspense) that vary among audience members. The only exception is comedy, which is clearly a genre, but, as will be discussed later, is not presently ready to be defined objectively.

Genre is not the only way of categorizing movies. One can also speak of styles of film, such as film noir (discussed under crime films). Another example of a cinematic style is the indie film. "Indie" was originally short for independent, and it just meant a film that was made outside the big-budget constraints of the studio system. But it came to have connotations of a certain cinematic style: quirky, character driven, low key, and, of course, low budget. A horror example is *May* (2002), the story of a young woman, May (Angela Bettis), who is a perennial misfit with violent tendencies.

Science Fiction

Most genres can be defined loosely or strictly, depending on whether you want to include everything vaguely related to the genre or only its undeniable core members. The definition of horror films as having the primary purpose of DDB presentation is a strict definition; and indeed, for any strict definition of a genre, the teleologic language of "primary purpose" is useful.

The loose definition of a science fiction film is that its action is contingent on a postulated but not presently actual scientific discovery or creation. This definition includes many films that have science fiction elements but do not seem exactly like science fiction, such as *Superman* (1978) and *The Nutty Professor* (1963). A strict definition is that the primary purpose of a science fiction film is to present a world that is contingent on a postulated but not presently actual scientific discovery or creation, where "world" may be a society, a planet, a solar system, a galaxy, or the whole universe. This leaves out *Superman*: the primary purpose is to present Superman himself, not the world that is contingent on him. And *The Nutty Professor* is primarily about Jerry Lewis and his comic antics, not how society is altered as a result of his character's personality-changing formula.

Real science fiction films, strictly speaking, have as their main purpose the presentation of worlds. *2001: A Space Odyssey* (1968) might almost be thought a horror film, because its computer, the HAL 9000, which runs amok and kills several astronauts aboard a spaceship, is a clear example of a DDB. However, HAL is a subplot in *2001*; the primary purpose of the film is not to present him but to present the world of 2001, a world in which scientific discoveries (such as an alien monolith and a journey beyond the infinite) and creations (such as a moon base) that had not yet come to pass when the film was released in 1968 were actualities. Similarly, *Blade Runner* (1982), *Star Wars* (1977), and *Forbidden Planet* (1956) primarily exist to present their respective worlds—Los Angeles of the future; a galaxy far, far away; Altair IV—not the DDBs within them (respectively, replicants, Darth Vader, and the Monster from the Id).

This does not mean that horror films cannot benefit from the imaginative equipment that the science fiction genre can provide. The link between the two genres is strong: science fiction offers scientific discoveries and creations that are not actual; horror aims to present DDBs, beings that are not actual and are frequently fantastic, but must somehow be discovered or created. The postulated science of science fiction is the perfect mechanism to account for the origin of many fantastic DDBs. Accordingly, many horror films use science fiction to explain their DDBs, including *Frankenstein*, *The Thing from Another World* (1951), *Alien*, and *The Fly* (both versions). Because these films have the primary purpose of presenting a DDB, they are horror films, not (strictly speaking) science fiction films, but they have science fiction elements.

This distinction between horror and science fiction may clarify the status of two subcategories of films: the giant monster and alien invasion films of the 1950s. During this period, the DDBs of many films were oversized creatures created or discovered by science—giant ants in *Them!* (1954); a giant spider in *Tarantula* (1955); a giant dinosaur in *Gojira*. Other DDBs were invaders from outer space, such as in *Invasion of the Body Snatchers, It! The Terror from Beyond Space* (1958), or *I Married a Monster from Outer Space* (1958). Because scientific means were used to generate these menaces, Worland lumps all such movies as science fiction rather than horror,[3] and follows Vivian Sobchak in arguing that science fiction films involve a social, collective threat, whereas in horror the menace is personal and individual.[4] However, to the contrary, Worland includes in the horror genre films in which the monster is generated by scientific means, such as *Frankenstein* and *Alien*, making it inconsistent to exclude giant monster films and alien invasion movies just because the monsters were generated the same way. As for the claim about social vs. individual menace, that too is inconsistent. In *Frankenstein*, the monster threatens not only individuals but society as a whole, which is why the villagers try to burn him down in the windmill. And the Monster from the Id in *Forbidden Planet* threatens only one girl and the crew of one ship, no more than are endangered in *Alien*. Yet *Frankenstein* is generally a considered a horror film and *Forbidden Planet* a science fiction film.

The distinguishing question to ask of border-straddling horrific movies is whether their primary purpose is to present a DDB. That was the case with the giant monster movies of the 1950s; therefore they are horror movies. Alien invasion movies are different, and should be examined case by case. In *The Day the Earth Stood Still* (1951), the primary purpose is not to present a DDB but to present a scenario of world-changing effects based on an alien visit, making this science fiction. But in *Invasion of the Body Snatchers*, a horror film, the main interest is not presenting a world but presenting a DDB: the pods and the rapidly proliferating pod people.

Fantasy

When a horror film has a fantastic DDB that needs to be explained, there are two avenues of recourse: science fiction, as just described, and fantasy. In a fantasy movie, strictly defined, the primary purpose is to present a world contingent on non–natural and non–scientific mechanisms, such as magic and the supernatural. Horror films frequently borrow such mechanisms from the fantasy genre to account for the origin of DDBs like ghosts, demons, vampires, some zombies (those not explained through science fiction), and werewolves.

Fantasy films, strictly defined, include films such as *The Wizard of Oz* (1939), *The 7th Voyage of Sinbad* (1958), and the *Harry Potter* series. Few films are sufficiently close to the border between fantasy and horror for the issue of how to distinguish them to arise. In *The 7th Voyage of Sinbad*, for example, it is clear that although the film contains monsters such as a Cyclops and a fighting skeleton, the monsters alone are not the focus of the movie. Rather, the entire fantasy milieu, including a genie and a miniaturized princess, is what is being presented. For more of a border-straddler, one needs to look to *The Company of Wolves* (1984), a retelling of the Little Red Riding Hood story that also includes werewolf themes. However, the fantasy elements predominate, enough to make this a fantasy with horror elements rather than a horror film with fantasy elements.

Crime

The crime genre provides a third source for the origins of horror movie monsters. DDBs

James Arness plays the title character in *The Thing from Another World* (1951, RKO).

are supposed to represent forms of being that are outside the audience's normal world; when this takes a fantastic turn, science fiction and fantasy can supply it, but when a naturalistic monster is desired, one that is abnormal but could be explained by natural mechanisms, crime is available.

The crime film can be strictly defined as a film whose primary purpose is to present the underworld of criminals living outside of and in conflict with the law. The genre includes a variety of subgenres, such as the gangster film (*Little Caesar* [1930]) and caper film (*How to Steal a Million* [1966]), as well as many examples of the style of film noir, a morally dark, visually shadowy mode of cinematic narrative often used in crime films (*The Killing* [1956]). The crime film's chief contribution to the horror film is the character of the psychopathic killer. Although this character often plays only a supporting role in crime films—such as the giggling maniac Tommy Udo in *Kiss of Death* (1947), who shoves an old woman in a wheelchair down a flight of stairs—in the horror film the psychopath is typically the DDB, the focus of the story.

In *This Gun for Hire* (1942), the hit man Philip Raven is a clear example of a DDB, and yet the film is not a horror film. Raven has a physical deformity—a warped left wrist—which was caused by abuse as a child, and which appears also to have warped him into a cold-blooded killer, establishing the deformity-destructiveness causal chain. However, he is redeemed by the friendship of a good woman and ends up working for the government to expose a nest of spies before he is killed for his past crimes. The film is therefore

A skeleton fights Sinbad (Kerwin Mathews) in the fantasy film *The 7th Voyage of Sinbad* (1958, Columbia).

not a horror film but a crime film about the underworld of spies and hitmen in which he made his living. Authentic horror films with crime film elements include *Psycho, Halloween,* and *The Silence of the Lambs.*

Action

The primary purpose of the action film is to present a hero who overcomes physical obstacles to defeat an adversary. It is sometimes called the action-adventure film, in deference to the strong elements of excitement and danger in it, elements associated with the idea of adventure. However, so many different types of movies contain elements of excitement and danger—horror, science fiction, fantasy, crime, action, comedy, and more—that the notion of an adventure genre separate from the others is theoretically unstable. It is better to think of adventure as a component in a range of genres rather than as its own genre. Action, on the other hand, as strictly defined above, is a clearly identifiable genre, in films such as *Gunga Din* (1939), the James Bond series, and the *Die Hard* series.

Horror films often have elements of action. *Jaws*, for example, gives its

Laurie (Jamie Lee Curtis), confronts her opponent, psychopathic killer Michael Myers (not pictured), in *Halloween* (1978, Compass International Pictures).

hero, Chief Brody, plenty of physical obstacles (the boat sinking; having to target a small cylinder of compressed air with his rifle) to overcome to defeat the shark. Nevertheless, the primary focus of *Jaws* is not the chief but the shark, making it a horror movie with action elements.

The reverse happens in *Aliens*. As a sequel to the horror film *Alien*, *Aliens* might have been expected to be a horror film as well. But the focus of the film is on Ripley as action heroine, backed by a squad of space marines, overcoming obstacles to save the little girl Newt from the nest of aliens, particularly the giant alien queen. At the film's climax, Ripley dresses in battle armor (a yellow loader) to equalize the fight with the queen and settle their differences with punches. *Aliens* is one of the best action movies ever made, but it is not a horror movie. It is an action movie with horror elements.

Comedy

The primary purpose of a comedy film is hard to define objectively. Subjectively, it is easy: it is a film primarily designed to get laughs. However, if one tries to define in the abstract what objective properties are likely to get laughs—i.e., be funny or humorous—one gets a confusing array of answers, from Aristotle's view that comedy is "an imitation of men worse than the average"[5] to the idea that humor is based on incongruity,[6] to the theory that humor stems from surprise recognition of patterns.[7] None of these explanations is sufficient, because none, if applied, guarantees laughs. If I show you a series of pictures of red objects, then show you a blue object, that is incongruous, but it is not funny. Until this issue is settled, I will rest with the subjective definition: the comedy film is a film whose primary purpose is getting laughs. In this respect, comedy is something like pornography, whose primary purpose is sexual arousal, even if opinion varies as to what will elicit that response.

The horror film, as noted in Chapter Three, frequently provokes laughter, whether intentional or unintentional. But if the deliberate courting of laughter becomes the film's primary goal, it becomes a comedy with horror elements, like *Ghostbusters, Abbott and Costello Meet Frankenstein* (1948), or *Zombieland* (2009). Films that primarily exist to present the DDB, with humor secondary, are horror films with comedy elements, such as *Re-Animator*. Close calls can be determined by careful scrutiny of such details as the closing credits. In *Jennifer's Body*, the closing credits roll not with humorous outtakes or other material typical of comedy end credits, but with stills of a rock band murdered by Jennifer's friend Needy. It is not particularly funny, but it does make a good horror film frisson, suggesting that Needy is taking over Jennifer's role as killer demon. Thus, *Jennifer's Body* is a horror film with comedy elements.

Horror comedies of whatever sort have an often fatal weakness. Consider *Zombieland*, a commercial success that made $60.6 million in 17 days to become the highest-grossing zombie movie up to that point.[8] It was also a critical success, attaining a score of 73 (generally favorable reviews) on the criticism Web site Metacritic.com.[9] Yet it is a prime example of the problem with horror comedies. Too often, as in this case, they are not very scary and they are not very funny.

Let us assume, as seems to be the case, that *Zombieland* is attempting to be a comedy with horror elements. Then it should be judged primarily by its success at getting laughs, and it is not a big laugh-getter. The biggest laugh, Bill Murray's cameo as himself in zombie makeup, is over quickly; the rest of the humor comes largely from the slapstick of killing zombies, which is dulled from the memory of having seen it many times before in other zombie movies. Even the motif of having a set of rules to survive among the monsters (e.g., "Cardio") has been seen before, in *Scream*.

Suppose *Zombieland* is actually intended to be a horror movie with comedy elements. Then it is even worse. The zombie attacks are extremely pale copies of copies of better zombie attacks in the George Romero *Living Dead* series. Cues in the film quickly make it clear that none of the four main characters is going to die, eliminating genuine destructiveness as a possibility. These zombies are not DDBs, just deformed clowns; in fact, one of them actually *is* a deformed clown.

Could it be that *Zombieland* intends to be primarily both horror and comedy? That is a logical impossibility: primarily means first, and one cannot be two things first. But even if it were the case, it still does both things badly, making it a bad film. This is not unusual for horror comedies. The lightness of the humor tends to undercut the horror, and the repulsiveness of the horror tends to reduce the humor. It is hard, though not impossible, to make a good horror comedy, and *Zombieland* fails at it.

Romance

The primary purpose of the film romance is the presentation of a love story, and the horror film borrows much from this genre, because nearly every horror film contains some kind of love story subplot. Yet it is rare when the love story become truly central to a horror movie. For example, the marital fondness between Chief Brody and his wife in *Jaws* is just supporting background, neglected once the story moves to the final battle with the shark. But in *The Fly* (1986) and *Bram Stoker's Dracula*, the love story between the DDB and a normal woman is so important that it is the woman who, at the DDB's request, kills the monster in the final battle, though it pains her. Nevertheless, even in these films, the love story is subordinate to the presentation of the DDB.

As noted in Chapter One, *Twilight* goes the other way, making presentation of the romance between the vampire boy and the human girl the purpose of the film, and leaving DDB presentation to the side. Thus, *Twilight* is a romance with horror elements.

Horror films can easily mix more than two genres. An example is the horror film *Jason X* (2002), in which Jason Voorhees, DDB of the *Friday the 13th* series, goes to space, gets fantastically resurrected, is surrounded by the usual sex-hungry young people, perpetrates murders, and keeps everyone fighting him, all in an air of utter ridiculousness—making this a horror movie with science fiction, fantasy, romantic, criminal, action, and comedy elements. Yet there is no doubt what audiences came to see: the same psychotic slasher they had sought out multiple times before. Horror movies often mix with other genres, but the primary purpose of the horror film is usually clear despite the mixing.

11

History: Beginnings to the 1950s

Up to this point, I have discussed DDBs almost ahistorically, as if they transcend time. But in fact they are created in time, growing out of preexisting cultural influences and social conditions, as well as those artistic mutations that we know as originality. If a DDB is sufficiently forceful — if, in particular, it is original and memorable, along with being plausible, coherent, and horrifying — it has a chance to come back in sequels and influence later DDBs and even the culture at large. The DDB can be considered one of the memes Richard Dawkins postulates[1]: a unit of cultural transmission that arises by evolutionary modification of earlier memes and may be passed on, depending on its perceived cultural value, in more or less modified form.

Many horror movies allude implicitly to the times in which they are made. *Invasion of the Body Snatchers* is imbued with the paranoia of the 1950s; *The Last House on the Left* with the 1970s fear of crime and anxiety about youth culture. Occasionally horror movies even make a public historical event explicitly central to the plot. *The Return of the Vampire* (1943) does so with World War II, *Deathdream* (1972) with the Vietnam War.

Of course, not every DDB is an original creation. The history of horror films is an oscillation between attempting to repeat DDB presentations that were previously proven effective and trying to generate distinctively new DDB presentations. The urgency of the latter stems from the very purpose of presenting DDBs, which is to let audiences see new kinds of being they would otherwise have little chance of encountering. If they have every chance of encountering the same being in sequel after sequel, the value of the horror film is diminished. The box-office receipts concomitantly decline, giving filmmakers financial incentive to create new DDBs, or at least "reboot" the series with an appropriately modified DDB.

The dulling of the DDB due to repetition accounts for the phenomenon that older horror films seem not to be as scary. The movies may have been scary once, but they have been seen so much that the DDB no longer has the same emotional effect. Even if they have not been reseen, they have often been parodied and merchandised into contexts that take away their edge of reality, and therefore of horror. For example, Jack Pierce's makeup for the Universal Frankenstein monster, originally worn by Boris Karloff in *Frankenstein*, was powerfully scary once. The *New York Times* critic wrote at the time of *Frankenstein*'s release that the monster was "hideous" and the film "spine-chilling" and "disturbing."[2] But this monster has now been parodied in everything from the situation comedy *The Munsters* to the breakfast cereal Frankenberry to Mel Brooks's movie and Broadway musical *Young Frankenstein*. It takes an effort of imagination to watch these older films freshly, and even then it may be impossible to restore completely the horror, and the sense of original encounter with a DDB, they once generated.

Since horror films are always getting dulled, there is a strong impetus to find new sources of horror, new DDBs, or at least to modify old ones in such a way as to make them like new. If nothing else, the "anxiety of influence," as Harold Bloom calls it,[3] is always driving DDB creation in fresh directions. This chapter and the next tell the story of ten such new or "like new" DDBs, one from each of the ten decades from the 1910s to the 2000s. The goal is to show the sources from which each DDB arose, and the modifications that made it original and memorable, as well as the cultural influence it went on to have. In this manner, the existence of DDBs as cultural artifacts that arise through cultural evolution will be made clear. The ten DDBs have been selected not necessarily because each is the most important or characteristic of its period, but because each has a different and interesting cultural history.

Between the stories of the DDBs are transition accounts of how the horror film genre had developed up to that point. Because of space constraints, these accounts of the genre at large necessarily amount only to brief sketches. For more detail, the reader is encouraged to consult more comprehensive histories of the horror film genre.[4]

Beginnings: Origins to 1910

The first horror films drew on the tradition of horror fiction and drama. A particularly important influence was Gothic fiction, which emerged in the eighteenth century and was marked by a taste for setting its stories in decaying castles, abbeys, old dark houses, and other buildings more or less of the Gothic style of architecture prevalent in late medieval Europe.[5] The novels *Frankenstein* (1818) and *Dracula* (1897) and the novella *The Strange Case of Dr. Jekyll and Mr. Hyde* (1886), all in the Gothic tradition, had a strong influence on the screen, not only through direct adaptations of those books but through sequels, imitations, and indirect borrowings. Another key influence on movie horror was the Grand Guignol Theater in Paris, which exhibited gory, bloody plays from 1897 to 1962, rife with realistic depictions of murder, mutilation, torture, rape, and other vile acts.[6] The Grand Guignol has had a long influence on horror movies, even stronger since the collapse of Production Code censorship in the 1960s made it permissible to show the graphic gore that previously could only be suggested.

In the silent film era that began in the 1890s, horror films developed along several lines. The so-called trick films of French filmmaker Georges Méliès included supernatural beings such as ghosts and devils.[7] Adaptations of literary horror classics provided further evolution toward cinematic horror. The first film version of *Dr. Jekyll and Mr. Hyde* was produced by Chicago's Selig Polyscope Company in 1908. Then, in 1910, the Edison Company released the first film version of *Frankenstein*, directed by J. Searle Dawley with Charles Ogle as the creature.

Frankenstein (1910)

Considering that the 1910 *Frankenstein* is silent and runs only about twelve minutes, it is surprisingly faithful to the essence of Mary Shelley's novel. Frankenstein, a student, becomes obsessed with the creating of a human being, but when he first beholds the creature he has brought to life he is horrified and abandons it. The creature pursues him and threatens his forthcoming marriage to Elizabeth. All this is from the novel. The monster is destroyed and the marriage saved, events that are not in the novel but establish the long-lived precedent of closing a horror movie with a happy ending for a heterosexual couple. In a sense, this was a "Hollywood" ending, although this was before Hollywood, or at least before Hollywood had become the capital of the U.S. motion picture industry.

What is left out in the transition from book to movie is instructive. All of the creature's murders have been deleted, so that the DDB — a large, shaggy thing with big head and shoulders, long arms, and skinny legs — is destructive only in the effect he has on the peace of mind of Frankenstein and Elizabeth. Edison publicity materials said that the film "carefully tried to eliminate all the actually repulsive situations" and to focus on "mystic and psychological problems."[8] Thus, the Edison Company was practicing an early form of self-censorship, toning down material that audiences might find too disturbing at the same time that it was introducing something disturbing — the Frankenstein monster. This would be a perpetual problem for horror filmmakers: how to bring horrific content to audiences while toning down the most potentially objectionable aspects. Yet the Edison Company had struck on the essentials of DDB theory. Its *Frankenstein* was a horror movie because its primary aim was to present a deformed being that was destructive (at least psychologically) as a result of its deformity.

The Edison *Frankenstein* was influential in several ways. Though the creature was never imitated in precisely the same form, the idea that he was big and wild-looking, with a high forehead, thick shoulders, and long arms, became the template for many future *Frankenstein* movies, including Karloff's incarnation for Universal in the 1931 *Frankenstein*. And although the novel had been vague about how the monster was created, Edison's *Frankenstein* recognized that a vivid creation sequence was needed, in this case a fascinating episode in which the monster is cooked from chemicals in a vat, gradually forming from a skeletal mess. Future versions would also emphasize the creation sequence, although they would use lightning and other effects. Finally, the novel had allowed the monster to get away without dying (although he promised to kill himself), whereas in Edison's film the monster is destroyed with the aid of a mirror that causes him to disappear. Later versions would also end with the destruction of the monster.

The Edison *Frankenstein* was different from its chief predecessor, the novel *Frankenstein*, and had an influence on future versions of the *Frankenstein* story. In those respects, it presented an original and memorable DDB.

Transition: 1910–1925

After Edison's *Frankenstein*, the horror genre developed rapidly. In Germany, *The Cabinet of Dr. Caligari* (1919), the story of an evil hypnotist who controls a somnambulist, and *Nosferatu* (1922), an unauthorized screen version of Bram Stoker's novel *Dracula*, were seminal horror films that had a wide influence. Both were German Expressionist films that used distorted sets, exaggerated lighting, long shadows, and stylized acting to produce horrific effects — techniques that would be used in many later horror films. In the United States, the films of actor Lon Chaney and director Tod Browning, who sometimes collaborated together on films that emphasized deformity and crime, also influenced the development of the horror genre. However, one seminal horror film was a production that starred Chaney but was not directed by Browning: *The Phantom of the Opera*.

The Phantom of the Opera (1925)

An actor who did his own makeup, Chaney was famous for his elaborate, grotesque makeup designs, which earned him the moniker, "Man of a Thousand Faces." He was particularly noted for his makeup as the title character in Universal's *The Hunchback of Notre Dame* (1923). This was not a horror film, because Chaney's hunchback Quasimodo was deformed but not particularly destructive; still, the hunchback had a horrifying makeup worthy of a

DDB: bulging eye, swollen cheeks, misshapen back. The film was a commercial success, and Universal looked for another property that could star Chaney as a grotesque. They found it, and it was even set in Paris, just as *Hunchback* was: *The Phantom of the Opera*, a 1910 novel by Gaston Leroux.

As filmed by Universal under the direction of Rupert Julian, *The Phantom of the Opera* is a horror movie, with Chaney as the DDB, Erik the Phantom, a hideously disfigured individual who inhabits the catacombs of the Paris Opera House. Devoted to the beautiful singer, Christine (Mary Philbin), he abducts her, taking her to his subterranean lair where she rips off his mask, revealing his skull-like face. Erik's DDB attacks follow, until he is hunted down by an angry mob and drowned in the Seine River.

Phantom had lavish sets and Technicolor inserts, but its greatest asset was Chaney's makeup, and the greatest moment — the one that everyone remembers — is the unmasking. The sudden uncovering of that skeletal visage is still one of cinema's most effective shocks. It helps that the makeup is linked to a fine, nuanced performance by Chaney that depends heavily on pantomime,[9] an art that was especially important in the silent era. Chaney's Phantom was clearly a person of culture and breeding, and that he should have been reduced to madness and hiding underground was tragic. Numerous horror films since then have borrowed from Erik's unmasking, including *The Mystery of the Wax Museum*, *The Abominable Dr. Phibes*, and *The Funhouse*.

No explanation was given in the film for the Phantom's deformity, which may have helped intensify its otherworldliness. On the other hand, David Jo Skal has argued that the unexplained face may have plucked "at the culture's rawest nerves" by reminding them of the scarred and maimed veterans of the recent Great War.[10]

Phantom was a box-office hit that contributed greatly to the developing horror genre. It had the sympathetic monster, who was at once deformed but yearning for human affection (in this case, Christine's). It had the heterosexual couple, Christine and her boyfriend Raoul (Norman Kerry), who survive the monster's demise. And in a scene that did not appear in the book, it had an angry mob destroy the DDB, as they would six years later in *Frankenstein*. Thus, *Phantom* helped to solidify the final battle as a key structural element in horror films. *Phantom* was often remade — in 1943, 1962, 1989, and 1999. In addition, it was made into a rock film, *Phantom of the Paradise* (1974), and a Broadway musical that itself spawned a film adaptation (2004). Yet the 1925 Chaney adaptation remains the definitive film version.

Transition: 1925–1933

Despite the importance of silent films, it took the advent of sound (in the late 1920s) to establish the horror genre as we know it today. The early 1930s, from 1931 to 1935, was the period in which the horror genre flourished as never before or since. In those years, Universal produced a series of great horror movies, including *Dracula, Frankenstein, The Mummy, The Invisible Man, The Black Cat, Werewolf of London* (1935), and *Bride of Frankenstein*, introducing or developing many of the types of DDBs that would be perpetuated in years to come. Influenced by German Expressionism as well as by its own *The Phantom of the Opera*, Universal's shadowy, foggy, foreign-set house style in turn influenced other horror filmmakers. To try to pick up on some of Universal's commercial luck with the genre, other studios hurriedly issued their own contributions, some of which also became classics, such as *Freaks* (1932), *Dr. Jekyll and Mr. Hyde* (1932), and *Island of Lost Souls* (1933). Other countries released their own horror films in this period, such as Germany's *M* (1931), Britain's *The Ghoul* (1933), and the French-German *Vampyr* (1932).

Wearing makeup of his own design, Lon Chaney plays Erik the Phantom in *The Phantom of the Opera* (1925, Universal).

Back in the United States, one of Universal's rival studios, RKO (then releasing films as Radio Pictures), produced the remarkable film *King Kong*.

King Kong (1933)

King Kong was remarkable because of its originality. Until *Kong*, no one had seen on a movie screen a gorilla the size of an apartment building. It was a new idea, one of the great ideas in DDB creation. It had antecedents and influences, but it was a new and successful type of being that had a powerful influence on future DDBs.

Kong has suffered from one thing: disagreement as to whether it really is

11. History: Beginnings to the 1950s   123

The giant gorilla Kong fights a pterodactyl to protect Ann Darrow (Fay Wray) in *King Kong* (1933, RKO).

a horror film. Sometimes it is characterized as a fantasy film, adventure film, romance, or all three. Chapter Ten offered criteria that clear up this issue. The primary purpose of *Kong* is to present Kong, who is deformed with respect to size (he is much too large for a gorilla) and as a consequence is destructive, killing many people and wrecking much property during his various rampages. Therefore Kong is a DDB and *Kong* is a horror film. It has elements of fantasy (the giant gorilla), science fiction (the realistic dinosaurs), adventure (the dangerous island), action (Kong's fights with dinosaurs, airplanes, and others) and romance (Kong's love for Ann Darrow). The seamless richness of its generic affiliations—as opposed to the more cluttered mix of genres in *Jason X*—is part of what makes the film great, yet it belongs primarily to the horror genre.

In *Kong*, filmmaker Carl Denham travels from New York to remote Skull Island in search of material for a movie. There the natives kidnap Denham's leading lady, Ann, and sacrifice her to the giant gorilla Kong, who keeps her captive and falls in love with her. Denham and his men, including Ann's beloved, first mate Jack Driscoll, struggle with dinosaurs to find Kong and bring him back captive to New York. There Kong breaks free and carries Ann to the top of the Empire State Building. Airplanes equipped with machine guns kill him and his body falls to the street. Ann is saved, and Denham reiterates a theme of the film, saying in the last line, "It was beauty killed the beast."

Kong had a number of antecedents, none of which jointly or singly could have predicted this precise DDB, but all of which contributed to his creation. *Kong* is a journey story, a type of narrative that is at least as old as Homer's *Odyssey*, in which sailors land on a strange island and fight their own giant monster (the Cyclops). By the sixteenth century, there was an extensive travel literature, some of it real, some fictional, documenting the voyages of European exploration and colonization. As Africa was colonized in the nineteenth century, it began to gain particular interest, with readers mesmerized by nonfiction narratives such as Richard Francis Burton's accounts of his explorations and novels such as Henry Rider Haggard's *She* (1887).

She was part of a growing subgenre of travel books in which explorers discovered fantastic lost domains deep in uncharted areas. In the novels *The Lost World* (1912) by Arthur Conan Doyle and *The Land That Time Forgot* (1918) by Edgar Rice Burroughs, the domains were overrun with prehistoric animals. *Lost World* had a strong influence on *Kong*. Filmed for the first time in 1925, the cinematic *Lost World* featured dinosaurs animated by special effects pioneer Willis O'Brien, who would later create the effects for *Kong*. O'Brien's stop-motion animation techniques—moving a puppet a minute amount, filming it, stopping the camera, moving the puppet a little further, filming it, and so on, thus creating an illusion of fluid motion upon playback—were used for both *Lost World* and *Kong*.

The film *Lost World* influenced *Kong* not only in its special effects but in its plot, which involved a journey to a remote dinosaur-ridden area and the abduction of one of these beasts to a major city (London) to be put on display, where the dinosaur ran amok and assaulted a landmark (London Bridge). This idea inspired Kong's capture on Skull Island and display in New York, where he ran amok and assaulted his own landmark, the Empire State Building. *Lost World* also featured an ape man, a simian creature similar in some respects to Kong, although much shorter.

The film *Lost World* was part of a larger genre at the time that may be called travel films, which picked up on the popularity of travel books that were similarly about wild, remote places. Merian C. Cooper and Ernest B. Schoedsack, co-directors and, with David O. Selznick as executive producer, co-producers of *Kong*, had broken into cinema on the crew of several travel films.[11] Frequently taking the form of a "jungle quest" in which explorers venture into the tropics on a scientific mission, travel films were sometimes documentaries (*Nanook of the North* [1922]), sometimes fiction (*Lost World*), and often a bit of both. Cooper and Schoedsack modified the authentic documentary aspects of their Thai jungle film, *Chang* (1927), with a fictional plot. *Kong* itself is a meta-movie—a film about filmmaking—in which the filmmaker, Denham, is making his own quasi-documentary: filming authentic footage of Skull Island but with plans to introduce Ann as a fictional love interest.

A number of travel movies featured monkeys or apes of some kind, in keeping with a general interest in simians on film. The most pertinent of these movies for *Kong* was the gorilla in *Ingagi* (1930), a film that purported to be an actual documentary and ended with a woman being sacrificed to a gorilla, much like Ann would be to Kong. With its implied mating of a woman and an ape, *Ingagi* was a tremendous hit, though it was forced to close its run early because of the interference of the censors. The studio that had distributed *Ingagi*, RKO, saw potential in another story about a woman sacrificed to a gorilla. Thus *Kong* was approved for production.

Kong, then, came into being as a DDB from multiple lines of influence: travel films and literature; the film *Lost World*, with its dinosaurs achieved through O'Brien's stop-motion techniques; the notion from *Ingagi* of an ape receiving a woman as a sacrifice. What made the brew original—what unified it into a new horror film with a new DDB—was, first, the magnification of the gorilla into a monster as big as a dinosaur (and more powerful than a dinosaur), and, second, Kong's falling in love with the woman so that he selflessly protects her, seeks her, and finally dies for her. Within the film, credit is explicitly given to the fairy tale Beauty and the Beast as yet another influence on *Kong*—it is, as Denham says, the "angle" that explains Kong's love for Ann.

Kong had another distinction that made it stand out from other horror movies of the time. Nearly all horror movies of the 1930s were set wholly in a foreign land, usually Europe, sometimes a tropical island. The effect was to soften the horror—and, in part, explain it—by making it seem more remote. Much of *Kong*, too, was set on remote Skull Island, but the film's opening and closing scenes are set in New York. Warner Bros., in an effort to distinguish its horror films from the European-based ones of Universal, set *Doctor X* (1932) and *Mystery of the Wax Museum* in New York around this time.[12] But *Kong* did a great deal more to capture the feel of Depression-era New York in its depictions of a soupline, the hungry Ann, the bustling theater where Kong is exhibited, and the newly completed (1931) Empire State Building, then the tallest building in the world. The effect was to give this exceedingly fantastic story a realistic edge, grounding it in everyday reality.

Kong was a smash hit and had a long influence. It generated one direct sequel, *Son of Kong* (1933; much inferior, and too sweet-natured to be a real horror film); a follow-up that resembled it in some respects, *Mighty Joe Young* (1949; also too sweet-natured to count as horror); and all the giant monster films of the 1950s and afterward, including Japan's *Gojira*, who fought Kong in *Kingu Kongu tai Gojira* (*Kong Kong vs. Godzilla*; 1962). Later there were two remakes of *King Kong*, in 1976 and 2005. But none of the sequels, remakes, or imitations could match the blend of innocent love and horrific destruction that the original *King Kong* had achieved.

Transition: 1933–1942

After the mid–1930s, the horror film became less rich with new ideas. Declining box office, censorship issues, and a general unwillingness of studios to invest in A horror productions led to fewer original DDBs. There were plenty of sequels: Universal made new *Frankenstein*, *Dracula*, *Mummy*, and *Invisible Man* films into the 1940s. They also started a new franchise with *The Wolf Man*, although that was in many ways a remake of the earlier *Werewolf of London*. The first hint of a different direction in horror came from RKO, the studio that had produced *King Kong*.

Cat People (1942)

Val Lewton was an RKO producer assigned to deliver a series of low-budget horror films with prespecified titles. One of these titles was *Cat People*. This was a clear gambit to imitate the success of *The Wolf Man*, presumably by making a similar film, only with hybrid cat-humans instead of wolf-humans. It is startling to think how dreadful this film could have been, with actors wearing furry makeup designed to make them look like they were half-tabby. But Lewton had his own ideas about how to make a horror movie. Although *Cat People* is about a woman who apparently can turn into a panther, she never wears monster makeup, and there are no special-effects-heavy transformation scenes. All the horror is accomplished through suggestion and mood.

Set in contemporary New York City (itself still an unusual setting for a horror film at this time; *The Wolf Man* was set more traditionally in England), *Cat People* was directed by Jacques Tourneur and starred Simone Simon as Irena. Believing that an ancient curse has doomed her to turn into a panther if sexually aroused, Irena declines to consummate her marriage to Oliver (Kent Smith), who turns for affection to Alice (Jane Randolph). Irena becomes jealous and it appears that she turns into a panther. Before the movie is over, she kills her psychiatrist and is killed herself.

With its psychiatrist character, Dr. Judd (Tom Conway), and its themes of repressed sexuality and hidden rage, *Cat People* is overtly Freudian, more so even than *The Wolf Man*, which had borrowed the name of one of Freud's most famous cases. Where *The Wolf Man* talked the language of good and evil, *Cat People* focused more on the psychological makeup of the individual monster, Irena. Where *The Wolf Man* left no doubt that the title character really was a werewolf, *Cat People*, for the most part, kept the reality of Irena's catness vague and open to question. Eventually, a real panther is shown, but the sighting is not enough to eliminate a feeling that Irena's transformation is deeply inside her head as well as strangely visible to the eye. The techniques used to suggest Irena as cat person are mostly subtle and creepy, particularly when Alice is swimming in a darkened hotel pool, menaced offscreen by an unseen, snarling animal.

Cat People was a great success for RKO, earning $4 million on an investment of $118,948.[13] Lewton went on to produce eight more horror films for the studio, characterized by the same low-key, suggestive qualities. They included a sequel, *The Curse of the Cat People* (1944), and titles such as *I Walked with a Zombie* (1943), *The Seventh Victim* (1943), and *The Body Snatcher* (1945). *Cat People* itself was remade in 1982 with decidedly more explicit sex and violence and much more expensive special effects, but much less satisfying results.

The original *Cat People* had a powerful influence on many later horror filmmakers who preferred the implicit style to the explicit style. Later films that have adopted this approach include *The Innocents* (1961; discussed in the next chapter), *The Haunting* (1963), *The Sixth Sense*, and *The Others*.

Transition: 1942–1958

In the 1950s, the horror genre's fortunes took another turn with the use of giant monsters (e.g., the giant ants in *Them!*) and evil aliens (e.g., *The Thing from Another World*) as DDBs. Japan launched a long-running cycle of giant monster movies with *Gojira*. Britain's Hammer Films inaugurated the Quatermass series of horror-science-fiction movies, in which the intrepid scientist Bernard Quatermass battled aliens three times: in *The Quatermass Xperiment* (U.S. title *The Creeping Unknown*; 1955); *Quatermass 2* (U.S. title *Enemy from Space*; 1957); and *Quatermass and the Pit* (U.S. title *Five Million Years to Earth*; 1967).

However, the DDBs of decades past—the vampire and the Frankenstein monster—seemed hopelessly outdated. Even the Italian film *I vampiri* (*The Devil's Commandment;* 1956) was not quite a vampire movie, concerning a duchess who keeps herself young with the help of a mad scientist and other women's blood. *I vampiri*, with unaccredited co-direction by Mario Bava, did have the distinction of being the start of Italy's golden age of horror, which would continue in the 1960s with films openly directed by Bava.

The British studio, Hammer, made an effort to revive the classic monsters of the 1930s with *The Curse of Frankenstein* (1957), a remake of the Mary Shelley novel. The results were successful, and Hammer tried its approach again with, logically enough, the story of Dracula.

Dracula (Christopher Lee) preys on a victim, Mina (Melissa Stribling), in *Horror of Dracula* (1958, Hammer).

Horror of Dracula (1958)

Like *Nosferatu* and Universal's *Dracula* (1931), Hammer's *Horror of Dracula* (or just *Dracula*, as it is known in the United Kingdom) was based on Bram Stoker's nineteenth-century novel. In that sense, it is the same old thing: evil vampire Count Dracula bites people on neck, turns them into vampires, is destroyed. But Hammer had new ideas about how to tell horror stories on film. For one thing, *Horror of Dracula*, like *Curse of Frankenstein* before it, was in color, an attribute that made for a brighter, visually richer world. For another, *Horror of Dracula* was much more explicit about showing blood and gore — in bright red, thanks to the use of color — and was more open about sexuality. Crosses burned skin; old vampire bodies decayed when destroyed; bosoms heaved. Censorship was more lax than it had been in the days of Bela Lugosi, but it still limited how far the film could go in the direction of either sex or violence; even so, Hammer pushed as far as it could. The actual plunging of a stake into the heart of vampire woman Lucy is not shown, but deft editing — the stake coming down, Lucy reacting — make it seem as though it has been shown. Similarly, *Horror of Dracula* features no graphic sex or nudity, but the famously chesty Hammer women do their part to bring sexuality to the proceedings. The breasts of Carol Marsh, the actress who plays Lucy, are prominently erect even while she lies in her coffin getting staked.

The plot of *Horror of Dracula* was changed significantly from either the novel or the previous film versions, with a view to emphasizing action and confrontation. Jonathan Harker, previously (in the novel) an unwitting victim of Dracula's malice involved in helping the count relocate to England, is now, from the earliest sequence, a vampire hunter working with Dr. Van Helsing to destroy the count. Dracula kills Harker early on rather than leaving him alive, providing an early first blood. Mina, who in previous versions had been Harker's fiancée, is now married to Arthur Holmwood, and Lucy is Holmwood's sister and Harker's fiancée, providing a direct link for Dracula between his scenes with Harker and his stalking of Lucy, a link that previously had been indirect. After Mina is bitten, she has Dracula live for a while in secret in her cellar, an act of human-vampire cohabitation that would have been too daring in previous versions. Dracula does not move by sea from his native land to England, but only crosses a land border between his native country and the site of Mina and Arthur's home, which appears to be a German-like nation. This allows for action to happen more swiftly; for example, it permits an exciting chase scene by horse-drawn carriage across the border near the end, as Van Helsing and Arthur try to outrace Dracula back to his castle before the sun rises. In the final battle, Van Helsing and Dracula have a physical fight, which ends with Van Helsing bounding across a table to tear down drapes that allow the sun to turn Dracula to dust. This climactic confrontation is more dramatic and visceral than in either of the previous film versions of the story.

The most important change in *Horror of Dracula* is the casting of Christopher Lee as the count. Tall, thin, and very British, with a clipped, aristocratic way of reading his lines, Lee looks and sounds different from any previous incarnation of Dracula. He is most fascinating when he is moving: athletic when fighting, swift and expressive when walking. Terence Fisher, director of *Horror of Dracula*, wrote of his star: "Lee is a mime expert; he studied ballet at one time, and he can express emotions eloquently in the simplest physical movements, just in his walk."[14] Lee's athleticism, which fits the action-oriented world of *Horror of Dracula*, differs markedly from the stationary mesmerism of Bela Lugosi's Dracula or the creepiness of Max Schreck's Count Orloc in *Nosferatu*.

Lee is also more bestial than his predecessors, with a strong sense of the animal underlying the aristocrat. He has visible fangs, which Lugosi did not have in *Dracula*, and is always ready to sink them into necks. And he is sexual. Women swoon at the sight of him, and when he prepares to bite Mina, he searches her face hungrily as though smelling her.

Despite the many differences between *Horror of Dracula* and previous versions, it is recognizably the same story: evil vampire Dracula attacks and gets destroyed. The same story audiences had enjoyed before was told again, but with changes that made it fresh and vigorous—color; greater explicitness, action, and physicality; and a new variation on an old DDB. The film was a great commercial success, and spawned a series of Hammer *Dracula* movies, most of them starring Lee. It also cemented Hammer's place as a prominent horror film studio and helped lead them to make many other horror movies. The influence of *Horror of Dracula* was widespread, feeding the growing trend toward explicit sex and violence in horror films. In addition, it affected the tone and style of many later vampire films, including yet another version of the Dracula story, Jess Franco's *Nachts, wenn Dracula erwacht* (*Count Dracula*; 1970), which starred, not surprisingly, Christopher Lee.

12

History: 1960s to the Present

This chapter continues the history of the horror film that was begun in the previous chapter, this time spanning the period from the 1960s to the present.

Transition: 1958–1961

The history of the horror film in the brief period from 1958 to 1961 was most prominently marked by Alfred Hitchcock's *Psycho*. This film continued the movement toward increasingly explicit violence and sex already seen in the Hammer films, and in low-budget exploitation films such as *I Was a Teenage Werewolf* (1957), made by the enterprising American International Pictures, which specialized in such fare. *Psycho* used a knife-wielding, psychopathic serial killer as its DDB, an idea that would later become the basis for the slasher film.

Another influential horror film of the time was the French-Italian *Les Yeux sans visage*, about a surgeon kidnapping young women to steal their faces in an effort to replace that of his daughter, disfigured in an accident. Similar stories were told in later films, such as the Spanish-French *Gritos en la noche* (*The Awful Dr. Orloff*; 1962).

The movement toward greater gore was not the only trend in horror films of the time. There was also an effort to recover the DDBs of the past and remake them for a new time, as Hammer was doing with Frankenstein and Dracula. Mario Bava did this with his new take on an old belief, witchcraft, in *La maschera del demonio* (*Black Sunday*; 1960). In a different way, this kind of recovery and remaking was what *The Innocents* did.

The Innocents (1961)

The haunted house subgenre was about as old as horror films, and had already become a joke by the time the horror comedy *The Cat and the Canary* was filmed in 1927. To take this tired old subject—creaking doors, lurking ghosts—and do something new and even adult with it required a completely new approach. The makers of *The Innocents* found that approach by going back to one of the classic literary versions of the haunted house—Henry James's 1898 novella *The Turn of the Screw*.

James's novella, in which a governess is tormented by the idea that her young charges, a boy and a girl, are menaced by ghosts, had been staged in 1950 as a Broadway play, *The Innocents*, by William Archibald, with Beatrice Straight as the governess. This play became the basis for the movie, *The Innocents*, but not before it received a rewrite. The screenwriters were Archibald, John Mortimer, and, of all people, Truman Capote. One of the finest writers of his day, Capote contributed something to *The Innocents*, though it is hard to say what: perhaps the vaguely southern mood that hangs over the film's old English country house; perhaps the strong emphasis on the governess's repressed sexuality. In any case, Capote is said to have called *The Innocents* "his best film script."[1]

The plot of *The Innocents* is similar to James's novella, although there were changes. In the film, unlike the novella, the governess, admirably played by Deborah Kerr, receives a name, Miss Giddens. In the film but not the book, the governess kisses the boy, Miles, on the lips, a scene sexually charged. But much of the film resembles the book. The governess is still obsessed with the two ghosts, Quint and Miss Jessel, who may be real or may be products of her insane imagination. She still thinks she has to rescue the children, Miles and Flora, from the ghosts. And in the end, she presides over the death of one of the children, Miles, whom either she or Quint, or both, have killed.

Just as Hitchcock had gone back to black and white for *Psycho*, director Jack Clayton shot *The Innocents* in black and white, which, by 1961, had the curious effect of intensifying drama while creating distance between audience and characters. Clayton shot it in the widescreen Cinemascope process, not because he wanted to but because the studio, 20th Century–Fox, insisted on it. Cinematographer Freddie Francis reported that he devised special filters to blur the sides of the frame to make the film more claustrophobic and add an element of mystery as to what was lurking in the corners.[2]

Whatever the process by which it was created, the result was an enduring gem of a ghost movie. Its ghosts could appear anywhere: out in the bright sunshine; in a reflection; deep in the house. The suspense of when the ghosts would appear next was equaled by the suspense of whether and when the governess would go completely mad. It remained ambiguous to the end whether the governess was the DDB (though that makes the most dramatic sense.) The tongue-in-cheek clichés of the haunted house movie and the heavy furniture of most classic literary adaptations had been overcome. *The Innocents* was at once a haunted house movie for adults, and a literary adaptation that was fun.

The Innocents does not fit in the grand narrative of gory horror films, the one that leads from *Psycho* to slashers, but it does not need to do so. It has its own chain of influence. It borrowed from the school of suggestive horror in which Val Lewton had specialized, and from the evil child subgenre that had begun with *The Bad Seed*, and contributed to the continuation of both lines. (Miles and Flora appear to Miss Giddens, at least, to be possessed by the ghosts, and thus qualify as evil children.) Most notably, *The Others*, with its tale of a mother trying to protect her two children from what she supposes are ghosts, would not exist without the influence of *The Innocents*.

Transition: 1961–1979

For the American horror film, the most important development of the period 1961 to 1979 was the collapse of the Production Code, with its tight rein on depictions of violence and sex. As social mores changed, it became clear that a new system was needed for regulating film content. In 1968, the Motion Picture Association of America inaugurated the ratings system, which permitted all sorts of violence and sex to be depicted on screen as long as each film was rated to provide guidance to the public about its suitability for younger audiences.

As censorship relaxed, a level of onscreen horror movie mayhem that had been previously unimaginable became not only permissible but de rigueur. *Blood Feast, Two Thousand Maniacs!, Night of the Living Dead, The Last House on the Left, The Exorcist, The Texas Chain Saw Massacre* (1974), *Jaws, The Omen, Carrie,* and *Halloween* presented ample blood and gore, often laced with sex, and there was never any guarantee, as there had been in Production Code days, that the story would work out and the DDB would be destroyed. The frisson became a common component of horror films. Whether low-budget or high-budget, these horror films were often of a very high quality, part of a wider Renaissance of film taking place in the late 1960s and 1970s as commercial filmmakers experimented fruitfully in ways that befit their changing times. Horror auteurs such as George Romero, Wes Craven, Tobe Hooper, and John Carpenter emerged.

Horror flourished abroad as well. In Britain in the 1960s and 1970s, Hammer continued making its traditional Frankenstein and Dracula movies, even as competitors arose, such as Amicus Productions, specialists in the horror anthology (e.g., *Dr. Terror's House of Horrors*). In Canada, David Cronenberg started making grotesquely horrific films such as *They Came from Within*. In Italy, Bava continued to make innovative horror films and new horror directors emerged, such as Dario Argento (*Suspiria* [1977]) and Lucio Fulci (*Zombi 2* [*Zombie*; 1979]).

Although the focus of this book is on films made for theatrical release, horror has always had a place on television as well. The 1970s were a period when the format of made-for-television movies was in its prime, and some of these were horror movies of high quality. There was *Duel* (1971), an early Steven Spielberg effort that pitted man against truck, and *Gargoyles* (1972), which pitted people against living gargoyles, and featured early creature makeup work by Stan Winston. In Britain, *The Stone Tape* (1972), an ingeniously high-tech haunted house film, was broadcast with a script by Nigel Kneale, creator of the Quatermass series of films, including *Five Million Years to Earth*. Frankenstein and the vampire both got effective TV treatments in, respectively, *Frankenstein: The True Story* (1973) and *Salem's Lot* (1979).

While the horror genre was flourishing in the 1970s, there was one frontier that had been little explored. Monsters of the period had invaded small towns, housing developments, and archeological ruins, but they had rarely reached outer space. This opened a niche for *Alien*.

Alien (1979)

In 1977, *Star Wars* became a tremendous hit, and studios throughout the movie industry looked to imitate it with their own space-based science-fiction films. 20th Century–Fox greenlit a property that had already been in development: *Alien*.

Alien, the story of an extraterrestrial that gets aboard a spaceship and starts killing the crew, was an original script by Dan O'Bannon, from a story by O'Bannon and Ronald Shusett, but it was influenced by many sources.[3] Foremost was the work of Swiss surrealist artist H.R. Giger, whose biomechanical paintings, combining elements of the mechanical and organic, directly inspired the idea of the alien and got Giger hired as the alien designer. The alien turned out to be a marvel of design, with three distinguishable phases in its life-cycle — the crab-like facehugger that leaps onto a human face and clings there until it implants its larva; the chestburster that burrows its way out of a human body and explodes free; and the full-grown alien, with its long, phallic head, double jaws, and a body equal parts insect, reptile, and machine.

The movie's other influences were many, among them *The Thing from Another World*, with its monster picking off residents of an isolated army base; *Forbidden Planet*, with its radioed warning not to land on a dangerous planet; and *Terrore nello spazio* (*Planet of the Vampires*; 1965), with a giant alien skeleton that inspired the derelict spaceship scene in *Alien*.[4] The movie *They Came from Within*, which features parasites that jump on faces and burst from bellies, is another plausible source,[5] as is the movie *It! The Terror from Beyond Space*, with its own monster aboard a spaceship. A.E. Van Vogt's novel *The Voyage of the Space Beagle* tells the story of another monster on a spaceship, a creature that lays eggs in its victims; Vogt, in fact, sued the makers of *Alien* and won an out-of-court settlement.[6]

However, the strongest inspiration for *Alien* may have come down to the line with which it was pitched to studios: "*Jaws* in space."[7] At a time when horror films such as *Jaws* were a highly successful genre, and *Star Wars* had proven the box-office power of space films, nothing was more natural than to mix the two genres with a horror film set in space.

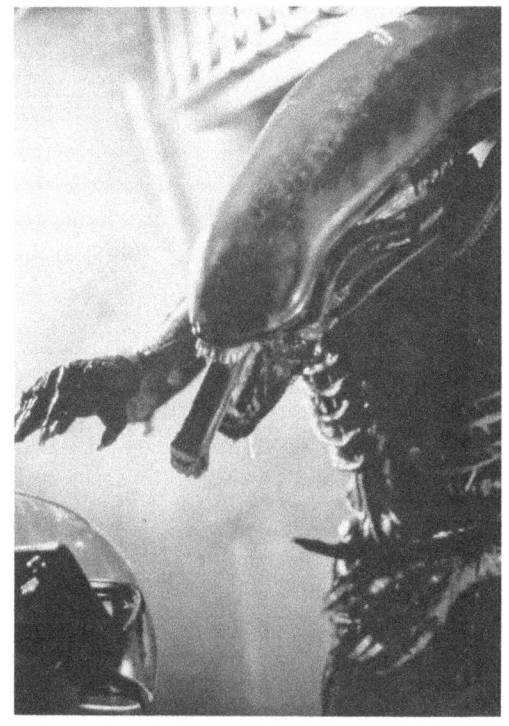

The full-grown alien (Bolaji Badejo) is on the rampage in *Alien* (1979, 20th Century–Fox).

Social trends also affected *Alien*. The influence of feminism may have affected the decision to cast a female performer, Sigourney Weaver, as the lead character, Ripley. As the only crew member who survives until the end, and who engages in single combat with the alien in the final battle, Ripley can also be seen as an example of the final girl, a type that was developing in horror films of the time, such as *Halloween*, released a year before *Alien*. The subplot of the corporation treating the crew as expendable, as part of a secret mission to bring a potentially lucrative biological weapon (the alien) back to Earth, fit in with post–Watergate/Vietnam paranoia about government lies and the military-industrial complex.

Alien has had extensive influence, spawning three direct sequels and numerous imitations about horrific beings from or in space: the *Predator* films; the *Alien vs Predator* films; the *Species* films; *Event Horizon (1997)*; and so on. It also influenced the developing slasher subgenre, which was usually earthbound but was similar to *Alien* in that it featured a DDB picking off a small band of people one by one, leaving the final girl at the end.

Transition: 1979–1985

The influence of movies such as *Halloween* and *Alien* led to a series of slasher films in the late 1970s and 1980s, in which a stalker hunted people, usually teenagers, and usually with a sharp weapon. When successful, these films often gave rise to series of sequels: for example, the *Halloween* series, the *Friday the 13th* series, the *Nightmare on Elm Street* series, and the *Prom Night* series. Critics bemoaned the decline of the horror film into such a tired and repetitive formula, particularly one that appeared to have so little in the way of redeeming social value. But audiences kept attending.

Some horror movies of the 1980s went in different directions. The werewolf was resurrected in *The Howling* (1981) and *An American Werewolf in London* (1981); the vampire came back in *Fright Night* (1985). *The Evil Dead* (1983) featured demonic forces in a cabin isolated in the woods. The novels of Stephen King inspired adaptations, including *The Shining*, *Christine* (1983), and *Cujo* (1983). *Re-Animator* went back to a source somewhat further in the past: the writings of H.P. Lovecraft.

Re-Animator (1985)

The early twentieth-century American horror writer Lovecraft was a prolific and imaginative creator of monstrous fiction. By the 1980s, his influence had already been felt on screen, notably in such film adaptations of his works as *The Haunted Palace* (1963) and *The Dunwich Horror* (1970). Lovecraft himself, of course, had been influenced by others, and his short story, "Herbert West — Reanimator," about the title character's experiments in bringing the dead back to life, bore the clear imprint of Mary Shelley's *Frankenstein*. This Frankensteinian element was what originally attracted Stuart Gordon to adapt Lovecraft's short story as *Re-Animator*, which Gordon directed and co-wrote.[8]

Despite its deep literary roots, *Re-Animator* was a child of its cinematic times, influenced most markedly by the contemporary zombie horror tradition that had begun with George Romero's *Night of the Living Dead*. In makeup design and acting performances, Gordon's living dead strongly resembled Romero's living dead, though cranked to a more manic, sometimes more comic level as crossed with the influence of Sam Raimi's *The Evil Dead*. Richard Band's musical score is strikingly similar to Bernard Herrmann's score for *Psycho*. *Re-Animator* had the gross-out makeup and gory special effects of other 1980s horror films, such as *The Thing* (1982) and *The Howling*. And it had youthful premarital sex and helpings of nudity in keeping with the slasher tradition from which it otherwise provided a break.

When all the elements were stirred together, *Re-Animator* was thoroughly original. It did not even adhere closely to Lovecraft's source, which is more a

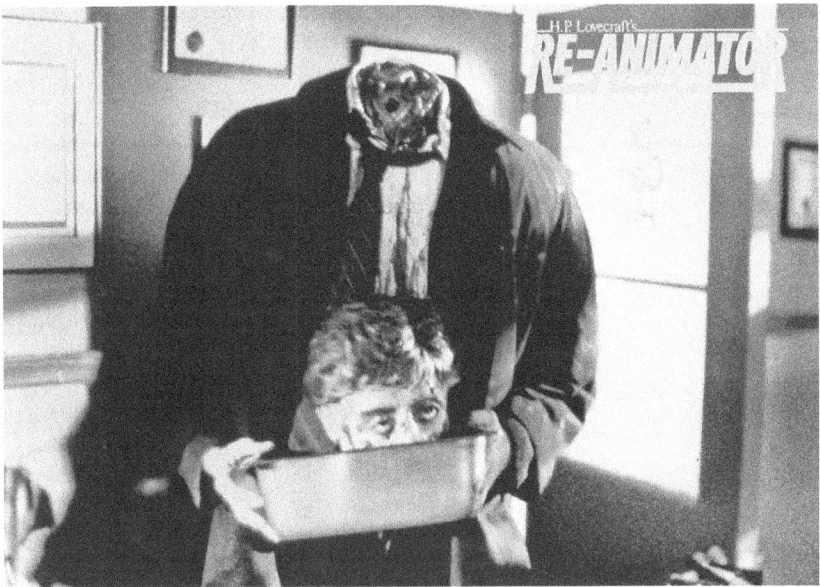

Dr. Carl Hill (David Gale) becomes a headless body carrying his own head in *Re-Animator* (1985, Empire Pictures).

collection of horrific anecdotes about West than a coherent story. The basic idea was preserved: West is a medical student at Miskatonic University who tries to bring dead humans back to life, with the help of a fellow student, given the name Dan Cain in the movie, and over the opposition of Halsey, the medical school dean. But the filmmakers fleshed out, so to speak, this outline by adding a love interest for Dan (Barbara Crampton as the dean's daughter, Megan Halsey) and a more menacing nemesis than the dean, Dr. Carl Hill, who threatens West's work and Megan as well. West figures out how to resurrect corpses, although they tend to behave badly once they spring to life, and even resurrects Hill after beheading him. Hill becomes an even more powerful adversary as a headless body carrying around his head, and abducts Megan and tries to rape her. The spectacle of Hill's head making lascivious advances on the naked, bound, screaming Megan is both outrageously comic and insanely horrific, representing the peak moment of the film. And then things get wilder, with more zombies entering the fray and a new peril for Megan: Dan's desire to resurrect her after she is killed.

Holding this lurid horror show together is the performance of Jeffrey Combs as West. Lovecraft called the character "an ice-cold intellectual machine,"[9] and that is just how Combs plays him, bizarrely steely, a mad scientist with all the ambition of an '80s yuppie but with an old-fashioned '60s-like devotion to a cause. Combs balances horror and humor in his performance without ever sliding so far into humor as to make West a caricature. This is central. The beheaded Dr. Hill is a formidable DDB, but the dominant DDB in the film, the amoral maker of all the chaos, is West. Without West's essential seriousness, *Re-Animator* would not be a horror movie.

Because of its outrageous nature, *Re-Animator* was released unrated, a move that usually bodes poorly for the box office. But the film made money and became a cult favorite. It spawned two sequels, *Bride of Re-Animator* and the made-for-TV *Beyond Re-Animator* (2003), as well as another Lovecraft adaptation, *From Beyond* (1986), also directed by Gordon. Its energetic zombies influenced later zombie films, and its blend of gross-out horror and comedy emboldened other filmmakers to try the same thing.

Transition: 1985–1996

Casey Becker (Drew Barrymore), moments before her untimely death, in *Scream* (1996).

By and large, the period from the late 1980s to the early 1990s was not a great one for horror. There were a few highlights, such as *Misery* (1990), which, with a capable William Goldman script from a Stephen King novel, told the claustrophobic story of an injured novelist trapped by a psychotic fan. *The Fly* (1986) was excellent and inventive, as were *Evil Dead II* (1987) and Peter Jackson's *Dead Alive* (*Braindead*, 1992). But most of the horror films of this period were sequels to slasher films: *Friday the 13th Part VI: Jason Lives* (1986), *Hello Mary Lou, Prom Night II* (1987), *Halloween IV: The Return of Michael Myers* (1988), and so on. It seemed that horror filmmakers, for the most part, had lost their ability to do anything but the same old slasher film. Then, in 1996, a different sort of slasher film appeared.

Scream (1996)

The key innovation in *Scream* was that it was a slasher movie in which the characters had seen slasher movies and were familiar with their clichés—

even though their familiarity did not prevent them from getting slashed. With a script by Kevin Williamson and direction by horror veteran Wes Craven, *Scream* was full of ironic wit and postmodern references to other horror movies—even references to references. One of the main characters is named Billy Loomis, a reference to the use of the name "Loomis" in *Halloween*, which in turn was a reference to its use in *Psycho*. Thus, *Scream* drew an implicit line of slasher descent for itself. It did so even more boldly by killing off its apparent star, the blonde Drew Barrymore, in the opening scene, just as *Psycho* had killed off its star, the blonde Janet Leigh, early in that film.

Scream was also marked by an elaborate mystery plot as to who the killer might be. In the film, a killer clad in a stretched-out ghost mask (whose design recalls Edvard Munch's painting *The Scream*) and a black Grim Reaper costume is stalking and murdering people in and around a high school. Suspicion falls on various characters, but finally it is revealed that the murders have been committed by two people working in concert, Billy and Stu. The final girls (there are two of these as well), a teenager played by Neve Campbell and a reporter played by Courteney Cox, finish off the killers.

Consistent with its postmodern style, there is little of genuine originality in *Scream*. Even the idea of having characters be familiar with horror movies had been done before. In *Halloween*, Laurie and the children she is babysitting are watching *The Thing from Another World* and *Forbidden Planet*, and in *Fright Night*, the teenage hero's familiarity with vampire movies gives him an edge over actual vampires. The "surprise" ending of the double murderer is at least as old as *Sei donne per l'assassino* (*Blood and Black Lace*; 1964), a Mario Bava film that influenced the slasher subgenre. What was new in *Scream* was to bring self-referentiality to the slasher film in such a thoroughgoing and playful way. This tended to undermine its strength as a horror movie: the characters' awareness of the artifice of their situation made it less real, and therefore undercut the authenticity of the DDB, to know whom is the main purpose of any horror film. *Scream* was entertaining, but its DDB was a relatively faint copy of copies. Regardless, *Scream* was a box-office smash and a critical favorite, and breathed new life into the tired slasher subgenre. It led to a series of sequels and many imitators, including *I Know What You Did Last Summer* (also scripted by Williamson) and *Urban Legend* (1998). It was the main subject of the parody in *Scary Movie* (2000). To this day, whenever a character in a horror movie says something like, "This is just like what happens in horror movies," the success of *Scream* is behind it.

Transition: 1996–2007

Scream had both parodied and perpetuated the slasher subgenre, but there was room in the horror genre as a whole for new directions in DDBs. More suggestive horror appeared in films such as *The Blair Witch Project* (1999) and *The Sixth Sense*: in the former, the DDB was only hinted at, never quite seen; in the latter, the lead ghost turned out to be the hero, a child psychologist played by Bruce Willis, who had not been aware he was dead. Creepy, evocative Japanese horror films of the 1990s, such as *Ringu*, led to American remakes in the 2000s, such as *The Ring*.

The 2000s also saw the introduction of the torture porn subgenre with films such as *Saw*, *Hostel*, and *Turistas* (2006), in which the emphasis was on the DDBs' brutal torture of the victims. Gore was the international language in many countries: in the French slasher film *Haute tension (High Tension*; 2003); the Australian serial killer film *Wolf Creek*; the Canadian werewolf film *Ginger Snaps*; and the British creature film *The Descent* (2005).

Despite the repetitiveness of many horror movies of the period, every once in a while there was a decidedly original film. Such a film was *Stuck*.

Stuck (2007)

Of the ten films profiled in these two historical chapters, only one director has helmed two of them: Stuart Gordon, who directed both *Re-Animator* and *Stuck*. Gordon is so spotlighted not because he is the horror genre's greatest director (although he is very good), but just to show how different the movies of a single director can be; indeed, the two films are so different that their analyses present little chance of repetition. *Re-Animator* is a zombie/mad scientist movie, and *Stuck* is—well, *Stuck*.

Many horror films claim to be based on a true story, but *Stuck* actually is. On October 26, 2001, a car driven by Texas woman Chante Mallard, who was then under the influence of drugs and alcohol, struck a homeless man, Gregory Biggs, who became lodged in her windshield.[10] Rather than seek medical care for him, she left him to die in her garage. With the help of a former boyfriend and a cousin, she hid the body in a park. Mallard was later arrested, convicted of murder, and sentenced to fifty years in prison.

Stuck retains only the basic premise of this story: intoxicated female motorist smashes into homeless man who gets stuck in windshield; she keeps him in her garage, hoping he will die. The rest of the story is considerably altered. In real life, the motorist was black and the homeless man was white; in the film, both are white, as if to eliminate racial overtones. However, there are hints of blackness in the character of Brandi, the motorist played by Mena Suvari, including her hairstyle (cornrows) and her black boyfriend; thus, a suggestion of the actual racial context of the story remains. What is mainly different is what happens after the homeless man, Tom, played by Stephen Rea, gets stuck in the windshield and parked in the garage. Instead of dying quietly, he fights to escape and get to a hospital. Brandi resorts to ever more

12. History: 1960s to the Present   141

aggressive murder attempts, finally trying to set him ablaze. Instead she is set ablaze and dies, while Tom escapes and gets the help he has been seeking.

In addition to being inspired by a true story, *Stuck* is clearly influenced by *Misery*, which itself is part of a tradition of invalids trapped under the cruel attentions of an insane person. *What Ever Happened to Baby Jane?* (1962) is an earlier example; more recently, in *Ôdishon* (*Audition*; 1999), a man is paralyzed and tortured by a young woman. *Stuck* also draws on old traditional stories of the dire consequences that await a person who is inhumane to a stranger: in the fairy tale Beauty and the Beast, for example, a prince is turned into an ugly Beast for refusing to give a fairy shelter from the rain. As noted in Chapter Six, the horror film often punishes characters who exhibit lack of charity.

Stuck is distinctive, however, largely because of how it uses a double DDB. At first, Brandi does not seem like a DDB: she is a normal person, a nurse's aide at a nursing home, who wins audience sympathy for the care she gives to her patients and her understandable ambition for promotion. This part of the story is cross-cut with that of Tom, who also is sympathetic, a man who has only just become homeless and is trying to get a job. When she crashes into him, both have been presented as decent human beings. But once Tom is stuck in her windshield, his head protruding into the front passenger seat and his legs into the air, the glass caught in his abdomen, he is a DDB to her: a horrible thing, barely living, even undead. He is also a threat to her, an agent of destruction, because of what might happen to her promotion if word gets out of the accident. When she decides to cover up the accident and let Tom die in her garage, Brandi becomes a DDB to him: an outwardly normal-looking but psychopathic killer without human feelings. Thus, together they are a mutually destructive double DDB.

In the course of the movie, Tom's point of view becomes more commanding, with the audience rooting for him as innocent victim to survive the depredations of Brandi (which he does). But the impression that they are both DDBs never goes away completely, and establishes a social significance to the story. In *Stuck*, the pressures of capitalism cause classes to be in conflict, including the classes at the bottom of the social ladder — the woman with the low-rung job and the unemployed, homeless man. Instead of joining together to fight the system, they fight each other for basic survival, and so see each other as DDBs.

Also making *Stuck* distinctive is the unique sensibility of Gordon, who brings to this film the same mix of gore and dark humor he brought to *Re-Animator*. In one of the most memorable scenes, a gay neighbor's fluffy little dog finds Tom in the garage and starts chewing at his raw flesh. The world of *Stuck* is literally dog-eat-dog, in which marginalized creatures fight each other for the essentials of life.

Stuck was not widely released and did not become a box office hit, but it was well reviewed. It may have influenced *Drag Me to Hell*, which had similar themes in its story of a young professional who gets in trouble for her inhumanity at a time when she is seeking a promotion. Whether *Stuck* will have more long-range influence remains to be seen.

Transition: 2007–Present

There have been a few horror movies of note since *Stuck*: *Drag Me to Hell, Paranormal Activity, Deadgirl* (2008), *Orphan, The House of the Devil, Splice,* and *The Human Centipede (First Sequence)* (2009) are among them. There has also been the usual crop of sequels and remakes, most of them tending to the undistinctive. What the future holds for the horror film genre is uncertain. But probably the genre will continue to thrive, as it has almost without interruption for about a century. And probably it will continue to evolve, developing its DDB presentations in ways subtle and pronounced, through the oscillation between cultural imitation and striving for originality that has marked its history all along.

13
Reputation

To many people, horror movies are an embarrassment, and DDB theory makes it clear why. On the surface, horror movies are about deformity and destructiveness, and from a superficial perspective it seems that only sick or twisted people would want to see such awful things. Now that DDB theory has clarified that horror movie fans are ontologists who want to know being, and in particular new forms of being that would be inaccessible if they were real, perhaps the cultural stock of horror movies will go up. But probably not. The reputation of the horror movie as, at best, a form of juvenilia, and, at worst, a sadistic showcase for gratuitous deformity and destructiveness, is too deeply engrained.

Even in writing this book, I found that when people asked what I was working on and I answered, "I'm writing a treatise on horror movies," almost everybody smiled. It seemed a joke that anything so weighty as a treatise would be produced about something so flimsy as horror movies. If I had said I was writing a treatise on eighteenth-century painting or modern poetry, I doubt that anyone would have smiled.

On the other hand, people would probably have been less engaged as well. Their smiles were a bit mocking, but also expressed a certain pleasure at an art form that most people have enjoyed at one time or another. Even the person who says, "I hate horror movies," has usually seen at least one. Horror movies are popular, indulging something almost everyone, at some point, wants to do: safely see a DDB. But only the devoted horror fan does this repeatedly and unabashedly. Horror movies are a pleasure, but for many, they are a guilty pleasure, something they are vaguely ashamed about liking.

In this chapter, I trace some key moments in the reputation — or disreputability — of horror movies.

The Production Code Era

By the time *Dracula* inaugurated the American sound horror film in 1931, there was already a bias among the country's moral authorities against some of the basic components of horror films. This was expressed in the Production Code, which brought nationwide, self-imposed censorship to the American film industry. Created in 1930 and enforced from 1934 into the 1960s, the Production Code had many provisions that affected horror films:[1]

- "[T]he sympathy of the audience should never be thrown to the side of crime, wrongdoing, evil or sin." This provision clashes with the horror film's frequently sympathetic presentation of evil, undertaken to improve the audience's knowledge of the DDB.
- "Revenge in modern times shall not be justified." Revenge is one of the key motives of DDBs.
- "Brutal killings are not to be presented in detail." This provision retarded the development of onscreen gore for decades.
- "Brutality and possible gruesomeness" must "be treated within the careful limits of good taste." Another roadblock in the development of gore.
- "Complete nudity is never permitted." Though not essential to a horror film, nudity is often helpful to maintaining audience attention and setting up a DDB attack.
- "Excessive and lustful kissing, lustful embraces, suggestive postures and gestures, are not to be shown." See nudity, above. Sex is one of the basic themes of horror films; the more excessive, the better.

The Production Code was not explicitly aimed at horror films, although many of its provisions clearly militated against them. In Britain in 1932, the British Board of Film Classification went further, creating a certificate, H for horrific, that restricted admission to those aged sixteen or over.[2] The press also tended to be biased against horror films. Norbert Lusk, reviewing *Dracula* for the *Los Angeles Times* on February 22, 1931, wrote:

> "[T]he story of human vampires who feast on the blood of living victims is too extreme to provide entertainment that causes word-of-mouth advertising. Plainly a freak picture, it must be accepted as a curiosity devoid of the important element of sympathy that causes the widest appeal."[3]

Note that Lusk does not argue here that *Dracula* is a bad example of a horror film; rather, horror films themselves appear to be bad. A story —*any* story— of human vampires is "too extreme" to be successful. It is a "freak picture," a "curiosity."

Fortunately for the horror genre, Lusk left the door open to empirical refutation. He claimed that a picture such as *Dracula* could not get good word-of-mouth or have wide appeal. In fact, *Dracula* was a box-office sensation. In its first domestic release, it grossed nearly $700,000, close to double its investment; its worldwide take by 1936 was more than $1 million.[4] Of course, financial success is not the same as aesthetic success, but in the movie business it is a marker for audience tastes. With *Dracula* and other early 1930s horror movies, the audience showed that it liked horror films. These films were popular; they had a good reputation among movie-goers. Thus the divide began between the public's attitude toward horror movies and that of various public figures, such as censors and reviewers.

A clear example of this divide occurred when *Dracula* and *Frankenstein* were re-released in 1938. The re-release was a commercial success, but Joseph Breen, head of the Production Code Administration, which administered film censorship, was gloomy about the situation. He received a letter from a school administrator who reported how severely agitated a boy of nine had become over the Frankenstein monster's drowning of the little girl, Maria, in *Frankenstein*. Breen replied:

Dracula (Bela Lugosi) displays his mesmerizing stare in *Dracula* (1931, Universal).

> "Personally, I dislike these pictures very much. Like yourself, I can hardly sit through them.... It goes without saying that these pictures are not intended for exhibition before children. The best that can be said for them is that they are 'adult fare'—for the kinds of adults who like them."[5]

Much can be said about this reply. Breen squarely situates the issue around two factors: his personal "dislike" of horror films, and the impropriety of showing them to children. He then goes further and implies there is something wrong with "the kinds of adults who like them." He has thus gone from a personal distaste and a desire to protect children to a vague condemnation of horror movie fans. It is possible that this is a typical movement in the building of the disreputability of horror movies and their audiences.

Oddly, children and young people are among the greatest aficionados of horror films. A 1941 *New York Times* report by Elizabeth R. Valentine on whether movies were good for children noted that some children watching horror films "hide their heads and whimper, but it is doubtful if any could be persuaded to leave the theatre short of force."[6] At the same time that horror movies attract young people, they also attract criticism from people who worry about their effect on young people. Valentine went on to describe psychologists and educators who thought it was bad to "subject a child to unnecessary horror or excitement, especially if he or she is nervous already."

In the 1950s and 1960s, as old horror movies were broadcast on television, a new generation of horror fans sprang up. Often they read *Famous Monsters of Filmland*; launched in 1958, this was a magazine devoted to the genre and memorable for its emphasis on what the horror fan most wanted to see — the monsters, the DDBs. The young horror fans might also watch *The Munsters* and *The Addams Family* on TV, two situation comedies that featured funny DDBs, and build model kits of the Universal monsters so they could look at them some more. At the same time, disapproval of horror films and their viewing by young people was common. A small example is a letter to the editor, published by the *New York Times* on November 3, 1963, that, in an incidental remark, condemns the "'horror' films to which our youth is exposed."[7]

After the Production Code

As horror movies became characterized by greater violence and sex, particularly after the Production Code collapsed in the 1960s, the amount of onscreen brutality to which youth was exposed became even greater. In the 1950s and 1960s, they could see it in the open air, at drive-in theaters; from the 1970s onward, at shopping mall theaters and video stores; from the 1990s onward, rented or downloaded online. Although some of these movies were big studio productions, many more were low-budget, independently made films with poor production values, increasing the sense that the horror film was a low, vulgar art form that was a danger to the nation's youth.

Yet young people in particular kept flocking to horror movies. Even when the movies were rated "R," requiring children under seventeen to be accompanied by an adult, lax enforcement ensured that those younger than seventeen still managed to find a way into *The Exorcist*. That movie was reportedly the first horror film to rank as number one at the box office for its year (1973),[8] and it would be surprising if the nation's youth did not play a part in *The Exorcist's* success. Similarly, the profitability of slasher movies, gory as they were, was driven predominantly by teenage males.[9]

There is some question as to why young people and males in particular should like horror films. Unfortunately, the empirical evidence is lacking to make a definite determination about this. This does not stop critics from speculating. For example, James B. Twitchell supposes, on the basis of what is apparently anecdotal or personal evidence, that adults are not interested in stories "about the vampire, Frankenstein monster, or werewolf," and that their recollections about such things are entirely from their late childhood or adolescent years.[10] This, he argues, is because horror stories serve the function of conveying modern codes of sexual behavior, an important lesson for the young but, once learned, no longer relevant. By implication, adults who keep liking horror movies (such as this writer and perhaps some readers of this book) have been stunted or twisted; they never learned the appropriate sexual lessons.

If others can speculate without evidence, so can I. I speculate that the young are naturally more curious about being, since they must absorb a vast amount of information about the beings in their environment during their formative years. This is why children love to explore and engage in imaginative play. They will take toys, cartoons, monsters, anything — just so that they get to know every being they can. For them, getting to know DDBs is just part of getting to know being. Adults who continue to like horror movies as they grow older exhibit a somewhat uncommon but valuable property: an undiminished, youthful interest in being.

As to the issue of why males particularly want to know DDBs, it is possible that there is a deep evolutionary psychological basis: that males in prehistory were more likely to fight the predators and human enemies — the real DDBs of their time — and therefore that it was important for males to be interested in DDBs. But without evidence, this too seems like a "just so" story, concocting an origin tale without having to prove it. Until more evidence appears, all that can be said is that males seem to like horror films for the same reason females seem to like romantic films: their respective fantasies of choice satisfy something deep inside them. And there is nothing to stop some females from liking horror films, nor some males from liking romantic films. Sometimes the two genres blend, as in the horrific romance of *Twilight* and the romantic horror of *Bram Stoker's Dracula*.

Oscars and Horror Films

The ultimate mark of reputation in Hollywood is the Academy Award. By the 1970s, the only horror movie to have been awarded one of the three top Oscars (Picture, Actor, Actress) had been *Dr. Jekyll and Mr. Hyde* in 1931–1932, and even that had been only half an Oscar: *Jekyll's* Fredric March shared the Best Actor Oscar for that year with Wallace Beery for *The Champ*. The scarcity of Oscar victories for horror films indicated the low status in which the genre was regarded.

Then, in the Oscar race for 1973, *The Exorcist*, a film about a girl possessed by a demon, received ten nominations, including Best Picture and several other top awards. Perhaps the film was helped by its literary origins (it was based on a best-selling novel by William Peter Blatty) and major studio bankrolling (Warner Bros.), or its grand themes of good and evil. Perhaps the

Academy was simply ready to recognize a film that contained projectile vomiting.

But not that ready. When the awards ceremony was held in 1974, *The Exorcist* lost for Best Picture to *The Sting*, a more traditional Oscar bet that featured a historical setting, a well-groomed cast, top stars, and no projectile vomiting. Ellen Burstyn, Linda Blair, and Jason Miller lost all the acting awards for which *The Exorcist* was nominated (respectively, actress, supporting actress, and supporting actor) and William Friedkin lost for Best Director. The cinematography, art direction-set decoration, and editing awards were also lost. Still, *The Exorcist* won two awards, for Best Adapted Screenplay (Blatty) and Sound (Robert Knudson, Chris Newman).

Anthony Hopkins won a Best Actor Oscar playing cannibalistic psychiatrist Hannibal Lecter in *The Silence of the Lambs* (1991, Orion).

Nearly two decades passed before a horror film won any further Academy Awards—Kathy Bates won the Best Actress Oscar for her role in 1990's *Misery*. Then, the following year, something remarkable happened to a horror film, perhaps because the Academy seemed uncertain whether the film really counted as horror. *The Silence of the Lambs* could pass as a police procedural, crime thriller, or other more innocuous entity. But most horror fans recognized it as one of their own. In the ceremony for the films of 1991, *The Silence of the Lambs* won five Oscars, including the highest one, Best Picture, as well as Actor (Anthony Hopkins), Actress (Jodie Foster), Director (Jonathan Demme), and Adapted Screenplay (Ted Tally).

Since then, another long stretch has passed without a major award. The Oscar ceremony honoring the films of 2009 featured a montage of horror film clips saluting the genre. It was not an award, but it was better than nothing.

Continuing Reputation Uncertainty

As the popularity of horror films continued unabated in the 1970s, they began to gain some respectability in scholarly circles. Film historian William

K. Everson devoted a history to them, *Classics of the Horror Film* (1974),[11] and a selection of scholarly essays about them was published in *Focus on the Horror Film* (1972).[12] Over the following decades, a horror film critical industry sprouted, sometimes lambasting the films but often treating them with respect and even admiration. For example, some critics considered slasher films, with their bloody attacks on women, to be anti–woman. In 1980, Gene Siskel and Roger Ebert devoted an episode of their *Sneak Previews* television program to the "disturbing new trend" of "women in danger" films. However, in 1992, critic Carol J. Clover pointed out contrary evidence to the charge of anti–womanism: the importance of male audience identification with the resourceful, heroic final girl.[13]

Yet even as some critics began to appear to take the side of horror films, the increasing goriness of the genre kept others away. Critic Walter Kendrick wrote almost apologetically:

> "For literal-minded fools—among whom, regrettably, I include myself—the spectacle of heads split open, innards ripped out, and livers flying through the air is intolerable, because we cannot resist the illusion that such atrocities are really taking place."[14]

Kendrick somewhat misses the point here. The difference between him and a fan of horror, gory or otherwise, is not that the fan *can* resist the illusion and Kendrick cannot. The fan does not *want* to resist the illusion; the illusion is necessary for knowing the DDB. Rather, as Stephen King, a champion horror fan, wrote, effective horror films "are those films which hold their spell over us in spite of all we can do, even including the recitation of that most magic spell-breaking incantation, 'It's only a movie.'"[15] The difference between the horror film fan and the person who does not care for horror films is that the horror film fan can tolerate and even seeks and enjoys the illusion that the DDB exists, whereas other people find that illusion, as Kendrick calls it, "intolerable." Horror film fans, as Breen sneeringly put it, are "the kinds of adults who like" these films, in contrast to people like him, who "can hardly sit through them." And then there are the people in the middle, who like an occasional horror film but may be vaguely ashamed about seeing it.

Perhaps because of this underlying psychological divide between those who like and those who do not like (or are ashamed about liking) horror films, there continues to be a tendency to belittle or condemn the genre. Some of these condemnations have been noted in earlier chapters—the coining of the term "torture porn" to malign horror films that featured torture; the efforts to censor the trailer for *Orphan*. In addition, consider this line from a *Hollywood Reporter* review of *The Human Centipede (First Sequence)*: "Crosses the line from horror to just plain sick."[16] The claim here is not that the film crosses the line from good horror to bad horror; that would be an aesthetic objection. Instead, the objection is psychiatric: the idea is that horror exists along a continuum of mental health, with sick being the worst and horror being next to worst. To be a little better than sick is to be a horror fan.

By and large, horror fans do not mind. They know that there is something pleasurable and important in their search for DDBs, and to have it be considered sick or low or harmful only helps restrict it to the relatively small (absolutely, quite large) number of true devotees—as Shakespeare would put it, "We few, we happy few." There may come a time when society as a whole honors the horror film the way its fans do. But probably not. Society as a whole is concerned with the beings whose existence and worth it acknowledges, the beings it regards as real, well-formed, and constructive. The horror audience is concerned with the rest—the fictional, deformed, and destructive, whose cinematic existence offers new possibilities for the searcher after being.

14
Taxonomy

The taxonomy, or classification, of DDBs is a difficult business. It is hard enough with real, biological beings, which at least have a single organizing principle to draw upon: evolutionary descent. No such principle applies to DDBs, among whom it is not clear whether zombies or vampires came first, and whether one spawned the other (probably not). Why, anyway, does one need a taxonomy of DDBs? Such a taxonomy is useful for comparing, analyzing, and discerning the significance of the various types of monsters. That is how taxonomy will be approached in this chapter, and it will require a classification scheme that begins with the division between the undead and the living.

The Undead

The undead are perennially popular as DDBs because they provide us with beings we cannot possibly see in real life, beings that should not even have being. Once an organism dies, it ceases to be; it is replaced with a corpse, which quickly decomposes. But in many horror movies, death is just the beginning. The corpse stirs, and a being comes to a kind of life we could make no sense of if it were not a DDB.

The undead, if presented well, are uncanny: they give you a sense that a forbidden border has been crossed, two types wrongly mixed, which is close to the definition of positional deformity (Chapter 1). Yet it is delightful to see the undead in the safe environs of a movie theater, and not only because of the pleasure of knowing being that underlies all horror films. There is probably also an element of wish-fulfillment in our desire to see the undead — we want to believe death is not the end — but, to keep the psychological books balanced, we punish ourselves for the wish by imagining that the undead would not be very pleasant company: they would, in fact, want to destroy us. The menace is most clear with the undead who want to consume us. These are the hungry undead, those who live off the living: the vampires and zombies.

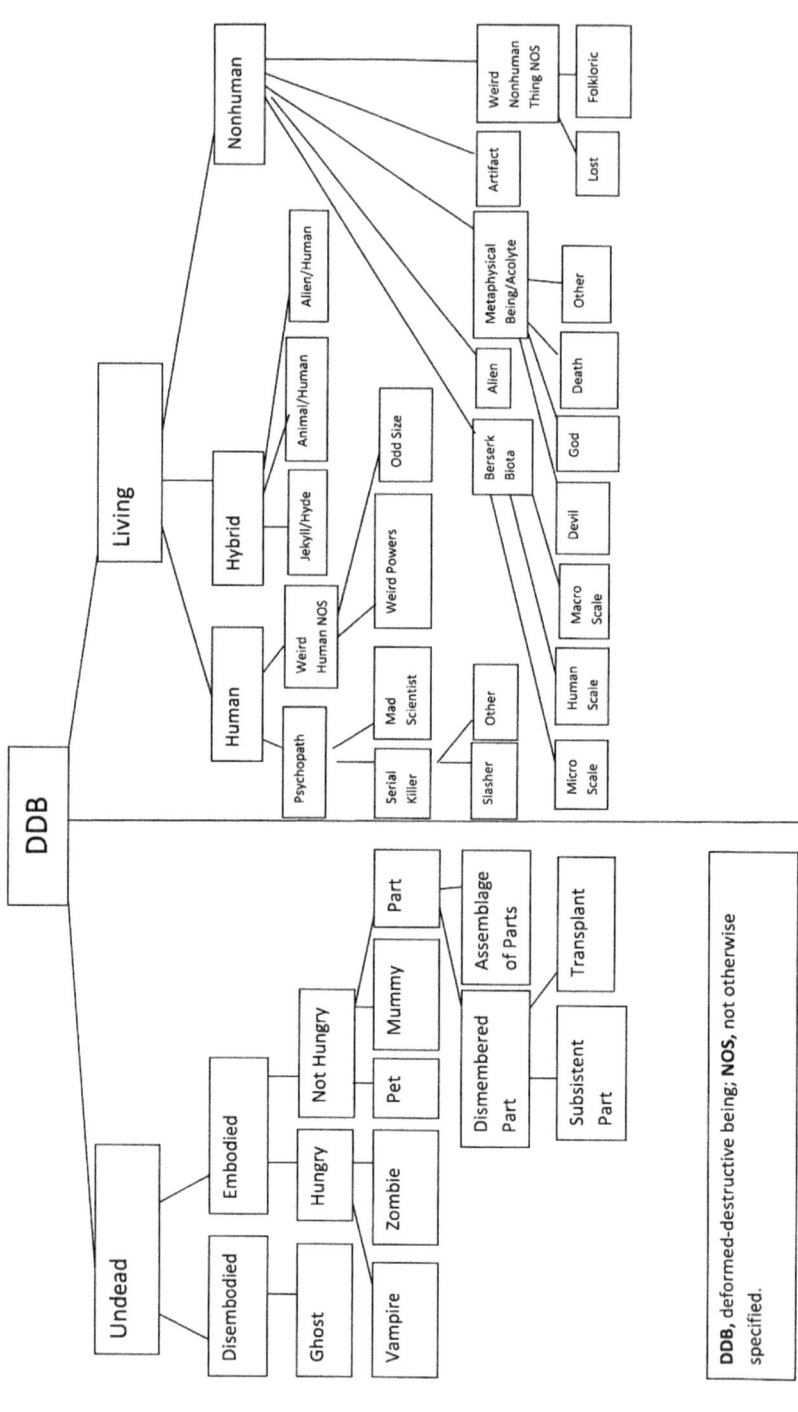

14. Taxonomy

THE HUNGRY UNDEAD

Vampires[1] and zombies[2] (at least, the breed of zombies that emerged in the 1960s with *Night of the Living Dead*) are undead who share in common a ravenous hunger for human beings. Additionally, in most versions of their stories, they are contagious: when they feed, they pass their status to their victim, who dies and becomes one of them. They are thus almost perfect in their destructiveness: they not only kill you, but transform you postmortem into another vampire or zombie.

The principal difference between vampires and zombies is that vampires want only to drink human blood, whereas zombies want to eat human flesh, including tissue, blood, and all. A whole set of opposing characteristics consistent with this difference further distinguishes the two. The vampire, at least in his incarnations from the various film versions of *Dracula* up through such movies as *Count Yorga, Vampire* (1970) and *Underworld* (2003), is aristocratic. Traditionally clad in a cape and tuxedo, he is wealthy, cultured, refined, articulate, and intelligent. Sexually predatory, he favors the blood of beautiful young women. The motif of the aristocratic vampire began to decline in the 1980s, but even then the vampire appeared to have some money, whether he was middle class (*Fright Night, The Lost Boys* [1987]) or working class (*Near Dark* [1987]). In contrast, the zombie is destitute. Homeless, clad in rags, abjectly poor, stupid, mute, asexual, the zombie is the emblem of the bottom of society as the vampire, in his classic incarnation, embodies the top.

Small wonder that their table manners are so different. The aristocratic vampire is a connoisseur of human fare who wants only the best and most refined portion, the blood, sipping it as if it were a fine wine. Like a gourmet who favors caviar, the vampire takes only the fish eggs and leaves the fish. When the vampire is done, the only sign that he has dined are two discreet holes in the neck. The zombie, however, has terrible table manners. Animal-like, he bites and tears off any part of his prey that he can reach. He is indiscriminate: he will eat the intestines with as much elan as the shoulder meat. His face is frequently smeared with blood and gore, whereas the vampire will have at most a little trickle coming from his fangs.

The vampire and zombie present two types of class fear. The vampire speaks of an origin in the imaginations of a peasant class about the aristocrats who preyed on them. The zombie originated in the nightmares of a middle class about the destitute who might rise up to overthrow them. However, because viewer identification in a horror movie can be with the DDB as well as the normals, one might also speculate that early moviegoers wanted to fantasize about being powerful aristocratic killers, and the middle class of the 1960s, fed up with their problems, fantasized about an apocalyptic collapse

Opposite page: This diagram presents the taxonomy of DDBs.

that could leave them as destitute zombies, with nothing to worry about but eating.

Both the vampire and zombie have changed over time, and will probably change again. The vampire, as noted, has lost his exclusive association with the aristocracy, and now sometimes has table manners as vile as the zombies: in *30 Days of Night* (2007), the vampires tear at their food with the ugly vigor of feral dogs. In *Daybreakers* (2010), almost everybody on Earth is a vampire, making the condition democratic compared to the old days of Count Dracula.

The zombie, for his part, has come up in the world since the days of *White Zombie* (1932), *I Walked with a Zombie*, and *The Plague of the Zombies* (1966), when zombieism was exclusively associated with voodoo and involved absolute obedience to a master, without even the reward of dining on human flesh. This weak state was mocked in the Bob Hope comedy *The Ghost Breakers* (1940), when a character describes zombies by saying, "A zombie has no will of his own. You see them sometimes walking around blindly with dead eyes, following orders, not knowing what they do, not caring." Hope replies, "You mean like Democrats?" However, since *Night of the Living Dead*, the zombie has become an anarchic force, obeying no one, untied to voodoo or any other religion, and eating the living. It is as if the vampire has descended in social status at the same rate as the zombie has climbed, so much so that it can sometimes be difficult nowadays to tell them apart.

Distinguishing the two used to be easier because the vampire had so many rules. As befit his fussy aristocratic origin, he was an obsessive-compulsive, always checking to see if it was day out (sunlight would kill him), and seizing up at the smell of garlic or the sight of a cross or a mirror (he was allergic to them all). He had to sleep in his native soil in a coffin, wait for an invitation before entering a house, and die if someone drove a wooden stake through his heart. You could not even count on him to remain in human form: he might turn into a bat or a mist or something if humanity became too much trouble. Some recent vampire movies have rewritten these rules, dispensing, for example, with the power of the cross in an effort to downplay the Christian associations. But the vampire remains, in most versions, a peculiarly fragile monster considering that he is supposed to have superhuman strength.

The zombies, as befits their proletarian style, are a hardier lot. Individually, they are not strong, and can be killed by piercing their brains with a bullet or a crowbar or the like, but when amassed in large numbers they can be invincible (again, suggesting their origin in fears or fantasies of class revolution). Crosses, mirrors, and other fey artifacts hold no terrors for them. They are traditionally slow, but have been getting faster in movies such as the *Dawn of the Dead* remake (2004).

Occasionally animals get zombified, such as the cats in *Re-Animator* and *Pet Sematary*, and they often have much worse tempers when undead than when alive. But they are not a major figure on the undead stage.

Mummies

The mummy is taxonomically related to the vampire and zombie in that all three are whole beings who live on after death, ontologically identical with what they were before death, although altered in monstrous ways. Strictly speaking, the mummy may not be undead in the same sense: mummy movies sometimes make a point of describing the mummy as someone who was buried alive and then kept alive through the eons via the aid of a mystical device such as tana leaves (the favored McGuffin of *The Mummy's Hand* and its sequels). But since he *was* buried and his life seems to go on and on afterward, it is fair to call the mummy undead.

The mummy is typically safeguarding a tomb from desecration. When the desecrators inevitably arrive, he rises from his sarcophagus and kills them by strangulation or other means. Thus, he is something like the voodoo-governed zombie, who does the bidding of his master, except that, even after thousands of years, he can work on his own initiative, like an undead subcontractor. (Sometimes a priest from an ancient order assists him.) Often, he is in love with the princess whose tomb he guards, and may search the earth for her reincarnated form, whom he usually finds, by good luck, in the movie's heroine.

The mummy is typically a sexual transgressor of sorts: he either loved a forbidden person, or committed sacrilege in trying to resurrect his dead beloved, or both. For this, he is punished with being mummified alive, sometimes with his tongue cut out or other barbarities perpetrated against him. He therefore projects the usual conservative-radical double message of horror films: follow the rules or be punished, but if you do not follow the rules, you will become strong and immortal and get into the movies. Most mummies stay wrapped in bandages for the entire film, although some take more or less human, unmummified form, as in both versions of *The Mummy* (1932, 1999).

The mummy film almost always concerns ancient Egyptian mummies, and this limits the monster, since there are only so many fresh ideas one can get out of ancient Egypt. In Mexico, a series of Aztec mummy movies, beginning with *La Momia azteca (The Aztec Mummy*; 1957), tried to widen the genre, and there have been scattered similar attempts, but for the most part the mummy is attached to Egypt.

Undead Parts

To qualify as a DDB, a monster must be a being, a subsistent entity, not just an attached part or a broken-off fragment of an entity. However, in horror films, even a fragment can become subsistent. This is the case with dismembered parts that somehow acquire independent life and persist as undead, and usually powerful and malevolent.

The best known example may be the hand cut by the intrepid Ash from his own arm in *Evil Dead II*. Ash does this because the hand is possessed, but afterward things get worse, with the hand continuing to live its demonic life, scuttling around and causing mayhem. *Donovan's Brain* (1953) is a brain that would not die, whereas *The Brain That Wouldn't Die* is actually a head that would not die, and that causes great trouble for the man who removed it from his wife. *Re-Animator* also features a malign undead head, carried around like a trophy by the undead body to which it was once connected.

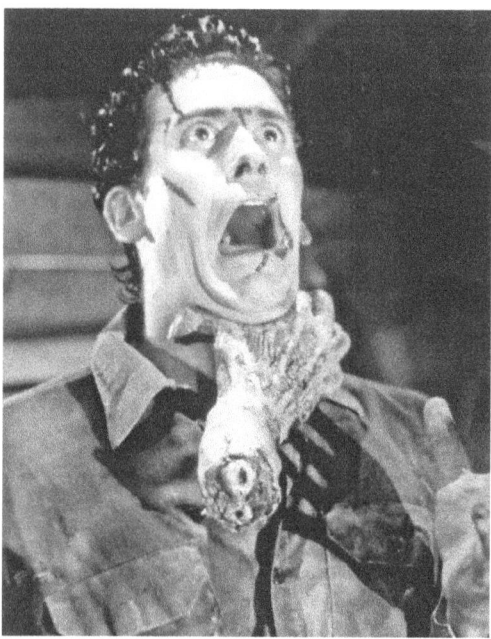

Ash (Bruce Campbell) is struggles with his own dismembered hand in *Evil Dead II* (1987, Rosebud Releasing Corp.).

A distinct subspecies of the undead part is the part that gets transplanted into a living body and behaves monstrously and even intelligently while there. A murderer's hands or brain (in, respectively, *Mad Love* [1935] and *Black Friday* [1940]) can get transplanted into an innocent patient and cause him to turn murderous. In *Gin gwai* (*The Eye*; 2002) and its American remake, *The Eye* (2008), a cornea transplant causes the victim to see ghostly things she would prefer not to see.

Undead parts have a profound positional deformity, because instead of being assimilated as subordinate components of a master being, they live independent of a master or, if transplanted, attempt to overthrow the master. Their deformity is so severe that they can seem comical, as with the fast-moving hand in *Evil Dead II*, or uncanny, as with transplanted evil parts.

Just as you can have undead parts, you can sew together a bunch of dead parts and then animate the whole package, resulting in an undead assemblage of parts. This concept is so closely associated with the Frankenstein monster, who came to life this way, that the term "Frankenstein monster" is more or less synonymous with this type of DDB. There have been, however, other undead assemblages, such as the title brides in *Bride of Frankenstein* and *Bride of Re-Animator*.

14. Taxonomy

As the prototype of the undead assemblage, the Frankenstein monster sets an example of superhuman strength, deformed ugliness, homicide, and a mix of pathos and horror. The source of the horror is obvious (deformity and homicide); the pathos comes from the fact that someone (Frankenstein) consciously assembled him, and why anyone would have thought it a good idea to do so makes us sad for the monster and angry at the creator—especially since the creator, in most cases, abandons him.

Versions of the Frankenstein monster have varied in how and when he got deformed. In the TV-movie *Frankenstein: The True Story*, the creature is handsome at the beginning, but gradually deteriorates into a hideous hulk. In *Mary Shelley's Frankenstein*, the monster is, following the novel, articulate, opposing the film tradition that, ever since Karloff in *Frankenstein*, has typically depicted him as mute or nearly mute.

The very artificiality of the undead assemblage makes him a metaphor of sorts for the DDB as a horror movie creation: every horror movie, so to speak, assembles its DDB from parts in the imagination, then brings it to life as a new being. For this, perhaps, and other reasons, the Frankenstein monster is perennially popular, and is often brought back for sequels. His undead nature makes it easy to explain his indestructibility. However, movie monsters in general, whether living or undead, can be brought back from the dead readily enough if the box-office potential is there.

Ghosts

So far, all of the undead described in this taxonomy have at least had bodies. Ghosts branch off from the embodied undead because they are disembodied: spirits or wraiths that fleshlessly haunt the living. In this respect, they resemble the undead part: a ghost is a sliver of itself, a fragment that has taken on subsistent being. Usually invisible, ghosts can manifest themselves to one or more people; when they do, they can be emotionally upsetting, even horrifying, but because of their disembodied nature it can be hard for them to put together a physical assault, let alone a murder. Still, they sometimes manage, especially if they can gain possession of a living person and use him as a tool, as the ghosts in the Overlook Hotel do with Jack Torrance in *The Shining*, or if they can scare someone into doing something foolish, like the hysterical Eleanor having a car accident in *The Haunting*. The ghost Freddy Krueger in the *Nightmare on Elm Street* movies does a lot of killing just by penetrating the dreams of his teenage prey: in his world, if you die in a nightmare, you die for real. Then there are certain ghosts who, incorporeal or not, seem to be able to kill directly, such as Samara in *The Ring* and Candyman in *Candyman*.

From some movies, such as *The Sixth Sense* and *The Others*, we have learned that ghosts do not always know they are ghosts, which can make for added creepiness. But the traditional depiction of ghosts, as handed down from literary works such as Shakespeare's *Hamlet* and Dickens's *A Christmas Carol*, is that they know perfectly well they are ghosts and generally do not like it.

Ghosts can appear in a variety of forms. The classic cinematic depiction was a double-exposed image that you could see through, but this got tired; Curtis Harrington pointed out in 1952 that this did not look so much like a ghost as like "a man double-exposed."[3] More recently they tend to be fully-fleshed in appearance, but with pale, zombie-like makeup and wounds from whatever way they died. One gets the impression they do not get out much: they tend to stick to whatever place they are haunting, and they hardly ever have sex. Perhaps for that reason, they are often angry, seeking vengeance or restitution for how they died. In some versions, the ghosts hope to progress from their exile on earth to enter paradise; others, like the ghosts at the Overlook Hotel in *The Shining*, seem content to stay where they are, but would like some company. This is frequently achieved by persuading a living person to join them, as the ghost girl does who demands a mother in *Honogurai mizu no soko kara* and its American remake, *Dark Water* (2005).

The Living

Living DDBs lack the uncanny characteristic of intrinsically violating boundaries that their undead colleagues have. Even so, there are many ways they can be deformed and destructive, and so qualify as DDBs. In addition, if their movies are successful, they often come back from the dead and carry out another installment of their adventures. This does not mean they should be classified as undead, because they are only contingently undead, for the sake of generating a sequel. But it does suggest there is some overlap among the taxonomic categories.

Living DDBs may be categorized as either human, nonhuman, or a hybrid. The human DDBs are generally insane, and are called here psychopaths.

PSYCHOPATHS

The simplest way to transform a living person into a DDB is to make him a psychopath, since all it takes is a slight abnormality in his brain circuitry, whether congenital or acquired. This method of DDB generation has been used in numerous films. There are two basic kinds of horror movie psychopaths: serial killers and mad scientists. Both are usually human, although there may be hints of something more diabolical about them. The serial killer Michael Myers in *Halloween*, for example, is, we are told, the bogeyman, and this, for all we know, is true. Serial killers and mad scientists are usually normal-looking, but they may be disfigured. Aside from that, they are, as a rule, physically ordinary human beings who happen to have serious psychoses.

The serial killer takes pleasure in killing people, and therefore does it over and over. The best known type, the slasher, appears to live only for killing.[4] He conceals his identity, usually behind a mask, stalks around silently, and prefers sharp objects (such as knives or power drills) that require him to get closer to his victim than, say, guns or explosives would. He preys on both males and females, often when they are having sex, but takes special delight in killing young women. However, the slasher is only one species in the menagerie of serial killers. Other types include those who kill mainly for revenge, often with an elaborate scheme in mind (such as the title character in *The Abominable Dr. Phibes*); killers driven by some compulsion more sophisticated than the typical slasher (such as the child murderer in *M* or the family-killing stepfather in *The Stepfather* [1987]); evil children (such as the youthful killers in *The Bad Seed* and *Orphan*); and killers who have some sort of theoretical point to make (such as those in *Seven* [1995] and the *Saw* franchise). There can even be a corporate killing enterprise, such as Elite Hunting, the entity that provides rich men and women the opportunity to torture and kill hapless tourists in the *Hostel* films.

Whatever their motives, serial killers are, in general, hopelessly middle class. The very poor do not become serial killers — presumably they cannot afford the knives — and the rich and aristocratic have better pleasures to entertain them. In the *Hostel* films, some rich people patronize the pay-for-torture service, but they appear to be mostly a *nouveau riche*, businessman lot, not old money, and the Elite Hunting enterprise itself is brashly entrepreneurial, and hence at heart middle class. We know exactly where *Halloween's* Michael Myers came from — that nondescript suburban house where he killed his sister. There can be blue-collar touches: Myers wears blue-collar clothes, but they are not his; he picked them off a victim, as if in rebellion against his class, just as the female college student killer in *Haute tension* prefers to imagine herself a male truck driver. Henry, the serial killer played by Michael Rooker in *Henry: Portrait of a Serial Killer* (1990) is solidly working class. In most cases, however, the horror movie serial killer is a middle-class concept.

Accordingly, serial killers act middle class. They kill other middle class people because that is all they know. They are usually sexually frustrated, which is why they keep penetrating teenage girls with their phallic knives, trying to achieve in blood what they cannot in sperm. They are unimaginative, repeating the same sort of crimes over and over. When they get fancy in their killing schemes, they are usually upper middle class — doctors, perhaps, like Dr. Phibes — so they can afford all that equipment. But even then, they suffer middle-class gaucheness, resorting to middle-brow ideas for their murders, such as the ten plagues of Egypt or the seven deadly sins.

Serial killers are almost always white, and so are most of their victims. This is because the killers live in segregated areas where they never meet a black person long enough to want to kill him. Also, black people, as presented in movies, are too cool to be serial killers. The movie black person would use a gun, not a knife, if he wanted to kill, and he would only kill for some good reason, and he would not do it out of sexual frustration because white people in movies are the sexually frustrated ones, not black people.

Mad scientists share with serial killers the characteristic of psychopathology — hence the epithet "mad"— but they are otherwise a distinct group.[5] They may be rich and aristocratic (such as Baron Frankenstein), but even if they are not, they are distinguished by their exceptional intelligence, creativity, and vision. Some may end up killing serially, but, unlike the traditional serial killer, they are not driven by an urge to kill; their primary aim is to achieve some great scientific feat, which often makes sense considered in the abstract: for example, to discover the secret of life, attain invisibility, teleport matter, explore space, or cure disease. But something always goes wrong: perhaps because the mad scientist violated the horror movie ethical rule against tampering with nature, and perhaps because he is mad. The mad scientist is usually mad in a specific way. He is, for one thing, grandiose, dreaming of being like God, changing the world as we know it, having power such as the world has never seen. When it all crashes and he succeeds only in creating a monster or making himself a monster, he is usually bitterly disappointed. In other words, the mad scientist is *bipolar*. Brilliant by nature, he climbs to heights of mania, crashes to depths of depression, and in the midst of it, creates or becomes a monster.

Like the serial killer, the mad scientist is frequently sexually frustrated, attached to a fiancée or girlfriend he cannot sleep with because he is so busy with his experiments. One wonders if he really wants the girlfriend, or if he is secretly gay, like the more openly gay Dr. Pretorius in *Bride of Frankenstein*.

The destructiveness of the mad scientist usually (but not always) is the result of the monster he creates or becomes. The mad scientist often feels remorse over what he has done, but not always: Peter Cushing's Frankenstein in the Hammer *Frankenstein* series is remarkably free of remorse. The mad scientist tends to be especially remorseful if he himself becomes the monster, because then he must suffer the burden of deformity rather than letting an outside party suffer it. If he becomes a monster, he is likely to gain special powers that improve his destructive capacity, such as invisibility in *The Invisible Man* or the power of lethal touch in *The Invisible Ray*. If he does not become the monster, the mad scientist is not necessarily a DDB. Provided that he is a decent, conscientious person who tries to destroy the monster and is otherwise non–destructive, he is not a DDB. But if he is destructive even before the monster comes into being, sides with the monster, or shows no remorse, the mad scientist is a DDB.

Whether the psychopathic DDB takes the form of the serial killer or mad scientist, the audience is likely to take pleasure in the flouting of the norms of cognition and behavior. Nearly everyone has it in them to act much more crazily than they permit themselves to, and horror movie psychopaths do just that. At the same time, normal people tend to be afraid of what might happen to them if other people started acting crazy—the premise of the two versions of *The Crazies* (1973, 2010)—and this accounts for the horror that is paired with wish fulfillment in viewing psychopathic DDBs.

Hybrids

At the edge between human and nonhuman living DDBs are the hybrids, who mix characteristics of both. This category includes the many versions of *Dr. Jekyll and Mr. Hyde*, the grandfather of hybrid stories. Strictly speaking, the Jekyll/Hyde character does not directly mix human and nonhuman; rather, the experiments of Dr. Jekyll demonstrate that humans are *already* a mix of human and bestial, or good and evil. What Jekyll invents is a chemical solution that will allow his bestial or evil side to rise to the top and become incarnate in the personality of Hyde. Indirectly, this makes it seem as if Jekyll, when he turns into Hyde, has mixed himself with something bestial. It is in this indirect sense that Jekyll/Hyde is a hybrid DDB. In addition, Jekyll/Hyde inspired numerous stories in which there is some direct mixing of the human and nonhuman, including the entire subgenre of animal/human films.

The mixing of animals and humans can occur from two directions: an animal can be made human-like and a human can be made animal-like. The prime example of the former is *Island of Lost Souls*, in which Dr. Moreau converts animals into not-quite-human creatures that stand on two legs and wear clothes but are deformed and excessively hairy. Like all hybrids, Dr. Moreau's creatures have a deep positional deformity, mixing categories that should not be mixed, as even they are aware. One of the animal-men, played by Bela Lugosi, accuses Dr. Moreau: "You made us things. Not men. Not beasts. Part men, part beasts—things!"

Much more common in horror movies are the humans who become animal-like. The most prominent example is the werewolf—a person who periodically becomes like a wolf, in movies from *Werewolf of London* to *Ginger Snaps*—though there have been other varieties, such as the woman who becomes a panther in *Cat People*, the man who becomes fly-like in both versions of *The Fly*, the man who becomes alligator-like in *The Alligator People*, the man who becomes snake-like in *Sssssss* (1973), and so on. In most such cases, particularly the werewolf, the transformation is for the worse. The hybrid is usually bad-tempered, homicidal, and grotesque, and the human who undergoes the transformation may suffer anguish and guilt for crimes committed while in the hybrid state.

Hybridization can also occur between extraterrestrials and humans, such as the teachers in *The Faculty* (1998), the pod people in *Invasion of the Body Snatchers*, and the female shape-shifter Sil in *Species* (1995). Like earthly hybrids, Sil is bad-tempered and homicidal, with the added feature of craving a man with whom to reproduce. The pod people are peculiarly even-tempered and polite, but they too are interested in spreading their kind, no matter how many normal people lose their invididuality along the way.

Despite the potential variety among hybrids, werewolves are by far the most common. Their popularity may stem from their resemblance to another popular beast, the dog. As man's best friend, the dog is docile, trustworthy, and treated to a special place in the movie audience's heart (see the analysis of *The Fly II*'s monster dog in Chapter Nine), and yet the dog is in essence a domesticated wolf. The idea that inside every faithful dog is a wild, ravening thing ready to tear apart and eat its owner may be disconcerting, but it is also attractive, because we humans are in essence domesticated apes, and we know what it feels like to have to push down the wildness every day. In the werewolf, then, the signs are crossed, and the human (who is generally docile and trustworthy, like the dog) becomes the wild beast he secretly always wanted to be (the wolf, the very animal that the dog would be if it had not become domesticated).

Indeed, for the makers of werewolf films, the major technical problem is to avoid having the werewolf look too much like a dog. That would arouse the wrong reactions, of cuteness and adorability, just when they were going for horror and shock. The trick is difficult because wolves *do* look like dogs, as befits their genetic connection. This is why the horror film has only rarely resorted to the seemingly obvious technique of using a trained wolf or a wolf-like dog to play the part of the werewolf. One such animal is used in *The Wolf Man*, but it only plays the role of a supporting werewolf, the one Bela Lugosi turns into, not the one that the star, Lon Chaney, Jr., becomes. It seems that a real wolf is just not monstrous enough to deliver the werewolf goods.

Instead, werewolves (like the one Chaney, Jr., played) are usually portrayed by an actor in makeup, or, in later times, by animatronics or computer-generated imagery (CGI). The creature never looks much like a wolf — that is the whole point, to transcend the wolf while invoking it — but in various ways it becomes a mix of human and wolf, or a wolf-like monstrosity. The anxiety of influence accounts for much of the variety: filmmakers are always worried about having their werewolf look too much like the last one, so they make this one look more wolf-like (e.g., the werewolf in *Van Helsing* [2004], the next one more human-like (e.g., the 2010 remake *The Wolfman*).

The hybrid raises themes common to many horror movies. Like vampires and zombies, werewolves spread their lycanthropy through contagion: if a werewolf bites you, you become a werewolf. Like Jekyll/Hyde, animal-man hybrids suggest the release of the inner beast, suppressed evil, or Freudian Id that dwells inside every person. Sometimes what is released is explicitly related to sexuality, especially when the transformed person is a woman, as in *Cat People, Species,* and *Ginger Snaps.*

Many animal-man hybrids hint at race mixing, particularly *Island of Lost Souls*, with its depiction of the hybrids as brutish natives oppressed under the slave-driving whip of the colonialist Dr. Moreau. Frequently, there is a simultaneous revulsion from and attraction to the idea of a human mating with the hybrid, as in the case of the sailor and the panther woman in *Island of Lost Souls.* The revulsion and attraction are both related to the idea of a new generation of DDBs being born, with still more possibilities for deformity and destruction.

Lon Chaney, Jr., played the screen's most famous werewolf, Larry Talbot, in *The Wolf Man* (1941, Universal).

Berserk Biota

Among living DDBs, psychopathic humans are most closely related to the hybrids, who share at least part of their humanity. Next closest are living creatures that have arisen naturally on earth, such as germs, sharks, and dinosaurs. With these organisms humans share at least an evolutionary heritage. From the perspective of the horror filmmaker looking for DDBs, the trouble with all such natural biota is that they are viewed more or less as safe. Germs still make us sick, but at known rates of prevalence and incidence; sharks rarely kill anyone; and dinosaurs are extinct. The whole natural order appears to be under human control. Therefore, to transform these organisms into DDBs, they must be made to go out of control — to become massively destructive as a result of a positional deformity in which they change their place in the order of being, becoming assailants of humans in ways previously unknown. The creatures must become berserk biota. This may happen as a result of their being trained, bred, mutated, or genetically engineered to go berserk, or there may be no explanation at all. They may look strange or deformed, or they may look normal. But they must attack humans, violently and usually repeatedly, to become DDBs.

As suggested by the examples of germs, sharks, and dinosaurs, berserk biota come on three scales: micro, human, and macro. On the micro scale are the germs, such as the invisible causes of the epidemic mayhem in *The Crazies* and *Cabin Fever*. Because germs are largely unseen, they are known less for being DDBs in their own right than for causing DDB behavior in those they infect. On the human scale are all the creatures visible to the naked eye and currently existing, from bugs to whales. These are the creatures we think we know, and, when they start misbehaving, may be horrified to find we do not. On the macro scale are creatures that have been elevated from the human scale — magnified in some way, such as by radiation or chemicals — so they are substantially bigger than we normally expect them. The macro scale includes large dinosaurs fantastically transported to our time, since they are bigger than any land animals currently ought to be.

On the human scale, there are two basic varieties of berserk biota: swarms of small creatures and large loners. These two categories are associated with the two great directors who did the most to make them plausible on screen: Alfred Hitchcock, director of *The Birds*, in which otherwise ordinary birds run amok, attacking the small town of Bodega Bay in swarms; and Steven Spielberg, director of *Jaws*, in which a great white shark runs amok, attacking the small town of Amity Island. Since *The Birds*, there have been other examples of swarms: *Willard* (1971) did it with rats, *Frogs* (1972) with frogs (and other animals), and one of the episodes of *Creepshow* (1982) with roaches. Since *Jaws*, other films have produced their own large loners, such as *Grizzly* (1976) and *Anaconda* (1997). But none of the imitators have been as effective as *The Birds* and *Jaws*. This suggests how difficult it is to make a human scale, berserk biota movie — hard enough that it takes a Hitchcock or Spielberg to do it well. The main trouble is that over-familiarity with human scale creatures makes it difficult to persuade the audience to accept them as DDBs; to overcome this obstacle effectively takes a rare combination of filmmaking skill and bravura.

The main wave of macro scale monsters occurred in the 1950s, when radiation provided a convenient explanation for how some of these creatures got so big. The giants included ants, a tarantula, grasshoppers, a gila monster, an octopus, and shrews (inflated only to about dog size, but big for shrews). They also included a variety of towering dinosaurs placed in modern times (*The Beast from 20,000 Fathoms* [1953]; *Gojira*).

The giant monster movie has turned up much less often since the 1950s, and when it does it frequently has tongue in cheek (e.g., *The Little Shop of Horrors* [1960], with a killer plant; *Tremors* [1990], with giant wormlike things;

and *Eight Legged Freaks* [2002], with killer spiders), as if there is something laughable about the whole thing. Yet in principle there is no reason a serious giant monster movie cannot work: the progenitor of them all, *King Kong*, is one of the great classics of the horror film. *Gwoemul* (*The Host*; 2006), a South Korean film about a giant fishlike amphibian, is moody with dark themes. The problem with giant monster movies may sometimes be that the filmmakers themselves find the concept ludicrous, and their skepticism gets translated into attempted or inadvertent comedy. There is no other explanation for the over-sized killer rabbits in *Night of the Lepus* (1972).

ALIENS

The berserk biota, psychopaths, and most of the hybrids share in common an origin on earth. Aliens, however, are extraterrestrials, and they have been serving as DDBs for many years. Strangely, though, it is difficult to put together a taxonomic category for them that stands on its own. Many aliens in horror movies take over human bodies, which put them in the category of hybrids (discussed above). Many other aliens belong in the genre of science fiction rather than horror, because their primary purpose is not presentation of the DDB but presentation of a world. The original *War of the Worlds* (1953), for example, had some nice Martian war machines and one interesting Martian, but the focus of the film was the cataclysmic clash of planets, not DDBs, so it does not count as a horror movie.

That leaves a relatively small group of alien DDBs who were not hybrids and presentation of whom was the purpose of their films—stand-alone aliens. They include the walking plant-based monster in *The Thing from Another World*, but not the creature in the remake, *The Thing*, which was a hybrid monster that liked to take over human bodies. *It! The Terror from Beyond Space* makes it in, as does the title creature in *Alien*.

Despite their different classifications, hybrid aliens and stand-alone aliens have something in common: they come from outer space and they cause trouble for humans. They express our strongest negative reaction to outsiders: they must be deformed and destructive because they come from far away.

METAPHYSICAL BEINGS AND THEIR ACOLYTES

This category includes devils, gods, and all other beings and forces that transcend the physical universe, are in a state of positional deformity, and may cause destruction on earth as a result. Because these beings are usually hard to see, the horror film that tells their story often includes some visible followers and maybe some possessed people, lumped together here as acolytes.

The horror genre is rife with stories of the Devil and his acolytes, whether Satan worshippers or the possessed girls in *The Exorcist*, *The Exorcism of Emily*

For obvious reasons, the lead Cenobite (Doug Bradley) in *Hellraiser* (1987, New World Pictures) is better known as Pinhead.

Rose (2005), and *The Last Exorcism* (2010). Much less common are films in which God is the DDB, as seems to be the case in *Frailty*, or Death personified, as in *Final Destination*. Alternative metaphysical beings include Pinhead and the other Cenobites in *Hellraiser* (1987); and H.P. Lovecraft's Old Ones, who combine features of devils, gods, and aliens; a cinematic example of a Lovecraftian film is *The Haunted Palace*. Witchcraft movies, such as *Operazione paura (Kill, Baby, Kill;* 1966) and *The Craft* (1996), usually belong in the metaphysical beings/acolytes category, as does any horror movie in which the characters spend a lot of time talking about vague dark forces that are not just ghosts or vampires.

Artifacts

Occasionally a nonhuman thing produced by human hands takes on deformed-destructive life, and then it falls into the category of DDBs that are artifacts. These may take the form of a menacing computer, as in *Demon Seed* (1977), or of something lower-tech, such as Chucky, the doll animated by the spirit of a dead murderer in *Child's Play*.

WEIRD HUMANS NOT OTHERWISE SPECIFIED

The taxonomy so far presented does not exhaust all the different DDBs that have been presented in horror films, but to avoid an infinite splintering of categories, two catchall categories are suggested: "Weird Humans Not Otherwise Specified (N.O.S.)" and "Weird Nonhuman Things N.O.S." The category of "Weird Humans N.O.S." includes people with weird powers not explained by the earlier categories. The title character in *Carrie*, for example, has telekinesis, but she did not get it by being a mad scientist or consorting with the devil; she was just born with it. It also includes odd-sized humans, such as giant people (*The Amazing Colossal Man* [1957]; *Attack of the 50 Ft Woman* [1958]), who, due to their origin as normal humans, do not belong in the *nonhuman* macro scale berserk biota category, but are macro scale nonetheless. An odd-sized human may also be small, such as the diminutive severed conjoined twin kept in a basket in *Basket Case* (1982). The Weird Humans N.O.S. category also includes killer freaks such as those in *Freaks*.

WEIRD NONHUMAN THINGS NOT OTHERWISE SPECIFIED

This category includes all sorts of fantastic living terrestrial creatures. They may be "lost" natural organisms that look bizarre only because it took us so long to discover them, such as the Gill-Man in *Creature from the Black Lagoon*, or they may be monsters from real or fabricated folklore, such as *The Gorgon* (1964), *Gremlins* (1984), *Pumpkinhead* (1988), *Leprechaun* (1993), and *Jeepers Creepers*.

That completes the taxonomy of DDBs as it presently stands. It is subject to revision as new films are made, new subgenres established, and old patterns uncovered.

15
Techniques

The horror movie does not just appear spontaneously before the audience. Like any art object, it is a constructed thing that must be made out of raw materials using human techniques. This is the technical context of the horror film.

The horror film uses a variety of techniques, all with the goal of presenting a DDB. The illusion of the DDB must include the DDB's deformity, its destructiveness, and above all its being—its presence and reality. In this chapter, I examine some of the most common techniques used by horror films to present the DDB, and I organize them by the film crafts with which these stratagems are most strongly associated. All together, these techniques help to create the distinct mise-en-scène of horror films—the cinematic world dominated by the DDB.

Sound Effects

In the world of horror films, it is common to have a period of tense silence followed by a loud, unexpected noise. The noise may be a crash, a shout, a scream, or some combination of all three. Of all the sound effects used to create the illusion of a DDB, or to prepare for one, the loud noise is the most useful. Humans have an instinctive fear of a loud noise, with its suggestion of something massive and powerful that has not yet been identified. The loud noise in horror movies is often used to fake viewers out and build tension: once the noise is identified it turns out to be a false alarm, but it leaves viewers jittery, and eventually one of the loud noises really is attached to the DDB.

Softer noises can also be effective. A creak, a thump, or a whisper is the surest sign that a ghost — or *something*— is unexpectedly in the house with the other characters. The soft sound of wolves howling in the night used to be a staple of horror films, then mostly fell out of fashion until it was revived in the 2010 remake *The Wolfman*.

Many sound effects track along with the action and are therefore expected, but can nevertheless be unnerving. The sound of a knife thrusting into flesh, or a blunt instrument cracking a head, can be as scary as or scarier than the actual sight of the action. In fact, the sound effect is sometimes substituted for the action, both to avoid censor trouble and because the mere noise can be powerful.

Fantastic DDBs may require some unusual sound effects. To supply the unearthly roar of the original King Kong, sound supervisor Murray Spivack played animal roars backward.[1] In *The Exorcist*, Mercedes McCambridge dubbed a peculiar voice for the demon who was possessing the girl played by Linda Blair—quite different from Blair's own voice. According to director William Friedkin, McCambridge chain-smoked, swallowed raw eggs, and was tied to a chair to produce the bizarre voice.[2] Animal noises and sounds were sometimes added to enhance the voice, but it was mostly McCambridge. "If you were going to say that there was a single element that really made the film," said Friedkin, "then it could well be the sound quality that she achieved."

Human DDBs may not require a fantastic sound, but they too can benefit from interesting sound effects. Michael Myers in *Halloween* never utters a line of dialogue, and for the most part is silent. But in the shots filmed from his point of view, the disturbing sound of his breathing behind his mask is audible.

Hair

Hair is an overlooked feature of horror film mise-en-scène. The Universal Frankenstein monster would be much less impressive without the close-cropped black hair accentuating his flat head; the traditional Dracula requires slicked-back aristocratic hair, the mummy dried-up, sandy hair. Wild hair or, paradoxically, a completely shaven head suggests a wild, uncontrolled personality, like those of the mutants in *The Hills Have Eyes*. Beards are generally menacing, and mustaches, such as that of Vincent Price, sinister.

Monstrous hair effects blend into makeup effects (see "Makeup," below), since both hair and flesh are common components of creature makeup design. The Wolf Man is practically all hair, and therefore the epitome of the wild, uncontrolled personality: hair is what primarily makes him animal. In one of the makeups in *Bram Stoker's Dracula*, Dracula sports a long, thick, gray ponytail that he seems to have been growing for centuries and that fits his antiquity as a vampire.

The hair of normals, too, can be important in a horror movie. Young women, in particular, have long, beautiful, alluring hair—the better to attract the DDB. The exception to the beautiful hair rule may be when the woman is the DDB. The title character in *Carrie* starts the movie with flat, stringy hair, then, as she strives to become more normal, develops the typical beautiful hair of horror movie teens—only to have it ruined with pig's blood as the result of a prom night prank, which triggers her explosive act of destructiveness against the school. It is a bad idea to mess with a DDB's hair.

Costumes

Two types of costumes are found in horror movies—the costume worn to represent the full body of a fantastic DDB, such as the monster suit of the title character in *The Creature from the Black Lagoon*; and the more ordinary clothing worn by either normals or DDBs. Creatures from the dinosaur star of *Gojira* to the extraterrestrial killer in *Alien* have been represented by monster suits. Nowadays, monster suits can be quite elaborate, incorporating makeup and puppet effects and enhanced by CGI, but in the old days they could be quite simple, or at least look that way. Monster suits tend to look fake if seen right away in full light: the Creature from the Black Lagoon's suit, prominently displayed early in the film, is obviously a suit, although it is so well designed and well constructed that the premature display does not hurt it much. Generally, however, it helps to hide a monster suit with shadow and build up to it slowly, as is done in *Alien*.

As important as monster suits are, ordinary clothing can be just as important to the success of a horror film. Human and undead DDBs can be defined by their clothing—the lab coat and snappy fedora of the mad scientist Dr. Pretorius in *Bride of Frankenstein*; the aristocratic cape of Dracula; the populist, beat-up clothing of the zombies in George Romero's *Dead* movies. Leatherface's slaughterhouse apron in *The Texas Chain Saw Massacre* defines him almost as much as his human leather mask.

The clothing of normal characters is vital to establishing the plausibility of the normal community with which the DDB clashes. The normals' clothing must be believable, true to the characters, pleasing to the eye without being so showy as to distract from the DDB. It must fit the era in which the film is set—usually the present, but in some cases another time, often the nineteenth century. An example of well-designed normal clothing is the fur-collared coat of vampire hunter Dr. Van Helsing in *Horror of Dracula*, which has the effect of softening a character who might otherwise seem overly stern. He even uses it to comfort a little girl menaced by a vampire; when placing it on her, he says she looks like a "teddy bear."

Underclothing is important in horror movies, too, particularly on women, who are frequently shown undressed, either when under attack by the DDB or, more or less arbitrarily, whenever the filmmakers feel like it. The effect is multiple: to suggest vulnerability; to implicate the monster and victim in a sexual relationship; and to titillate the audience. So common is this wardrobe choice that Manohla Dargis described Kate Hudson's character in *The Skeleton*

Key (2005) as yet another example of "the plucky-heroine-in-panties role."³ Women are often nude in horror movies as well, but even then there is usually some element of costume. In the extended chase scene in *My Bloody Valentine* (2009) in which Betsy Rue's character flees from the slasher, she is entirely naked except for one thing: her high heels. It is just enough to maintain her in character.

Every so often, the DDB in a horror movie requires clothing from the opposite gender. The best known example may be Tim Curry as Dr. Frank-N-Furter in *The Rocky Horror Picture Show*, who strutted around in lingerie through most of the film while preying on innocent Brad and Janet. However, *The Rocky Horror Picture Show*, despite its title, is not a horror film but a musical comedy with horror elements. In actual horror films, the DDB wearing transgendered clothing is not exactly common, but it is persistent. Women's clothing on a male DDB may make the DDB look weaker and sillier, not the effect usually desired for a DDB. On the other hand, if worn in the right context, it can enhance the sense that there is something creepy and twisted about the DDB, which increases its deformity and potential destructiveness. Transvestite clothing also increases the identification of the DDB with marginalized groups of people, part of the significance of horror films. Examples include *The Devil Doll* (1936), *Psycho*, *The Texas Chain Saw Massacre*, and *Dressed to Kill* (1980). In *The Silence of the Lambs*, serial killer Buffalo Bill goes even further, stitching himself a suit of women's skin so he can fully enflesh himself as a woman.

Production Design

The prototypical set of the horror film is the old dark house. It was already so well known in 1932 that the horror comedy *The Old Dark House* took it for a title even as it parodied films set in such a space. Old dark houses (or castles, cathedrals, or asylums) are shadowy places of some age, often in a state of decay but sometimes preternaturally well-preserved, and they are frequently the home of the DDB. They may be Gothic in design, but even when they are not, they are Gothic in inspiration, picking up from the Gothic aesthetic the idea of a place that has been bypassed or forgotten, a place that involves a journey back to an earlier period and from which it may not be possible to escape. Thus, in the 2005 remake of *House of Wax*, the DDBs live in an otherwise forgotten town from the 1950s, populated by wax figures. The old dark houses in *Candyman* are Chicago's crime-ridden Cabrini-Green housing projects, figuratively abandoned by the larger society. In *Psycho*, the old dark house is a gloomy Victorian edifice situated behind the brightly lit, modernistic Bates Motel. The idea of the old dark house is to increase the spatial and temporal distance between the world of the normals (represented by blandly normal

The titular creature carries off Kay Lawrence (Julia [Julie] Adams) in *The Creature from the Black Lagoon* (1954, Universal International Pictures).

architecture) and the world of the DDB (the old dark house), and to invest the DDB with the creepiness and psychological weight of something the audience once knew about but has forgotten, like a dream or a remote memory.

Spaces in a horror movie are typically confined spaces. Claustrophobia is a common fear, so horror filmmakers can draw upon it in increasing the scariness of the DDB. The worst such space is the coffin, with its accompanying fear of being buried alive, a fear that comes true in films such as *The Premature Burial* (1962) and *Spoorloos* (*The Vanishing*; 1988). Many other tight spaces figure in horror movies, such as the closet from which Laurie fights Michael Myers in *Halloween*, the parking garage in which the heroine is trapped with a psychopath in *P2* (2007), and the narrow areas of the abandoned asylum basement where the boys find the dead girl in *Deadgirl*. Locked doors help to confine spaces further; the locked doors variously block victims from escaping, conceal secrets related to the DDB, or keep a monster trapped, at least until later in the film, when he usually breaks free. Closed boxes or crates can be similarly effective, such as the crate loaded aboard a train and housing a creature from the remote past in *Horror Express* (1972).

Underground places figure prominently in horror films: basements, cellars, dungeons, and pits, like the victim-preparation pit maintained by Buffalo Bill in *The Silence of the Lambs*. The underground symbolizes the suppressed parts of the mind, the forbidden emotions or Freudian Id. Subways can be effective as underground dwelling places of DDBs, such as in *Five Million Years to Earth*, *Raw Meat* (1972), and *The Midnight Meat Train* (2008). Underwater places are used less often, mainly when the DDB is aquatic, such as in *The Creature from the Black Lagoon* or *Jaws*, but they too are useful in portraying that which is normally hidden in psychological life and is regarded as hazardous if released.

Vehicles can contribute to the mise-en-scène, whether it is a normal person's vehicle, such as the recreational vehicle in *The Hills Have Eyes*—which isolates the normals in the wilderness setting of the mutants—or the monster's creepy truck in *Jeepers Creepers*. Props are often vital to the presentation of the DDB. Weapons are usually needed, whether handled by the DDB, the normals fighting him, or both. These are usually sharp or blunt instruments, such as knives, razors, axes, drills, needles, wooden stakes, chainsaws, clubs, pipes, or the meat-and-bone cutting wire in *Ôdishon*. Guns are used less often, because they involve killing at a distance, which is less scary than a close-in kill; however, a gun is sometimes used by a normal person futilely trying to put down a monster who cannot be killed that way. Swords are rarely used; they carry too much of the sense of a historical action movie rather than a horror movie. An exception is *Captain Kronos— Vampire Hunter* (1974), which has elements of both genres. In a pinch, almost any prop can be turned into a weapon. In *Horror of Dracula*, Van Helsing grabs two candlesticks and clangs them into an impromptu cross to keep Dracula at bay.

Props that suggest the world of the normals are important too, though they are usually less dramatic. In *Frankenstein*, flowers are a significant prop: the orange blossoms that suggest normal fertility, given to Elizabeth on the occasion of her wedding to Frankenstein; the flowers that the little girl Maria shares with the monster before he kills her.

Cinematography

It is usually dark in the horror movie world. The time is night, the interiors are poorly lit, and the shadows are thick. A fog or mist may obscure the outside. The only light may come from candles or flashlights, or the occasional burning monster.

All this awakens another of humanity's basic fears—the fear of the dark, with the limits that darkness places on our ability to see potential dangers. Within the movie, darkness limits the vision of the normal characters as well, making them more prone to jump when something comes at them out of the shadows. As noted in Chapter Two, darkness is useful in the gradual unveiling of the DDB, the typical process by which the DDB becomes known; darkness also hides defects in the costume, makeup, or special effects used to create the DDB, allowing the viewer's imagination to fill in what might otherwise have looked fake.

Just because darkness is so common in horror movies, some horror filmmakers have deliberately shot extensive scenes in daylight or bright indoor illumination, to show that the monster can get you anywhere. The effect is subtly to increase the impact of the DDB, provided that the creature is otherwise well constructed. The zombies in the original 1978 *Dawn of the Dead* are effectively filmed in daylight and bright shopping mall light; the ghosts of the Overlook Hotel in *The Shining* are more chilling for being filmed in bright hotel light.

Horror films can be photographed well in either black-and-white or color. The Universal horror films of the 1930s set a standard for lush black-and-white horror cinematography; *Night of the Living Dead* achieved good effects with a very different style, a stark, crude black-and-white that emphasized the film's subversive nature. Hammer, beginning in the 1950s, introduced a drenched color style that emphasized a bright blood red, the most important hue in its arsenal. In the 1990s and 2000s, the colors of many horror films were much more muted, especially if they were American films based on Asian originals, such as *The Ring*, with its drab, rainy milieu.

The choice of lenses can be used to create chilling effects. In *The Haunting*, an extra wide, 30 mm lens that distorted the images of the interiors of the haunted house contributed to the unsettling atmosphere.[4]

Composition is important in a horror film. The monster often comes up from behind or to the side of the normal—we can see it coming but the normal cannot—generating suspense. Some compositions are pictorial in their beauty—for example, the scene in *Bride of Frankenstein* when the two mad scientists stand to either side of the monster's bride, dropping her hem in a gesture of unveiling. Some are savage, such as the shot of Leatherface, isolated against the morning sky, swinging his chainsaw at the end of *The Texas Chain Saw Massacre*. A particularly frightening sort of composition is the mirror shot, as in *Repulsion* (1965), in which the swinging of a mirror reveals an intruder in the glass whose presence had not been previously revealed.

One of the first principles of most cinematography is to keep the camera steady even when it is in motion, but several horror movies have fallen into the annoying habit of shaking the camera constantly to approximate the unsteadiness of amateur video. The result is not to thrill the audience but nauseate it with motion sickness. *The Blair Witch Project*, *Cloverfield*, *Paranormal Activity*, and *The Last Exorcism* have all been guilty of this nuisance.

Editing

Editing is easy to miss in horror films. If the arrangement of shots, scenes, and sequences is fluid enough, the focus of the audience is entirely on the action rather than on how the pieces of film were cut together to compose the action. Nevertheless, there are moments when the editing is clearly indispensable, such as complex attacks by the DDB. An example is the beheading sequence in *The Omen*, one of the best film beheadings of all time. The sequence begins with Gregory Peck as Robert Thorn throwing away knives intended for killing his adopted son, the son of Satan. From the moment Peck throws away the knives until the end of the sequence, about one minute elapses. During that time the photographer, Jennings, played by David Warner, tries to pick up the knives to continue the mission of killing the boy, but a truck's parking brake is mysteriously released and the truck rolls down a slope, spilling a sheet of glass that slices off Jennings's head. Thorn sees what has happened and realizes that Satan has staged yet another "freak accident" to kill an enemy.

In that minute of screen time, there are no less than thirty shots—one shot every *two seconds*—including numerous shots cross-cutting between the descending truck and the doomed Jennings, as well as other shots documenting the beheading from multiple angles. Each shot is so well timed and juxtaposed that the audience scarcely notices how the beheading effect is created (involving the substitution of a special effects head and body for Warner). All that registers is the horror.

Certain juxtapositions of shots are common in horror movies, such as the revelation scene, in which a normal sees the DDB for the first time. The DDB comes out of the shadows or is unveiled or unmasked — most famously in the silent *Phantom of the Opera*—then there is typically a cut to a reaction shot in which the normal, often a woman, screams or otherwise reacts with horror to the visage.

Editing contributes to pacing, the apparent speed with which a story moves along. A slow build is common in the early parts of horror movies, as the audience gets to know the characters and suspense is built, something like the slow uphill climb of a roller coaster. Later in the film, the pace often becomes breakneck, like the roller coaster's downhill descent and its twists and turns. Much of the first part of *Halloween* is slow build, as Michael Myers plays peekaboo with Laurie and her friends, but once the murders start the rest is almost pure roller coaster.

Marion Crane (Janet Leigh) is murdered in a motel shower in *Psycho* (1960, Paramount).

Music

Music in horror films is varied, depending on the setting and mood. Films set in the nineteenth century or earlier often have large-scale orchestral scores, as in *Bram Stoker's Dracula*. Films set in contemporary times typically have a more low-key sound, such as the synthesizer scores that John Carpenter composes for his own horror movies. Almost always there is a throbbing sound to build suspense, and something scream-like for the DDB attack—for example, the sound of violins screaming when Marion Crane is murdered in the shower in *Psycho*. The louder the better at such moments, following the rule that loud noises scare the audience.

Offbeat music can work well in horror movies. *Two Thousand Maniacs!* features a song called "The South Will Rise Again" that plays like a southern ditty and expresses the animosity of the Confederate ghosts toward the northerners. Though it sounds like an old standard, it was actually written by the film's director, Herschell Gordon Lewis. *The Abominable Dr. Phibes* mixes Dr. Phibes's maniacal organ music and popular dance tunes from the period of the film (1920s), melodies that come out haunting when played by his robotic dance band.

Makeup

Makeup in horror movies is often essential to portraying the deformity of the DDB. The names of many great makeup artists have been associated with such creature designs, among them Lon Chaney, who did his own monster makeup in films such as *The Phantom of the Opera*; Jack Pierce, who created the makeup of the Universal monsters of the 1930s and 1940s; Tom Savini, creator of the zombie makeup in *Dawn of the Dead* and *Day of the Dead*; and

15. Techniques

Sarah (Shauna Macdonald) emerges from her subterranean hell in *The Descent* (2005, Lions Gate Films).

Rick Baker, whose horror movie work has included *An American Werewolf in London* and *The Ring*. A good monster makeup can be tremendously useful in putting over the illusion of a DDB. The subterranean creatures in *The Descent*, known colloquially as crawlers, are revealed late in the film and would have spoiled it had they looked fake. Instead, because of well conceived and executed makeup design, they are a plausible colony of feral humanoids adapted to living in the dark, crawling on rock, and attacking wayward spelunkers.

Normals need makeup too, although for more pedestrian purposes. They need to look normal during the scenes establishing their characters, to provide contrast with the abnormality of the DDB. Once the normals are in conflict with the DDB, they need to look sweaty, bloody, grimy, wounded, and, in many cases, have their bodies ripped apart with special makeup effects that simulate guts, bone, and general gore. We may need to see what the normals look like dead — blue, bruised, and decayed — and if they have been bitten by the undead, they may come back as vampires, zombies, or other DDBs.

Special Effects

Special effects are central to the presentation of the DDB in many horror movies, particularly those in which the creature is of fantastic design. If the creature has superhuman strength, it must smash things and throw people around. Much of this mayhem can be done with mechanical effects, live effects such as walls that are rigged to break open or wires that are used to make people fly as if thrown. If the creature possesses invisibility, visual effects (based on altering the photographic image) rather than mechanical effects may be more important: for example, the matte work used to make Claude Rains invisible in *The Invisible Man*. If the creature is a shape-shifter, such as a werewolf, a variety of effects have been used for transformation: optical effects, such as a series of dissolves, with each shot showing a successive stage of transformation; mechanical effects, such as puppetry to make a snout grow longer or a limb become distorted; and CGI, in which computers are enlisted to morph the human into a werewolf.

CGI has been a mixed blessing for the horror film; the effects are sometimes believable, sometimes not. In *Piranha 3D*, the schools of computer-generated piranhas are fairly persuasive as they swarm over swimmers, particularly when seen in dim light underwater. But in *The Ring Two*, the herd of computer-generated deer that attacks Naomi Watts's car is palpably fake, partly because the animals are shot in full daylight, exposing their flaws; partly because many audience members are familiar enough with deer (more so than with piranhas) to know a fake when they see one. The scene would have been more effective in pre–CGI days, when the only way to produce it would have been to get some deer and train them.

However, special effects do not have to look completely real for the audience to accept the illusion and enjoy the horror film. The brain-shaped monsters in *Fiend without a Face* (1958) and the eye-shaped monsters in *The Crawling Eye* (1958) are not exactly realistic by today's standards, and were probably not much more convincing when the films appeared in 1958, but they are interesting, grotesque, and distinctive, enough to make the audience want to accept that such things exist in the world of the film. In fact, advances in special effects technology do not necessarily result in a better horror film. The CGI effects work used to bring to life the flying brides of Dracula in *Van Helsing* is undoubtedly more impressive than the rubber bat on a string used to represent Dracula as a bat in the original *Dracula* (1931), but *Dracula* remains a horror classic whereas *Van Helsing* is an overstuffed, plodding attempt to resuscitate the classic Universal monsters. Similarly, the effects in the 1988 remake of *The Blob* are superior to those of the 1958 original, but the original is still the one with Steve McQueen.

Still, too little attention to realism can leave the audience dissatisfied if it results in the feeling that the DDB is not an actual being even within the horror movie world. The monsters in *The Green Slime* (1968) are sufficiently fake that the movie is unwatchable except as camp.

Special effects in horror movies may focus on certain key scenes, such as destroying the monster. It is commonly thought that Van Helsing is the great nemesis of Count Dracula, but at least in the Hammer series in which Christopher Lee played Dracula, it was special effects artist Les Bowie. "[A] job I often do for Hammer is dispose of Dracula at the end of his films," Bowie once reported.[5] "I've lost count of the times I've killed Christopher Lee." A series of dummies and slow dissolves were typical for these sequences, but the specifics were individual to each film: for example, plaster ice mounted on pivots for the scene in *Dracula — Prince of Darkness* where Dracula falls through ice into deadly running water. "The methods vary, depending on whether he goes wet and bloody or if he is supposed to wither away into dust," said Bowie. At the beginning of the next film Bowie had an additional chore: resurrecting Dracula. These resurrections, he said, were "quite lengthy operations, almost animations really," that usually required him to sequester himself in a quiet room in the studio for a few days to work in peace.

Screenplay

Nearly everything that is visually displayed or said in a movie can be attributed in large part to the screenplay, since it includes not only dialogue but the description of action and character from which the director shoots the film. Yet, when considering the screenplay as a source of techniques for presenting the DDB, what is most clearly the contribution of the script are the lines the actors speak. In this respect, there are two types of DDBs: those that speak and those that do not. If they do not, they tend to be bestial, inhuman things, like dinosaurs, giant ants, werewolves, Satan, and zombies. If they do speak, they are more like us but their menace is more sinister and cruel, as if articulateness were a mark of both civilization and a greater capacity for evil. These creatures include the vampires, articulate serial killers (as opposed to silent ones), and mad scientists.

Normals usually speak, and their dialogue is important to establishing character and mood and explaining the origin of the DDB. Dialogue can provide comic relief or build tension; sometimes they even do both at once, as in Chief Brody's famous alarmed statement — "You're gonna need a bigger boat" — on his first glimpse of the shark in *Jaws*.

Sometimes the main function of a line of dialogue is to introduce a chill: "Do you spook easily, Starling?" the FBI supervisor Jack Crawford asks trainee Clarice Starling near the beginning of *The Silence of the Lambs*. When a DDB speaks dialogue, it can shade his character, as when, in *Bram Stoker's Dracula*, Dracula tells his beloved Mina, "I have crossed oceans of time to find you." Dialogue can get bogged down in boring details and pedestrian style, but sometimes even exposition about the DDBs — the most likely place for dialogue to become onerous — can be done deftly and succinctly. In *The Sixth Sense*, the line in which the boy reveals his gift for seeing ghosts — "I see dead people" — became the main catchphrase of the movie.

Acting

What the actors do onscreen is the most visible part of the horror film, and much of it can make a signal contribution to presentation of the DDB.[6] This is true whether the actors are speaking, fighting, looking afraid, looking menacing, killing, writhing, having sex, losing a limb, eating flesh, or looking afraid or menacing again. The actors' techniques include both the expression of emotion and physical action. Depending on whether they are cast as DDBs or normals, they may be called on to be diabolical or victims of the diabolical. The actors who play the DDBs are, of course, likely to have the more rewarding roles: whatever the billing, they are the real stars of the film and are likely to have more scenery to chew, whether it is Kathy Bates as the madwoman with a sledgehammer in *Misery* or Robert Englund as the jocular dream fiend in the *Nightmare on Elm Street* series. But the normals have their moments too. Amanda Seyfried delivered a nicely nuanced performance as the teenage friend of Megan Fox's demon in *Jennifer's Body*. And some actors get to play both the DDB and the primary victim, as Fredric March did memorably in the 1932 *Dr. Jekyll and Mr. Hyde*.

Sometimes even the small supporting roles can provide invaluable assistance to the presentation of the DDB. Richard Blackburn, the director and co-screenwriter of *Lemora, A Child's Tale of the Supernatural*, cast himself as the minister who takes care of the young heroine, Cheryl Smith's Lila Lee. Though not a big role, the minister, as played by Blackburn, exudes equal parts stern religiosity and repressed sexuality, forming an essential component of the background that drives Lila Lee into the arms of the vampire Lemora.

These are the principal crafts by which a horror film is put together, except for one—directing. The role of the director is both so pivotal and so difficult to define that it is left for its own chapter, coming up next. With that exception, these are the techniques by which the presentation of the DDB is made. Together, they yield what is seen and heard in the horror film, including most prominently the DDB itself.

16
Directors

The director is responsible for directing everything that is seen or heard in a horror film, and this involves overseeing the acting, cinematography, production design, and all the other film crafts described in the previous chapter. Because of the centrality of the director to all parts of DDB presentation, it is hard to specify what aspects of that presentation are peculiarly attributable to the director. However, there is one way to discern the director's contribution: look for resemblances among the various films the director has done.

In some cases, a director will do one horror film and no more, yet the director's signature may be evident across both horror and other films. Jonathan Demme, for example, has so far made only one horror film, *The Silence of the Lambs*, to which he brought the warm, humanistic sensibility evident in many of his other films. Stanley Kubrick, by contrast, brought his cold, misanthropic style to his single horror film, *The Shining*. In *The Exorcist*, William Friedkin exhibited the same clear-eyed professionalism and meticulous realism that he did in the police film *The French Connection* (1971). And in *Invasion of the Body Snatchers*, Don Siegel showed the same steady pacing and expert story-telling that he did years later in *Dirty Harry* (1972). Steven Spielberg only made one horror feature film, *Jaws*, although he delved into horror in his early television work, most notably the made-for-TV movie *Duel*. But the elements in *Jaws* of larger-than-life action and suspense, combined with small-town sentiment, are visible throughout his films.

Some directors have made a specialty of horror, at least for part of their careers.[1] In the work of these directors, it is easy to see the contribution a director can make to presenting the DDB. Below, in alphabetical order, are a dozen of the most notable horror directors of the past eighty or more years, with some of their principal distinguishing characteristics. Although these directors are selected for the signature qualities they brought to the horror genre, they are not necessarily the dozen best horror directors, if it were possible to make such a judgment. They are simply a group who have made a difference to the horror film. All are discussed with an eye to their individual style and the contribution they have made to the genre.

Director Tod Browning (top row, center, in sweater and tie) poses with the cast of his film *Freaks* (1932, MGM).

Mario Bava (1914–1980; born in Italy)

A cinematographer, Bava brought to his directing career an eye for lush, forceful compositions, whether he worked in black-and-white or color. This helped to make his horror films potent viewing experiences, even if they were hampered by low budgets and melodramatic acting. A spooky, oppressive atmosphere overlays his horror films, which are invested with a vivid visual imagination. There are the gold coins embedded in hearts in *Operazione paura*, a film that influenced later Japanese horror, or J-horror. And there are the eerie landscape and body-snatching inhabitants of *Terrore nello spazio*, a film that influenced *Alien*.

Witchcraft was an important theme in Bava's films, as in *La maschera del demonio* and *Operazione paura*, but he also dealt with modern subjects. An originator of the *giallo* film genre, which combines crime, mystery, sex, and horror, he contributed to it such works as *La ragazza che sapeva troppo* (*The Girl Who Knew Too Much*; 1963) and *Sei donne per l'assassino*; the latter featured a masked murderer who influenced the slasher subgenre. *Reazione a catena* (*Twitch of the Death Nerve*; 1971) also influenced the slasher films. In a bow to an earlier generation of screen horror, Bava's anthology film *I tre volti della paura* (*Black Sabbath*; 1963) featured the American horror star Boris Karloff.

Always stylish and inventive, Bava knew how to make the most of his cinematic resources. Probably his greatest special effect was the starkly beautiful Barbara Steele, who played a dual role in *La maschera del demonio* as the very wicked Princess Asa Vajda and her virtuous relative Katia Vajda. The opening of *La maschera del demonio* is typical Bava: flames, night, hooded inquisitors, intense music, and a woman strapped face down to a slanted wooden frame. The woman is branded in the back for being a slave of Satan, and only then does she turn, showing the defiant face of Steele. In elevated tones, she curses her brother who is condemning her and vows to return immortal for vengeance. Then a mask of Satan is nailed onto her face, and the credits roll. *All of that before the opening credits.*

Besides his other contributions, Bava made Italy a name in horror films, opening the way for such directors as Dario Argento, Lucio Fulci, and his own son, Lamberto Bava.

Tod Browning (1880–1962)

Browning ran away from home at sixteen to join a carnival,[2] and that experience influenced his horror film career, particularly his masterpiece, *Freaks*, which was set among the sideshow freaks at a carnival. Browning had a warped, twisted, carnival-inspired view of things that was evident in many of his films; the underside of life, human deformity, sexual strangeness, and dark irony all run through his work.

Much of Browning's best work was in collaboration with star Lon Chaney, although not all of these films can be considered horror films. Of those that can, one is now lost, *London after Midnight* (1927), in which Chaney played a toothy vampire. Another, *The Unknown* (1927), almost straddles the line between melodrama and horror, but just makes it across to the horror side because its primary purpose is presentation of a DDB, a deformed and destructive person named Alonzo who becomes even more physically deformed and destructive as the story develops. At a carnival, Alonzo pretends to be an armless performer to hide his murderous past, but when he falls in love with a woman (a young Joan Crawford) who has a phobia about arms, he has his arms amputated to try to win her — all for naught, because her phobia is cured and she falls in love with someone else. It is just the kind of thing that happens in Browning's world.

Browning's best known horror films are *Dracula* and *Freaks*. Except for the bravura first part in Dracula's homeland and castle, much of *Dracula* is talky and tame, although there is Browningian humor in Renfield's crazy appearances. For more characteristic Browning, *Freaks* is the film to see.

The lived-in quality of the carnival sideshow in *Freaks* bespeaks personal knowledge of this bizarre world. In one brief scene, conjoined twins Violet and Daisy Hilton flirt with a male colleague, chat about Daisy's impending marriage, and display their unusual property of being able to feel when the other is touched. The horrific scenes seem lifted from a nightmare, such as the armless, legless man crawling through the mud with a knife in his teeth, part of a mob of freaks bent on vengeance. Even a microcephalic person, presented earlier as gentle and playful, is now armed and on the attack. The rough justice of the transformation of beautiful Olga Baclanova, who has offended the freaks, into a legless chicken lady is the type of irony that fits Browning's milieu.

John Carpenter (1948–)

Carpenter's world is dark, mean, and biting. It is not surprising that the DDBs act that way, but even the normals have similar attitudes. In *Halloween*, the friends of Laurie make fun of her for being a virgin; in *The Thing*, Kurt Russell's character, R.J. MacReady, faces off against his fellow Antarctic researchers while trying to combat an alien invader. In *Vampires* (1998), James Woods's Jack Crow is one of the least appealing vampire hunters in memory. Carpenter's DDBs are even worse: implacable, gruesome, often silent as they go about their destructive business.

Carpenter has balanced his horror work with action (*Assault on Precinct 13* [1976]) and science fiction (*They Live* [1988]), or films that are a hybrid of all three (*Ghosts of Mars* [2001]). Nearly all of his films, whatever the genre, share the dark, mean, biting atmosphere, with undercurrents of left-wing social and political comment. (There is usually something wrong with society, authority, or both in a Carpenter film.) Nearly all these films are scored by Carpenter, with his tense, suspenseful, driving beats. Where the horror films differ from Carpenter's other films, as should be expected, is in the primary focus on the DDB. These DDBs are characterized by their imaginativeness and variety: the slasher of *Halloween*; the fog-bound ghosts in *The Fog* (1980); the shape-shifting alien in *The Thing*; the devil in *Prince of Darkness* (1987); the Lovecraftian menaces in *In the Mouth of Madness* (1995).

What makes a Carpenter horror film worth seeing, whatever its individual quality, is the intelligence he brings to the project. Even though *Halloween* contributed to the founding of the slasher genre, his DDBs are never just repetitive slashers, his normals never just empty-headed stock figures.

Consider the scene in *The Thing* in which MacReady administers a blood test to his colleagues at the Antarctic research station in an effort to uncover which of them are secretly aliens. The blood of a normal merely sizzles when touched with a hot needle; the blood of an alien DDB reacts violently, trying to escape the needle because each component of the alien is a self-centered individual with its own will to survive. The test on small dishes of blood proceeds tensely, with the men, who have been tied up by MacReady, questioning the test's validity and edgily waiting their turn. Then the blood of one of the men, Palmer (David Clennon), screams, surging away from the needle, and Palmer transforms into an alien, head bulging and turning blood-red, a tentacle shooting out on the attack. The scene is not only a vivid DDB presentation, but ripe with significance, because it suggests that every normal is that close to being a DDB, a self-centered thing that attacks when exposed. Such significance is always going on in Carpenter movies, expressed in images that stick, the products of a mind that thinks in horror.

Wes Craven (1939–)

Craven combines expert suspense-building, violent shocks, and imaginative DDBs with certain characteristic themes. His films often have an intense focus on the dark side of the family, beginning with his first film, *The Last House on the Left*, in which a middle-class family confronts a family-like gang of hoodlums. In *The Hills Have Eyes*, another middle-class family confronts an incestuous family of mutants, and in *A Nightmare on Elm Street*, yet another middle-class family confronts a ghostly child murderer who inhabits teenage dreams. In Craven films, American families are always meeting their monstrous counterparts, mirror images of themselves with the worst parts exaggerated. "The family is the best microcosm to work with," Craven has said. "If you go much beyond that you're getting away from a lot of the roots of our own primeval feelings."[3]

Another theme of Craven's is the instability of reality. There is a fine line, often violated, between dreams and reality in the *Nightmare on Elm Street* movies, between movie-making and reality in the *Scream* films and *Wes Craven's New Nightmare* (1994), and between voodoo and normal reality in *The Serpent and the Rainbow* (1988). If you think you are awake, you are probably dreaming, and if you think something only happens in movies, look around: it is probably happening now.

The DDBs in Craven movies are vivid and memorable, particularly Freddy Krueger in *A Nightmare on Elm Street*, with his burnt face, striped shirt, cocked hat, and blades on fingers. The burnt face is the image of monstrous deformity, the blades the image of destructiveness; the hat suggests old-fashioned masculinity, and the striped shirt a kind of childlike playfulness. Altogether, Freddy is a clownish, aggressively male, ruined, and anarchically destructive DDB — the kind of thing that would turn up in the dreams of teenagers as a vision of what the adult world is like and of a kind of furious revolt against it.

Craven has worked outside horror, as in the exceptional, claustrophobic airplane hostage film *Red Eye* (2005). But even in *Red Eye*, his skill at suspense

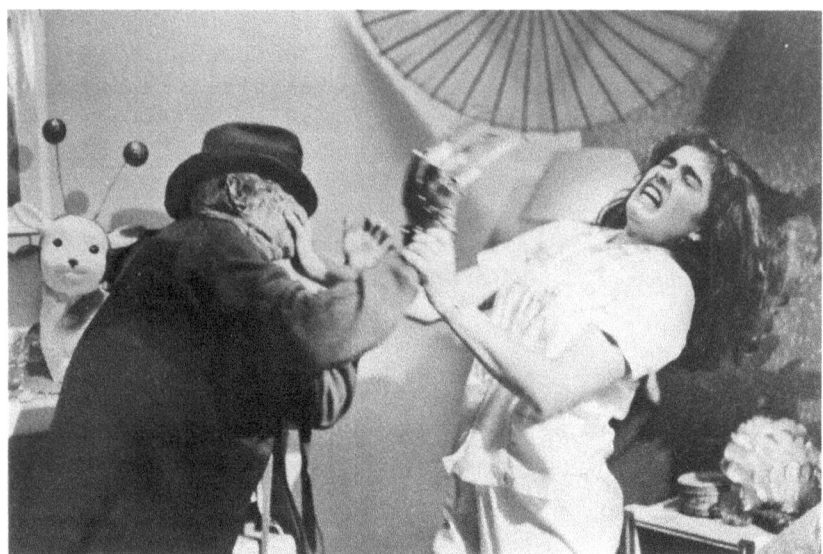

Dream monster Freddy Krueger (Robert Englund) fights teenager Nancy Thompson (Heather Langenkamp) in *A Nightmare on Elm Street* (1984, New Line Cinema).

and his penchant for making memorable monsters (here a terrorist played by Cillian Murphy) are evident.

David Cronenberg (1943 –; born in Canada)

Cronenberg's feature film horror career has so far lasted from the mid-1970s with *They Came from Within* to *The Fly* (1986); since then other types of stories, often violent and macabre but not quite horror tales, have occupied him. But the films he made during his horror period were highly influential and had a characteristic style. The horror films of Cronenberg emphasize body horror: something is always growing out of people (the appendages in *Rabid* and the insectoid mutations in *The Fly*) or making people change physically (the exploding head in *Scanners* [1981]; the videotape in the abdomen in *Videodrome* [1983]). Sex and reproduction are constant obsessions, beginning with the sex-crazed high-rise dwellers in *They Came from Within* and continuing to the weird offspring in *The Brood* and the dream sequence of the human-fly birth in *The Fly*. His films, Cronenberg has said, are "very conscious of physical existence as a living organism, rather than other horror films or science-fiction films which are very technologically oriented, or concerned with the supernatural, and in that sense are very disembodied."[4]

Cronenberg's horror films are rife with comment on the barrenness of modern society. His landscapes are bleak, shot in muted colors, whether they are nondescript cities or isolated modern buildings in rural areas. The major source of life in a Cronenberg movie comes from the DDBs, who at least are different, pulsing, and creative. In *Scanners*, one of them is even a sculptor. In *The Fly*, Seth Brundle is articulate and even poetic while he is being transformed into ever more hideous lumps of flesh. In a scene where he is beseeching his girlfriend Ronnie to leave, he talks about wanting to become the first insect politician, but doubts whether he can, because insects are so brutal. He says he is an insect who dreamt he was a man, "but now the dream is over, and the insect is awake." Finally he says simply, "I'll hurt you if you stay." This is a DDB who retains his humanity even as he becomes inhuman.

Cronenberg's DDBs typically originate from scientific experimentation, often of the careless and polluting variety. Not for Cronenberg ghosts, vampires, or other supernatural sources of horror; in his steadfastly nontheistic universe, whatever horrors occur are rooted in nature and manipulations thereof. This is consistent with the theme of body horror: materialistic dangers are the only dangers that count.

Cronenberg is a cunning story-teller, whose narratives creep up on the audience until, by the time of the final battle, they are intensely gripping. The final battle between two telekinetically-endowed scanners in *Scanners* is one of the best scenes of DDB-on-DDB violence in horror cinema. Violence and sex are almost always graphic in Cronenberg films, the better to emphasize the body whose fate is at stake in both settings.

Terence Fisher (1904–1980; born in the United Kingdom)

Terence Fisher made a variety of films, but is best known today for the horror films he made with Hammer from the 1950s to the 1970s. It was under his direction that Frankenstein, Dracula, the mummy, Jekyll and Hyde, the werewolf, and the Phantom of the Opera were reborn for a new generation, in, respectively, *The Curse of Frankenstein*, *Horror of Dracula*, *The Mummy* (1959), *The Two Faces of Dr. Jekyll* (1960), *The Curse of the Werewolf* (1961), and *The Phantom of the Opera* (1962).

In Fisher films, the color was saturated, the blood dripping, the bosoms heaving, the music swelling. The stories were usually on the fantastic side, set in a vaguely historical past, rather than being concerned with the modern psychopathic killer. The DDBs were often drawn from legend and mythology, such as the vampire and werewolf. The imagery was often Christian — Van Helsing with his crucifix, inimical to vampires — although Fisher could work in other traditions, as with his use of Greek mythology in *The Gorgon*.

Even in *The Gorgon*, with its offbeat pagan imagery, the characteristic

Fisher style was evident. The film opens ominously, with a title about a haunted castle, but quickly switches to a salacious tone, with a topless model being immortalized by her artist boyfriend. The lovers quarrel, and the girl runs out into the moonlit night chasing him. She is killed by something off-camera, and when she is wheeled into Peter Cushing's examination room one of her fingers breaks off: it is made of stone. The girl has become a statue. Fear, sex, Gothic atmosphere, Cushing calm, and a hint of a literally petrifying DDB have all been introduced in the opening minutes.

Hammer's leading horror director, Fisher collaborated often with their top stars, Cushing and Christopher Lee. Together they worked out much of what is now known as the Hammer style, which included a certain seriousness about the mayhem. In *Curse of Frankenstein*, which starred Cushing and Lee, Fisher wrote, "the great temptation was for the actors to try and send it up, to overdo things…. But once I'd told them to take it straight, they knew exactly what I was after."[5] The horrific seriousness, the emphasis on blood and sex, the animalistic vampire, the obsessed but cool mad scientist became powerful influences on later generations of filmmakers.

Alfred Hitchcock (1899–1980; born in the United Kingdom)

Known as the master of suspense, Alfred Hitchcock had a long career of scaring audiences with his films. Yet only two of these films could clearly qualify as horror films in the sense of having presentation of the DDB as their primary purpose: *Psycho* and *The Birds*. In *Psycho*, a homicidal maniac is the DDB; in *The Birds*, the title animals are the DDBs.

Both films are marked by Hitchcock's characteristic skill at suspense. In *Psycho*, for example, as elsewhere in Hitchcock films, the audience is made to side with a fugitive in situations where she seems about to get caught. Marion Crane, on the run with a bundle of stolen cash, successfully dodges a used car salesman and a policeman. But uncharacteristically for Hitchcock, she gets stopped by a danger she was not expecting: the psychotic Norman Bates and his alter ego, his mother. This surprise element goes against Hitchcock's usual dictum of preferring suspense to surprise,[6] but for that reason it works: it breaks the rules of what the audience can expect, creating a shudder of uncertainty and instability for the rest of the film.

Suspense also operates in the buildup to the avian attack at the school in *The Birds*, as children sing innocently inside the school while birds amass outside. When the attack comes, it is savage, airborne, coming at the town from all angles, in one of Hitchcock's great set-pieces. Spectacular set-pieces themselves are characteristic of Hitchcock: for example, the crop-duster attack on Cary Grant in *North by Northwest* (1959), culminating in the crop-duster/oil truck explosion.

Hitchcock's career-long interest in Freudian themes is visible also in his pair of horror films, most obviously in *Psycho*, in which a psychiatrist actually explains for us at the end the twisted passions that motivated Norman's crimes. (There is some ironic distance during this scene, so that it is likely the psychiatrist is being subtly mocked even as his explanation appears to fit the facts.) In *The Birds*, the tension between Melanie (Tippi Hedren) and her boyfriend's mother (Jessica Tandy) has Freudian overtones, and the omnipresence of the vicious birds suggests something out of a dream, a bad dream.

Tobe Hooper (1943–)

Hooper's first major feature film was *The Texas Chain Saw Massacre*, a horror classic that he never topped. Nevertheless, he has had an interesting career, generally marked by great skill with telling a scary story and a concern with destructive outsiders trying to break into normal middle-class life. In *Texas Chain Saw Massacre*, the outsiders are cannibals and ex-slaughterhouse workers; in his made-for-TV miniseries *Salem's Lot* they are vampires; in *The Funhouse*, bizarre carnival workers; in *Poltergeist*, ghosts; and in *LifeForce* (1985), space vampires.

Hooper's ability as a horror director is best seen in *Texas Chain Saw Massacre*, which has a slow build, generating heavy suspense, followed by a roller coaster of grotesque horrors once the travelers reach the cannibals' house. Leatherface has received a lot of critical attention, but the other DDBs are interesting too—the hideously old grandfather; the father who is by turns polite to his victim Sally and brutal to his sons; the hitchhiker who cuts himself, then cuts an unwilling victim.

We are made to side with the victims in *Texas Chain Saw Massacre*, but the sheer creativity and energy of the DDBs make it clear that they are the focus of attention. This is the case throughout Hooper's career. The blue vampires of *Salem's Lot*, the deformed carnival worker in *The Funhouse*, and the naked space girl Mathilda May in *LifeForce* remain in the imagination after other aspects of the films may have been forgotten.

From film to film, Hooper varies his styles and DDBs so that his movies sometimes do not seem to resemble one another. Even in the case of the sequel *The Texas Chainsaw Massacre 2* (1986), the new film is starkly different from the original. Whereas the lair of the cannibal family in *Massacre* is a house, the lair of the same family in *Massacre 2* is an elaborate underground network of tunnels, making for a more baroque, exaggerated atmosphere. *Massacre 2* has other new features, including Dennis Hopper as a crazed avenger stalking the cannibals, Leatherface falling in love, and Caroline Williams as a captive who not only flees the cannibals but picks up a chainsaw and fights back against them.

Hideo Nakata (1961–; born in Japan)

One of the masters of J-horror, Nakata specializes in the gloomy atmosphere and angry ghosts that are often found in this subgenre. Fear is built slowly in his films, with both natural forces (such as rain) and technology (such as videotapes) contributing to the growing tension. Nakata has had a broad influence: his *Ringu* and *Honogurai mizu no soko kara* were both remade into American films (respectively, *The Ring* and *Dark Water*), and he himself directed the American sequel *The Ring Two*. Other Nakata films include *Joyûrei* (*Ghost Actress*; 1996) and *Garasu no nô* (*Sleeping Bride*; 2000).

Behind Nakata's work, and J-horror generally, is a long tradition of religion, folklore, and literature in which ancestral spirits are omnipresent, and some of them hold a grudge or wish to avenge themselves.[7] Yet the horror in Nakata's films is found not simply in the vengeful ghosts, but in their collision with a modern world that is often bleak and isolating. It is as if modernity were recovering a forgotten piece of itself, a terrifying piece.

In *Honogurai mizu no soko kara*, the lost piece is a little girl, Mitsuko, who was abandoned by her mother and has been missing for some time. Yoshimi, a woman with a young daughter of her own, finds hints that Mitsuko's ghost dwells in the apartment building where Yoshimi has moved — brief sightings of Mitsuko; a red school bag that will not go away. Finally it emerges that Mitsuko was accidentally drowned in a water tower on the roof, and that she will not leave Yoshimi and her daughter alone until Yoshimi becomes Mitsuko's mother, which means Yoshimi too must become a ghost. To save her own daughter, Yoshimi complies. Near the end of the film, Yoshimi's daughter, years later, comes back to the apartment building and finds her mother still there. They have a brief, moving conversation, then the mother is gone again — another piece forgotten, recovered, lost again.

Nakata can handle the shock special effect — the girl ghost climbing out of the television in *Ringu* — but he is especially adept at subtler effects that add up to horror. His manipulation of the soundtrack, emphasizing long intervals and quiet sounds, is a case in point. "Other people tend to use different sounds altogether to express horror," he told an interviewer, "but I can increase the perception of it to the maximum by utilizing a very quiet sound."[8]

Sam Raimi (1959–)

Raimi's horror films, beginning with *The Evil Dead*, have been notable for their frenetic pace and wildly creative, often humorous imagination. *The Evil Dead*, for example, combines all the standard haunted house tricks — isolation in woods, fog, night, eerie voices, thunder and lightning — with devices that make the haunted house subgenre fresh. These include the Book of the

Dead (similar to Lovecraft's Necronomicon), zombies that demonically mock the living, vines that disrobe and rape a young woman, wild tracking shots through the woods, and body parts that stay alive even after being dismembered.

The first sequel, *Evil Dead II*, was perhaps Raimi's peak, with the bizarre contest between his hero, Ash, and Ash's hand, which has become possessed by a demon. When Ash cuts off his hand with a chainsaw to escape the hand's malevolence, and the severed hand just keeps coming, the audience has entered a strange new realm in which horror and laughter are one.

The third movie in Raimi's *Evil Dead* trilogy, *Army of Darkness* (1993), was already veering away from horror into something like medieval fantasy with elements of horror, action, and comedy. Indeed, Raimi is a restless director who has tried his hand at multiple genres—the superhero genre with *Spider-Man* (2002) and its sequels; noirish crime with *A Simple Plan* (1998); even baseball with *For Love of the Game* (1999). Whatever his genre, he is almost always a good story-teller, imaginative and surprising.

Raimi returned to the horror genre with *Drag Me to Hell*, which featured his characteristic blend of humor and fear. Again, as with the hand attacking Ash, the unstoppable demonic force (an old Gypsy woman) repeatedly attacked the virtuous protagonist (loan officer Christine). The surprise ending, in which the promise of the title is fulfilled, has the usual Raimi darkness and wit.

George A. Romero (1940–)

Rarely is a horror film director so closely associated with a single type of DDB as Romero is with the zombie. In *Night of the Living Dead,* Romero essentially created the modern zombie, the kind that wanders around on its own looking to eat the flesh of the living, as opposed to the less inherently violent, more supernaturally based Voodoo zombie who obeys the orders of his master. The Romero zombie spawned an industry of zombie films, most of them far inferior to his. Even a late, relatively weak Romero zombie film, such as *Diary of the Dead* (2007), is better than the best effort of most of his imitators.

Romero's films are generally exciting, suspenseful, and gruesomely shocking. Gore is abundant, yet much of the horror is suggested: for example, in *Day of the Dead*, the zombies wander half-visible in the underground depths, just out of reach of the soldiers charged with capturing them for medical experiments. There is always the terror of when the next attack will come, and who will die next. The zombies are horrible, clownish, and pathetic, dressed in rags of the clothing in which they died and drawn to memories of their former lives.

Social and political commentary is woven throughout Romero's films. *Night of the Living Dead* comments on racism, *Dawn of the Dead* on consumerism, *Day of the Dead* on militarism. His non–zombie horror films, such as *The Crazies* and *Martin* (1978), are similarly fraught with social concern. *The Crazies* depicts how easily a society can collapse; *Martin* the peculiarly normal existence of a young man who regards himself as a vampire even though he has to use a hypodermic needle and razor blade on his victims.

Despite his interest in social concerns, Romero never becomes only a social commentator. He is a maker of DDBs, and this is always foremost in his films. In the opening scene of *The Crazies*, for example, a father goes berserk, killing his wife and wrecking and burning the house, while his terrified children bear witness. The scene both sets forth the social theme of societal collapse and presents a well-wrought tableau of horror with a disturbing DDB.

James Whale (1889–1957; born in the United Kingdom)

Whale directed only four films on horror subjects—*Frankenstein, The Old Dark House, The Invisible Man*, and *Bride of Frankenstein*—but his influence over the horror genre is profound. Whenever Gothic castles are lit by lightning, or mad scientists play at being God, or cemetery graves are set at odd angles, or DDBs are sympathetic as well as destructive, the hand of Whale is at work. He was a genius at creating gloomy atmosphere and mood, laced with dark comedy and pointing toward cosmic themes.

Although his horror films were made in Hollywood, Whale was British-born, and his horror work has a British sensibility, even when it is supposed to be set in some vaguely central European country. Comic relief is often provided by character actors from the British Isles— Frederick Kerr playing the old Baron Frankenstein in *Frankenstein*; Una O'Connor playing Minnie the maid in *Bride of Frankenstein* and the innkeeper's wife in *The Invisible Man*. Lead actors such as Boris Karloff, Colin Clive, Ernest Thesiger, and Claude Rains were all British. Except for Karloff, whose job was to speak in grunts and monosyllables, these actors enunciated their lines with clipped authority and grandeur. Anglophilia was evident in Whale's non–horror work, too— *Waterloo Bridge* (1931), a film about World War I, was set in England; however, he could also go thoroughly American, as in his adaptation of the riverboat musical *Show Boat* (1936).

Whale is known for the mordant wit he brought to his horror films. The satirical flourishes in *Bride of Frankenstein* have already been noted (see Chapter Eight), from the Christ-iconography of the Frankenstein monster to the pricelessly arch dialogue of Dr. Pretorius. Humor is present in his other horror films as well, particularly *The Old Dark House*, really a comedy with horror elements.

The prototypical Whale horror movie character is the mad scientist, a role handled by Clive and Thesiger in the *Frankenstein* films and Rains in *The*

Invisible Man. The mad scientist is always reaching beyond where man should reach, and either creating or becoming a monster as a result. But in this reaching is the majesty and rebelliousness for which Whale seems to suggest everyone should aim, and the DDB that results is the emblem of the creative power humanity can have — the power to make new being.

The director's contribution of style, sensibility, and unifying vision is, in a sense, the most abstract of all the techniques by which the DDB is presented. Yet it touches on all the other film techniques that were discussed in the previous chapter. Together, the collaborative arts of the cinema — including the director's art — make the horror film what it is: a display in which the DDB seems actual, horrifying, and primary.

17

Stars and DDBs

The names Tom Tyler, David Peel, and Michael Villella may not mean much to most people. But all capably played prominent roles as DDBs, despite a lack of any great star power either before or since those roles. Tyler was the mummy Kharis in *The Mummy's Hand*; Peel was Baron Meinster, the principal vampire in *The Brides of Dracula*; and Villella (sometimes spelled Villela) was the serial killer in *Slumber Party Massacre* (1982). The names of these actors have gone down, for the most part, in obscurity, despite their contributions to the depiction of monsters.

From such examples, one might conclude that playing a DDB is a bad idea for an actor. But in fact, some stars, such as Boris Karloff and Bela Lugosi, made their careers by playing DDBs. Others, such as Bruce Willis and Nicole Kidman, were already stars when they appeared as DDBs in horror films, and did not appear to harm themselves by doing so. The effect of DDB portrayals on stardom is the subject of this chapter. The significance of the subject for DDB theory is this: DDB theory states that DDBs are pleasing to the audience as sought-after examples of otherwise inaccessible being. Therefore, DDB theory predicts that playing DDBs is, under the right conditions, a good career move for an actor. If DDB theory is incorrect and people are not pleased by seeing DDBs, then they would tend to punish actors who play DDBs by not buying tickets to their movies, and thus hurting their careers.

In fact, as this chapter shows, playing DDBs has been useful to the careers of many actors, either making them stars or helping them stay stars, and where it has been useless or harmful there are circumstances that explain why. My definition of "star" is the same as it is in Hollywood: someone whose name in the credits attracts an audience to the film, and who therefore is likely to be paid better and achieve more renown than other actors.

Not discussed in this chapter are the many actors who played normals but not DDBs in horror movies, even though some of them thereby achieved fame (Fay Wray for *King Kong*, for example) or were already famous when they played the roles (e.g., Dana Andrews in *Curse of the Demon*). That is because it is obvious that actors who play normal people in horror movies

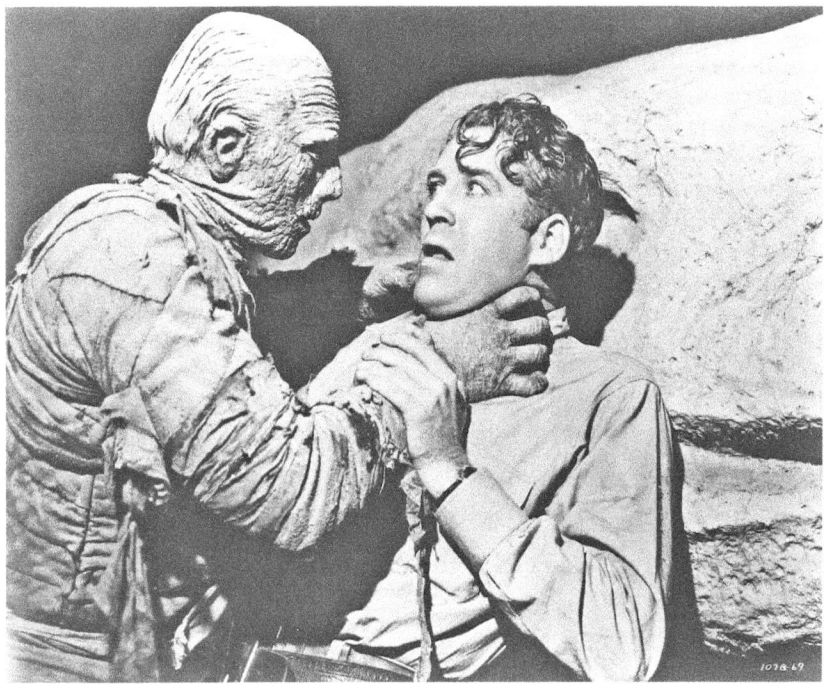

The mummy Kharis (Tom Tyler) attacks archeologist Steve Banning (Dick Foran) in *The Mummy's Hand* (1940, Universal).

should be able, at least sometimes, to attract the sympathy of normal audience members. The question at stake is whether playing a DDB also can win an audience. The main evidentiary base of DDB theory, as stated earlier, is how much can be done with it. But like many theories, it also makes empirical claims than can either be confirmed or disconfirmed. Some of these claims will be discussed in the next and final chapter; one, the relation between stars and DDBs, is discussed here.

Stars of the Horror Ghetto

The first great American horror star was Lon Chaney. People flocked to his movies to see what sort of grotesque character he would play next. Not all his films were horror films; they were not all primarily geared toward presentation of a DDB. But there was usually something odd, shady, or deformed about his characters, and some of these characters were DDBs. Playing DDBs and other grotesques did not hurt Chaney's career, but made it.

The same held true for the next generation of horror film stars, Karloff,

Lugosi, and Lon Chaney, Jr. It is doubtful that any of them would have become household names if not for their playing monsters—respectively, the Frankenstein monster, Dracula, and the Wolf Man, the roles that made them famous. They were all fine actors, especially Karloff, but something about them was just strange and menacing enough that they would probably have languished in small character roles if not for their star turns as monsters. Karloff admitted as much, stating of the Frankenstein monster, "I owe everything to him. He's my best friend."[1]

Some may consider this type of stardom typecasting, a strait-jacket that keeps an actor in the horror ghetto and prevents him from getting other, better roles. Lugosi, for example, appears to have always longed to appear in something other than horror films, but horror films were all he was offered. However, working actors know that any work is better than no work. For every Lugosi who had to "settle" for playing another vampire, there are many more actors who have no opportunity to work at all. To be a star in the horror ghetto was still to be a star.

Thus, for at least part of the careers of actors such as Karloff, Lugosi, and Chaney Sr. and Jr., horror movies provided a steady stream of roles. Audiences liked them as DDBs and wanted to keep seeing them that way, expressing their approval by buying tickets. Prominent supporting players also made a career in horror by having played DDBs: Lionel Atwill, for example, played the monsters in *The Mystery of the Wax Museum* and *Doctor* X, and afterward never lacked for work in horror films.

In later days, other actors similarly made a career in horror that started by playing DDBs: for example, Peter Cushing as Frankenstein and Christopher Lee as Dracula. Curiously, both actors later branched out to play villainous roles in the *Star Wars* saga: Cushing as Grand Moff Tarkin in *Star Wars* (1977); Lee as Count Dooku in *Star Wars: Episode II: Attack of the Clones* (2002) and *Star Wars: Episode III: Revenge of the Sith* (2005). Vincent Price went from supporting roles to horror leads after playing the DDB in *House of Wax* (1953). Robert Englund may not be a household name outside the houses of horror movie fans, but he has had steady work in horror films because of his star turn as Freddy Krueger in *A Nightmare on Elm Street*.

Horror Careers That Never Were

For every DDB portrayal that led to a long horror career, other performances did not. Three have been mentioned already: Tyler, Peel, and Villella. It would seem that these serve as counter-evidence against DDB theory.

However, in all such cases, there are reasons why the DDB performer did not become a horror star. Tyler fell victim to a rule against letting the makeup be too heavy. His mummy makeup encased his face, allowing it little expression, even less considering that the role demanded him to be stiff and emotionless. In these cases, audiences feel that any actor can play the role just as well, if they think about the actor at all. Indeed, after Tyler, Lon Chaney, Jr., took over the role of Kharis, adding some marquee value to the films' credits and without anyone much noticing the difference. Tyler's acting career did not suffer, however; he continued making a decent living in B westerns and serials.

Even more damaging to a DDB's potential stardom is a mask or a full-body costume. The title character in *The Creature from the Black Lagoon* was played by two actors, Ben Chapman on land and Ricou Browning, an expert swimmer, in the water. Because the creature was entirely covered by a mask and costume, no one could tell that two different actors were at work, and neither actor rose to stardom.

Similarly, the actors who have played Jason Voorhees, the psychopathic killer of the series that began with *Friday the 13th* (1980), have usually been hidden behind a hockey mask. With no way to see the actor's face, audiences have declined to grant stardom to this group, and producers have kept shuffling in new actors, since it hardly matters who plays the role. Only Kane Hodder has achieved any sort of continuity in the role, having played it in four consecutive films, from *Friday the 13th Part VII: The New Blood* (1988) to *Jason X*.

Heavy makeup by itself does not preclude stardom. Karloff and Englund both wore heavy makeup in their star-making roles. But the makeup must be such as to allow the actor to express emotion and thus maintain human connection to the audience, as was the case with, respectively, the Frankenstein monster and Freddy Krueger.

As for the other supposed counter-examples: Peel did a creditable job as the lead male vampire in *The Brides of Dracula*, but he retired from film shortly afterward, so the potential for his career will never be known. Villella was overshadowed by the women in *Slumber Party Massacre*, who not only wore skimpy clothing but banded together to defeat the killer. He was therefore a weak DDB, as well as a derivative one, his type of role having been played many times before. The chances for stardom are greater if the DDB is strong and original. This may explain why Richard Crane, lead alligator person in *The Alligator People*, never became a major star. Similarly, Glenn Strange, who played the Frankenstein monster in the late sequels of the Universal series, usually did little more than come to life in the last few minutes of the movie, making him a weak DDB in a highly derivative role.

Also important for actors who want to parlay a DDB role into a career is that the film be a hit. Eric Stoltz was relegated to small roles and indies after the bomb that was *The Fly II*. And the DDB should not be part of a DDB ensemble. The reason none of the zombies in the *Night of the Living Dead* series has become a star is that each zombie is a nearly indistinguishable part of a DDB mass. Similarly, the cannibal family members in *The Hills Have Eyes* are part of a family, and therefore not quite distinct enough to gain stardom.

Outside the Horror Ghetto

Several actors have used a DDB portrayal to win stardom outside the horror ghetto. Anthony Perkins became a household name with his performance as the deranged Norman Bates in *Psycho*. He went on to act in such mainstream films as *Catch-22* (1970) and *Murder on the Orient Express* (1974). Nevertheless, he was always best known as Norman Bates, which perhaps was why he returned to the role late in his career in the sequels *Psycho II* (1983) and *Psycho III* (1986), as well as the TV film *Psycho IV: The Beginning* (1990).

Kathy Bates made her name, and won a Best Actress Oscar, playing the deranged (just like Norman Bates) Annie Wilkes in *Misery*. She was exceptional at turning without notice from an apparently sweet, caring person to a creepy adoring fan to a malevolent psychopath. She went on to starring and supporting roles in such non–horror films as *Fried Green Tomatoes* (1991), *Dolores Claiborne* (1995), *Titanic* (1997), and *About Schmidt* (2002).

Then there is the type of actor who is already known to the public for non–horror work before his turn as a DDB, but who uses the DDB performance either to boost his non–horror career or just to continue it. Anthony Hopkins needed a boost when he appeared in *The Silence of the Lambs*. He had been on the fringes of stardom for years before that, familiar to many people from his roles in TV miniseries and feature films—Richard the Lionheart in *The Lion in Winter* (1968); Captain Bligh in *The Bounty* (1984)—but he was still not a major star. Then his portrayal of the deranged (again) Hannibal Lecter not only won him a Best Actor Oscar but made him a popular success.

There were so many nuances to Hopkins's performance as Lecter: the alert, expectant gaze with which he first greets Clarice; the droll way he pronounces the name of a wine in the phrase, "I ate his liver with some fava beans and a nice Chianti"; his perpetual look of intelligence and hunger; the loving creepiness with which he grazes Clarice's finger; the operatic viciousness of his attack on his guards; his final sashaying off into the crowd, on the hunt for his next victim. At last, Anthony Hopkins could open a picture. He went on to such non–horror films as *Howards End* (1992) and *Shadowlands* (1993), besides returning to the horror genre as the paternal werewolf in *The Wolfman* (2010).

Jack Nicholson has been in and out of horror films most of his career. He started off playing normals in low-budget Roger Corman movies such as the horror film *The Terror* (1963) and the horror comedy *The Little Shop of Horrors*, then became a big star in non–horror films such as *Five Easy Pieces* (1970) and *Chinatown* (1974), then went back to horror—but this time in a big-budget way. He starred as the deranged (yet again) Jack Torrance in Stanley Kubrick's *The Shining*. This DDB portrayal seemed to strengthen his already strong career, and three years later he appeared in *Terms of Endearment* (1983), for which he won a Best Supporting Actor Oscar (one of his three acting Academy Awards). Later he starred as the Devil in a horror comedy, *The Witches of Eastwick* (1987), and as a werewolf in *Wolf* (1994).

Bette Davis played the monstrously deranged Baby Jane Hudson in *What Ever Happened to Baby Jane?* The move helped extend her acting career pretty much until her death, in 1989, the year she appeared in the Larry Cohen horror comedy *Wicked Stepmother*.

Kathy Bates became a movie star, and won a Best Actress Oscar, playing the psychopathic Annie Wilkes in *Misery* (1990, Columbia).

By now, it will have been noted that the roles of deranged DDBs seem to be particularly good career moves for would-be or actual movie stars. There is a reason for this. The DDB whose deformity is psychological can often get away without having any physical deformity, as in the case of Norman Bates, Wilkes, Lecter, Torrance, and Hudson. This allows the audience to see the star without the distraction of grotesque makeup, and makes it more likely that the star can go on to play non–deformed roles, without being typed as ugly characters. Also, playing deranged requires a lot of acting, and this acting can attract attention and awards.

Other actors have discovered the benefits of playing a DDB without grotesque makeup, but have done so by portraying a spiritual rather than a psychological deformity. Bruce Willis in *The Sixth Sense* and Nicole Kidman in *The Others* both played ghosts who did not know they were ghosts—and did so without any physically deforming makeup. In an understated performance as a deceased child psychologist, Willis projected sadness, caring, inquisitiveness, humor, and fear, as well as stunned realization when he discovers that he is dead. He managed to portray all this despite the fact that most of his scenes are played either alone or with a child actor, Haley Joel Osment. Willis's career profited from his performance; as for Kidman, she was effective in her own right as a ghost, and went on to win the Best Actress Oscar shortly after *The Others*, for 2002's *The Hours*.

The exception that proves the rule was Robert DeNiro's turn as the Frankenstein monster in *Mary Shelley's Frankenstein*. The performance did nothing much to help his career, perhaps because he was concealed in a lot of disfiguring makeup and because the film was a bomb. On the other hand, the role did not hurt him either; he went on to better things in films such as *Casino* (1995) and *Meet the Parents* (2000). Another kind of exception was Terry O'Quinn as the deranged stepfather in *The Stepfather*. Although he gave a good performance in a deranged role free of grotesque makeup, he did not become a movie star; however, he has had a long career, mostly on television, playing, for example, John Locke on *Lost*.

As a rule, playing a DDB can be good for an actor's career, because audiences take pleasure in DDBs and associate that pleasure with the actor. This is evidence that the DDB is the thing horror film audiences want to see and delight in seeing. It helps if there is not so much makeup as to make the actor unrecognizable, if the DDB is strong and original, and if the film is a hit. With those caveats, the association between stardom and DDBness is pronounced.

18
Other Directions

DDB theory has potential applications to a number of areas besides those already mentioned. It connects to the larger field of aesthetics, to biology and evolution, to psychology, and to society. In all these areas, further study may prove fruitful.

Aesthetics

The teleologic approach to aesthetics is to ask of each art: what is its primary purpose? The prediction of DDB theory is that for each art, the primary purpose is the presentation of being. As Heidegger says, the nature of art is "the truth of beings setting itself to work."[1] This purpose is achieved through characteristic means. In the case of horror films, the being presented is deformed and destructive, and it is made known through cinematic narrative. The more general the art form, the more general the definition of being. For example, of films in general, one could say that the presentation of beings through cinematic narrative is the primary purpose. In the performing arts (which include film, as well as drama, dance, and music), the primary purpose is the presentation of beings through the acting bodies of artists. In art in general, the primary purpose is the presentation of being through constructed means. The appeal of art in general is to satisfy the human desire to know being, whether by presenting an imitation of actual being (a photograph of a city street), an original object (an abstract mosaic), or both (the photograph of the street not only represents the street, but is so composed from a specific viewpoint as to be an original object).

In some cases, the type of being presented is clear. In landscape painting, landscapes are presented. In other cases, the being is more abstract. In instrumental music, the notes as played on instruments form a temporal and sonic structure that is itself a type of being. When the first notes of Beethoven's *Fifth Symphony* are played, they are instantly recognizable to anyone who has heard them, suggesting that they possess existence as a kind of object, albeit an abstract object.

Joyce Webster (Beverly Garland) struggles with her husband-turned-unconvincing-alligator-man, Paul Webster (Richard Crane), in *The Alligator People* (1959, 20th Century–Fox).

All art, according to this approach, which may be called teleologic-ontologic theory or intended being theory (of which DDB theory is a special case), exists to present being through constructed means. In this specific sense, art may be regarded as that which primarily is presented to be beautiful — that is, to please when apprehended, as being does. This does not mean that art cannot have other purposes. Antique chairs on display in a museum were originally made for sitting. But they may have been made, even at the time of their construction, to be beautiful as well, and by the time they have reached the stage of display in a museum, they are being presented only for their beauty.

Should there be a God in anything like the Thomistic sense, he would be the ultimate artist, because he makes everything to be beautiful — to please himself when he apprehends it, and secondarily to please humans who are also apprehending — and what makes everything beautiful is that very being that God supremely possesses. Humans imitate God by making beautiful things of their own, and apprehending the beauty in the things they make and God has made; and in thus imitating God, they achieve their own purpose as creatures, which is to know and be like God and therefore be united to him.

Humans themselves are intended beings, works of art, and in fulfilling that purpose, they are happy.

Because the intended being approach unifies the arts, it also offers a unified method of aesthetic evaluation. In any art, that art object is good that seems to present a new being. Some of the criteria for evaluating the art object's success are universal: the art object must be original, memorable, and coherent, whether it is a sonata, a tapestry, or a poem. Others are specific to the type of means or type of being at issue: in imitative arts such as fiction or representational painting, the imitation must be plausible; in the horror film, the DDB must be horrifying. A creature such as the leading monster in *The Alligator People* fails at both. Plausibility and horror are not issues in other arts, such as flower arrangement, but in that case an issue such as focal point is.

For intended being theory to progress, formal accounts would be needed of how each art and genre fit within the theory, as this book has done with the horror film. This process would also permit the elucidation of counterexamples, if any, which, should they demonstrate weaknesses within the theory, would require the theory to be modified or abandoned.

Biology and Evolution

As noted earlier, DDB theory has strong connections to evolutionary theory. Everything living is a DDB, in the broad sense that it represents the deformation of something from which it evolved, and the concomitant destruction of other beings—both those that came before it and those rivals or enemies that must suffer from the superior fitness it attains through its evolution. When humans evolved, we represented a deformation of the hominin species that preceded us, and we made them obsolete and extinct. We also became a menace to species that would have had little to fear from, say, our Australopithecine ancestors: big and moderate-size game animals that ultimately went extinct, such as mammoths, and others that survived but are very nervous around us, such as deer. All living things, ourselves included, are deformed and destructive beings whose deformity causes destruction.

This conclusion should not come as news to evolutionary biologists, and is unlikely to alter their scientific methods. However, it may have more to say to the field of the arts. The inference to be drawn from DDB theory is that evolution itself—biology itself—is one long horror movie. It suggests a new approach to studying biology and evolution—as an aesthetic display, pleasing for its very horror. This type of display already exists in the work of artists such as Damien Hirst, whose tiger shark preserved in formaldehyde, *The Physical Impossibility of Death in the Mind of Someone Living* (1992), presents a biological specimen as art. Numerous other displays might be considered to fall under this category, from nature documentaries to ethological accounts of wild animal behavior to taxidermy to mounted dinosaur skeletons.

Yet there are two types of work missing from the genre of what might be called real biological DDBs: a systematic critical-historical account of all the different human-made works that have so far contributed to this realm of art; and systematic artistic efforts to present the horror of nature from many angles and at many levels, from the microscopic to the dinosaurian. Such systematic works would include not only presentation of static specimens—this or that tiger or dinosaur—but attempts to represent visually, musically, and verbally the dynamic evolutionary process by which one species gives rise to another, and some species fall into greater threat, through the natural unfolding of deformity and destruction.

Psychology

DDB theory offers a psychological hypothesis that can be tested empirically: that people want to see and take pleasure in seeing beings, and that they are particularly delighted in seeing beings that are new to them, even if those beings are in some respect deformed or destructive, provided that the beings pose no imminent danger to the viewers. Carefully constructed experiments to test this hypothesis could be done using psychophysical or neuroimaging methods, with test subjects exposed to stimulation from horror film DDBs that were new to them, while control subjects received either no stimulation or watched films of non–horror subjects either new to them or very familiar to them. Such experiments would shed light on the extent of human interest in being as such, as well as on the function of the horror film.

There are various ways to test whether DDB theory is correct, but here is one simple proposal. DDB theory claims that people who like horror movies seek them out for the pleasure of having a DDB presented to them. A "bait and switch" experiment will test this.

On a college campus, place an ad for volunteers for a psychological experiment, and specify that the volunteers must enjoy horror movies. Test the volunteers to make sure they are not lying: administer a questionnaire that requires them to be able to name some horror films they have enjoyed and that verifies whether they indeed take pleasure from such movies. For example, ask, "Do you take pleasure from the fear you feel at a horror film?" The right answer is yes.

Once you have a pool of authentic horror film fans, divide them into three groups. Inform all groups that they are about to watch a horror film and will be asked to rate it afterward on a liking scale, where 0 is "Did not like at all" and 5 is "Liked greatly." The first group will see a recent, well-reviewed, popular horror film with a clearly presented DDB. The second group will be told that the intended horror film was not available, but that they will instead see another film. This turns out to be a recent, well-reviewed, popular crime film with elements of action, in which there is roughly as much violence as in the horror film but no clearly presented DDB. The third group will also be told that the horror film was not available, and instead will watch a taped panel discussion in which members of the English department discuss the various meanings and significances of horror movies, including their social, political, and psychological import.

DDB theory predicts that when the liking scores are compiled, the group that saw the horror movie will have a mean score significantly higher than the mean score in either of the other groups. This will support the theory that horror movie audiences are interested in the presentation of the DDB, not merely violence or a good narrative (the crime film) or presentation of the meaning and significance the horror film is presumed to convey.

There is another area of psychology in which DDB theory might be especially informative: the study of nightmares, which have long been noted as being similar to horror films. Nightmare studies have been on the rise in recent years, and the five most common nightmare themes identified in one article — falling, being chased, being paralyzed, being late, and the deaths of close persons[2] — have clear analogs to horror film content. Four of the five themes are found obviously in many horror films; the fifth, being late, occurs whenever the normals are too late to stop another normal from being attacked by the DDB, as in the race to prevent a shark attack on the Fourth of July in *Jaws*. Comparative studies of nightmares and horror films might uncover a deep link between the two areas of experience. In a nightmare, the dreamer may be apprehending a DDB during sleep, principally for the pleasure of encountering the DDB, and even to the point of arousing painful emotions and disturbing sleep. It may even be that dreams in general have a hitherto unexplored function of allowing the exploration of being to occur during sleep.

Society

According to DDB theory, the horror film is primarily intended to please the audience by satisfying their desire to know new beings that would otherwise be inaccessible. However, a secondary purpose may be to educate — to show us what we have to face in the real world, and to prepare us to survive it. As noted, the horror film shows vividly what goes on in biology and evolution. It also shows what goes on in society.

In real life, there are no vampires, zombies, ghosts, or werewolves. There are psychopathic serial killers, but not that many, and there are people who seem to act as if they are the Devil's minions, though not that many outright Satanic cultists. Yet human evil is widespread. Criminals, dictators, terrorists, corrupt policemen, unethical soldiers, inept doctors, wife-beaters, child-abusers, bullies, and mobs routinely do cruel, violent, and sometimes homicidal things to their fellow human beings. They are all clearly monsters, deformed in their way of thinking and as a result destructive.

But there are also less obvious monsters. In our global society, many people are desperately poor, uneducated, uncared-for, hungry, or homeless. Sometimes it is not clear that anyone is to blame for the dire circumstances of these people; it is just how the world is. Yet on an individual basis, it would take no miracle to help any particular person in this group: just a little money, maybe with a few social services. Why then, with all the wealth that is available in some parts of the world (such as the more prosperous areas of the United States), do so many people suffer? Possibly, and in large part, because of the selfishness of the prosperous people. Their unwillingness to care about the poor amounts to cruelty and monstrousness. It makes them DDBs.

An example of how to live peacefully as DDBs: the blind hermit (O.P. Heggie) and the Frankenstein monster (Boris Karloff) in *Bride of Frankenstein* (1935, Universal).

I have described the horror film as both conservative and subversive, but it is also something else: potentially humanizing. Just because the horror film focuses on the worst things that can be done to a person — killing, torture, imprisonment, deprivation — it forces the audience to think, if only fleetingly, about the nature of evil. In the horror film, the perpetrators of evil may be fantastic or exaggerated, but the evils that they do are, for the most part, real evils, things that are done to humans by other, more pedestrian, agents. Not all of those agents are in human control — for example, earthquakes, famines, and germs. But many agents are in human control — in fact, many are humans themselves.

Earlier I noted that there is no conclusive evidence of the impact of horror films on society. But the potential of horror films to affect society is clear. They are about deformed and destructive beings attacking normals; we ourselves are both deformed and destructive beings and normals. We learn from the horror film that the DDBs are not always as bad as they seem, and the normals are not always as good. From this mix of ideas, it is possible that we could learn from the horror film how to be better DDBs and normals, so that we cause as little destruction as possible (like the Frankenstein monster and the hermit during their sojourn together in *Bride of Frankenstein*), while protecting ourselves rationally from the destruction others might wish to cause us. For this reason, further research on the social implications of horror films from a DDB perspective would be welcome, provided it is remembered that the main purpose of a horror movie is not to teach but to please.

Notes

Preface

1. Noël Carroll, *The Philosophy of Horror, or Paradoxes of the Heart* (New York: Routledge, 1990), 181.
2. James B Twitchell, *Dreadful Pleasures: An Anatomy of Modern Horror* (1985; repr., New York: Oxford University Press, 1988), 104.
3. Vincent Price, foreword to *The Horror Film: A Guide to More Than 700 Films on Videocassette* (Evanston, IL: CineBooks, 1989), vi.

Chapter 1

1. *The American Heritage Dictionary of the English Language*, 3rd ed. (Boston: Houghton Mifflin, 1992), 872, 1533.
2. *Webster's II New College Dictionary*, 3rd ed. (Boston: Houghton Mifflin, 2005), 546, 964.
3. Alain Silver and James Ursini, eds., *Horror Film Reader* (New York: Limelight Editions, 2000), 3.
4. Thomas Nagel, *The View from Nowhere* (Oxford: Oxford University Press, 1989), 14–15.
5. Richard Rorty, *Contingency, Irony, and Solidarity* (Cambridge: Cambridge University Press, 1989), 8–9.
6. Noël Carroll, *Philosophy of Horror*, 160, 158.
7. "Why are horror movies appealing? Adrenaline? Shock?" Fluther.com, November 3, 2009, accessed August 28, 2010, http://www.fluther.com/disc/60240/why-are-horror-movies-appealing-adrenaline-shock/.
8. Walter Kendrick, *The Thrill of Fear: 250 Years of Scary Entertainment* (New York: Grove Weidenfeld, 1991), xix.
9. Stephen King, *Danse Macabre* (1981; repr., New York: Berkley Books, 1983), 13.
10. Ernest Jones, *On the Nightmare* (1931; repr., New York: Liveright, 1951), 78.
11. David Punter, *The Literature of Terror: A History of Gothic Fictions from 1765 to the Present Day* (London: Longman, 1980), 351.
12. Robin Wood, "Return of the Repressed," *Film Comment* 14, no. 4 (July–August 1978): 25–32.
13. David J. Skal, *The Monster Show: A Cultural History of Horror* (1993; repr., New York: Penguin Books, 1994), 386.
14. Camille Paglia, *Sexual Personae: Art and Decadence from Nefertiti to Emily Dickinson* (1990; repr., New York: Vintage Books, 1991), 268.
15. Valdine Clemens, *The Return of the Repressed: Gothic Horror from the Castle of Otranto to Alien* (Albany: State University of New York Press, 1999), 1.
16. Carol J. Clover, *Men, Women, and Chain Saws: Gender in the Modern Horror Film* (1992; repr., Princeton: Princeton University Press, 1993), 229.
17. Rick Worland, *The Horror Film: An Introduction* (Malden, MA: Blackwell Publishing, 2007), 9.
18. Aristotle, *Metaphysics*, 7.7.1032b1–2.
19. Arthur O. Lovejoy, *The Great Chain of Being: A Study of the History of an Idea* (1936; repr., Cambridge, MA: Harvard University Press, 1982).
20. Noël Carroll, *Philosophy of Horror*, 32.

21. Aquinas, *Summa Theologica*, 1.5.1.
22. Ibid., 1.5.4; 1.88.3.
23. Aristotle, *Metaphysics*, 7.1.1028b1–5.
24. Aquinas, *Summa Theologica*, 1.49.2.
25. That a "warped" nature might establish a distinct species of creature is hinted at in Aristotle, *History of Animals* 8.2.589b25–30.
26. Aquinas, *Summa Theologica*, 1.49.2.
27. Ibid., 1–2.27.1.
28. Aristotle, *Poetics* 9.1452b1–5.
29. Aquinas, *Summa Theologica*, 1.39.8.

Chapter 2

1. Aquinas, *Summa Theologica*, 1.85.2.
2. Scott MacDonald, "Theory of Knowledge," in Norman Kretzmann and Eleonore Stump, eds., *The Cambridge Companion to Aquinas* (Cambridge: Cambridge University Press, 1993), 169, 184.
3. Aquinas, *Summa Theologica*, 1.84.6.
4. Ibid., 1.85.1.
5. Robin Wood, "An Introduction to the American Horror Film," in Bill Nichols, ed., *Movies and Methods*, vol. 2 (Berkeley: University of California Press, 1985), 203.
6. François Truffaut with Helen G. Scott, *Hitchcock*, rev. ed. (New York: Touchstone, 1985), 72–73.

Chapter 3

1. Aquinas, *Summa Theologica*, 1.78.1.
2. Ibid., 1.78.1.
3. "Death by Murder," Ben Best, accessed July 5, 2010, http://www.benbest.com/lifeext/murder.html#world.
4. Clover, *Men, Women, and Chain Saws*, 6.

Chapter 4

1. See, for example, the analyses at "Structure: Jaws," August 23, 2008, accessed September 25, 2010, http://thestorydepartment.com/structure-jaws/; and "What are Act Breaks, Turning Points, Act Climaxes, Plot Points? (Examples)," blog entry by Alexandra Sokoloff," April 13, 2009, accessed September 25, 2010, http://thedarksalon.blogspot.com/2009/04/what-are-act-breaks-turning-points-act.html.

2. Syd Field, *Screenplay: The Foundations of Screenwriting*, 3rd ed. (New York: Dell, 1984).
3. Noël Carroll, *Philosophy of Horror*, 99–108.
4. Carl Gottlieb, *The Jaws Log*, 30th anniversary edition (New York: Newmarket Press, 2005), 210–11.

Chapter 5

1. William K. Everson, *Classics of the Horror Film* (New York: Citadel Press, 1974), 3.
2. Curtis Harrington, "Ghoulies and Ghosties," in Silver and Ursini, *Horror Film Reader*, 12–13.
3. Leonard Maltin, ed. *Leonard Maltin's Movie & Video Guide*, 2004 edition (New York: Signet, 2003), 781.
4. Leonard Maltin, ed. *Leonard Maltin's 2011 Movie Guide* (New York: Signet, 2010), 772.
5. David Edelstein, "Now Playing at Your Local Multiplex: Torture Porn," *New York Magazine*, January 28, 2006, http://nymag.com/movies/features/15622/.
6. Dolf Zillmann and James B. Weaver, "Effects of Prolonged Exposure to Gratuitous Media Violence on Provoked and Unprovoked Hostile Behavior," *Journal of Applied Social Psychology* 21, no. 18 (1999): 1517–23.
7. L. Rowell Huesmann et al., "Longitudinal Relations between Children's Exposure to TV Violence and Their Aggressive and Violent Behavior in Young Adulthood: 1977–1992," *Developmental Psychology* 39, no. 2 (2003): 201–21.
8. Jonathan L. Freedman, *Media Violence and Its Effect on Aggression: Assessing the Scientific Evidence* (Toronto: University of Toronto Press, 2002), 201.
9. Clover, *Men, Women, and Chain Saws*, 21.
10. Skal, *Monster Show*, 312.
11. John McCarty, *Splatter Movies: Breaking the Last Taboo of the Screen* (New York: St. Martin's Press, 1984), 5.
12. Worland, *Horror Film*, 11.
13. Robin Wood, *Hollywood from Vietnam to Reagan* (New York: Columbia University Press, 1986), 78.

14. Clover, *Men, Women, and Chain Saws*, 35.

Chapter 6

1. Wood, "Introduction to the American Horror Film," 196–97.
2. See, for example, Frank Cioffi, *Freud and the Question of Pseudoscience* (Chicago: Open Court, 1998).
3. Clover, *Men, Women, and Chain Saws*, 124.
4. Noël Carroll, *Philosophy of Horror*, 28.
5. Aquinas, *Summa Theologica*, 2–2.64.3.

Chapter 7

1. E.D. Hirsch, Jr., "Objective Interpretation," in *Validity in Interpretation* (New Haven: Yale University Press, 1967), 209–44.
2. Terry Eagleton, *Literary Theory: An Introduction* (Minneapolis: University of Minnesota Press, 1983), 67–71.
3. François Truffaut, "Une certaine tendance du cinéma français," *Cahiers du Cinéma* 31 (January 1954); Andrew Sarris, "Notes on the Auteur Theory in 1962," *Film Culture* 27 (Winter, 1962/63): 1–8.
4. Vincent LoBrutto, *Stanley Kubrick: A Biography* (New York: Donald I. Fine Books, 1997), 412.
5. Cynthia A. Freeland, "Feminist Frameworks for Horror Films," in Leo Braudy and Marshall Cohen, eds., *Film Theory and Criticism: Introductory Readings*, 6th ed. (Oxford: Oxford University Press, 2004), 742–63.
6. Richard Rorty, "Nineteenth-Century Idealism and Twentieth-Century Textualism," in *Consequences of Pragmatism (Essays: 1972–1980)* (Minneapolis: University of Minnesota Press, 1982), 151.
7. "'Orphan' horrifies adoption groups," *The Hollywood Reporter*, July 17, 2009, http://www.hollywoodreporter.com/hr/content_display/film/news/e3ibdf529fl8374f6c9528143d2c418c203.
8. Joseph Carroll, *Literary Darwinism: Evolution, Human Nature, and Literature* (Florence, KY: Routledge, 2004).

9. Michael J. O'Neill et al., "Ancient and continuing Darwinian selection on *insulin-like growth factor II* in placental fishes," *Proceedings of the National Academy of Sciences*, 104, no. 30 (2007): 12404–9.
10. Douglas W. Mock, *More than Kin and Less than Kind: The Evolution of Family Conflict* (Cambridge, MA: Belknap Press, 2004), 4.
11. Alan S. Miller and Satoshi Kanazawa, *Why Beautiful People Have More Daughters* (New York: Perigee, 2008), 98, 119.
12. Kyle Buchanan, "Two-Minute Verdict," Movieline.com, April 2, 2010, accessed July 10, 2010, http://www.movieline.com/2010/04/splice-trailer.php.

Chapter 8

1. Rotten Tomatoes, accessed February 2, 2010, http://www.rottentomatoes.com.
2. Wood, "Introduction to the American Horror Film," 201.
3. Horror-Wood Webzine, accessed February 4, 2010, http://www.horror-wood.com/pretorius.htm.
4. Alberto Manguel, *Bride of Frankenstein* (London: British Film Institute, 1997), 47.
5. Ibid., 56.
6. Michael Brunas, John Brunas, and Tom Weaver, *Universal Horrors: The Studio's Classic Films, 1931–1946* (Jefferson, NC: McFarland, 1990), 120.
7. F.S.N., "At the Roxy," review of *Bride of Frankenstein*, *New York Times*, May 11, 1935.
8. Elizabeth Young, "Here Comes the Bride: Wedding Gender and Race in 'Bride of Frankenstein,'" *Feminist Studies* 17, no. 3 (1991): 403–37.
9. Gary Morris, "Sexual Subversion: The Bride of Frankenstein," *Bright Lights Film Journal* 19 (July 1997), http://www.brightlightsfilm.com/19/19_bride1.php.
10. Ibid.
11. Manguel, *Bride of Frankenstein*, 30.

Chapter 9

1. "*The Fly II*," accessed February 12, 2010, http://www.x-entertainment.com/messages/594.html.

2. "Horror Talk Review: *The Fly II* DVD Review," 2005, accessed February 12, 2010, http://www.horrortalk.com/reviews/The-Fly2/TheFly2.htm.

Chapter 10

1. David Bordwell, Janet Staiger, and Kristin Thompson, *The Classical Hollywood Cinema: Film Style & Mode of Production to 1960* (New York: Columbia University Press, 1985), 110.
2. John M. Swales, *Genre Analysis: English in Academic and Research Settings* (Cambridge: Cambridge University Press, 1990), 46.
3. Worland, *Horror Film*, 24, 77.
4. Vivian Sobchak, *Screening Space: The American Science Fiction Film*, 2nd ed (New Brunswick, NJ: Rutgers University Press, 1997).
5. Aristotle, *Poetics*, 5.1449a30–35.
6. Francis Hutcheson, *Thoughts on Laughter and Observations on 'The Fable of the Bees' in Six Letters* (1758; repr., Bristol: Thoemmes, 1989), 24.
7. Alastair Clarke, *The Faculty of Adaptability: Humour's Contribution to Human Ingenuity* (Cumbria, UK: Pyrrhic House, 2009).
8. Brandon Gray, "Weekend Report: 'Wild Things' Roars, 'Citizen,' 'Activity' Thrill," Box Office Mojo, October 19, 2009, accessed June 18, 2010, http://www.boxofficemojo.com/news/?id=2620&p=.htm.
9. "Zombieland," Metacritic.com, accessed June 18, 2010, http://www.metacritic.com/film/titles/zombieland?q=zombieland.

Chapter 11

1. Richard Dawkins, *The Selfish Gene* (1976; repr., Oxford: Oxford University Press, 2006), 192.
2. Mordaunt Hall, "The Screen," review of *Frankenstein*, *New York Times*, December 5, 1931.
3. Harold Bloom, *The Anxiety of Influence: A Theory of Poetry*. (New York: Oxford University Press, 1973), 5–6.
4. Skal, *Monster Show*; Worland, *Horror Film*; Everson, *Classics of the Horror Film*; Twitchell, *Dreadful Pleasures*; Charles Derry, *Dark Dreams 2.0: A Psychological History of the Modern Horror Film from the 1950s to the 21st Century* (Jefferson, NC: McFarland, 2009); Andrew Tudor, *Monsters and Mad Scientists: A Cultural History of the Horror Movie* (Hoboken, NJ: Wiley-Blackwell, 1991).
5. Kerr, *Thrill of Fear*, 67–99.
6. Worland, *Horror Film*, 36–37.
7. Ibid., 32–35, 41.
8. *Edison Kinetogram* 2 (March 15, 1910): 3–4.
9. Everson, *Classics of the Horror Film*, 13.
10. Skal, *Monster Show*, 67.
11. Gerald Peary, "Missing Links: The Jungle Origins of King Kong," 1976; revised 2004, accessed February 28, 2010, http://www.geraldpeary.com/essays/jkl/kingkong-1.html.
12. Bordwell et al., *Classical Hollywood Cinema*, 111.
13. Skal, *Monster Show*, 220.
14. Terence Fisher, "Horror Is My Business," in Silver and Ursini, *Horror Film Reader*, 71.

Chapter 12

1. "'The Innocents': Scared? You will be..." *Independent*, June 8, 2006, accessed July 1, 2010, http://www.independent.co.uk/arts-entertainment/films/features/the-innocents-scared-you-will-be-481537.html.
2. Ibid.
3. Paul Scanlon and Michael Gross, *The Book of Alien* (London: Titan Books, 2004).
4. David McIntee, *Beautiful Monsters: The Unofficial and Unauthorised Guide to the Alien and Predator Films* (Surrey, UK: Telos Publishing Ltd., 2005), 19.
5. Kelly Parks, "Shivers aka They Came from Within," 2002, accessed March 13, 2010, http://www.feoamante.com/Movies/STU/shivers.html.
6. McIntee, *Beautiful Monsters*, 19–20.
7. Matthew Hays, "A Space Odyssey," *Montreal Mirror* 19 (Oct 23–29, 2003), http://www.montrealmirror.com/ARCHIVES/2003/102303/film1.html.
8. Meredith Brody, "We Killed 'Em in

Chicago," *Film Comment* 23, no. 1 (January 1987): 74.

9. H.P. Lovecraft, "Herbert West: Reanimator," accessed July 2, 2010, http://www.dagonbytes.com/thelibrary/lovecraft/reanimator.htm.

10. "Motorist given 50 year-sentence in windshield murder trial," CNN.com, June 28, 2003, accessed March 13, 2010, http://www.cnn.com/2003/LAW/06/27/windshield.death/.

Chapter 13

1. "The Motion Picture Production Code of 1930 (Hays Code)," ArtsReformation.com, accessed July 3, 2010, http://www.artsreformation.com/a001/hays-code.html.

2. "Chronomedia," Terramedia, accessed July 4, 2010, http://www.terramedia.co.uk/reference/law/H_certificate.htm.

3. Cited in David J. Skal, *Hollywood Gothic: The Tangled Web of Dracula from Novel to Stage to Screen* (1990; repr., New York: W.W. Norton, 1991), 144.

4. Skal, *Hollywood Gothic*, 147.

5. Cited in Worland, *The Horror Film*, 127.

6. Elizabeth R. Valentine, "Are Movies Good or Bad for Them?" *New York Times*, March 30, 1941.

7. Celia Sachs, letter to the screen editor, "Movie Opinions," *New York Times*, November 3, 1963.

8. At least since 1939, per Susan Sackett, *The Hollywood Reporter Book of Box Office Hits* (New York: Billboard Books, 1990), 228.

9. Clover, *Men, Women, and Chain Saws*, 6.

10. Twitchell, *Dreadful Pleasures*, 66–67, 104.

11. Everson, *Classics of the Horror Film*.

12. Roy Huss and T.J. Ross, eds., *Focus on the Horror Film* (Englewood Cliffs, NJ: Prentice-Hall, 1972).

13. Clover, *Men, Women, and Chain Saws*, 5, 61, 64.

14. Kendrick, *Thrill of Fear*, 250–51.

15. King, *Danse Macabre*, 179.

16. Frank Scheck, "The Human Centipede—Film Review," *Hollywood Reporter*, accessed July 4, 2010, http://www.hollywoodreporter.com/hr/film-reviews/the-human-centipede-film-review-10040876 85.story.

Chapter 14

1. For a collection of writings about vampires that puts film vampires in context, see David J. Skal, *Vampires: Encounters with the Undead* (New York: Black Dog & Leventhal Publishers, 2006).

2. Peter Dendle, *The Zombie Movie Encyclopedia* (Jefferson, NC: McFarland, 2000).

3. Harrington, "Ghoulies and Ghosties," 9.

4. Adam Rockoff, *Going to Pieces: The Rise and Fall of the Slasher Film, 1978–1986* (Jefferson, NC: McFarland, 2002).

5. For a cultural history of the mad scientist, see David J. Skal, *Screams of Reason: Mad Science and Modern Culture* (New York: W.W. Norton, 1998).

Chapter 15

1. Andrew R. Boone, "Prehistoric Monsters Roar and Hiss for Sound Film," *Popular Science Monthly* 122, no. 4 (April 1933): 20–21.

2. "The Sound of Silence," accessed March 10, 2010, http://theexorcist.warnerbros.com/cmp/silencebottom.html.

3. Manohla Dargis, "Just in Time, a Southern Gothic Gumbo of Fluff and Horror," review of *The Skeleton Key*, *New York Times*, August 12, 2005.

4. Pam Keesey, "*The Haunting* and the Power of Suggestion: Why Robert Wise's Film Continues to 'Deliver the Goods' to Modern Audiences," in Silver and Ursini, *Horror Film Reader*, 305–15.

5. John Brosnan, *Movie Magic: The Story of Special Effects in the Cinema* (New York: New American Library, 1976), 101–2.

6. Mark Clark, *Smirk, Sneer and Scream: Great Acting in Horror Cinema* (Jefferson, NC: McFarland, 2004).

Chapter 16

1. Dennis Fischer, *Horror Film Directors, 1931–1990* (Jefferson, NC: McFarland, 1991).

2. Skal, *Monster Show*, 28.

3. Robin Wood, "Neglected Nightmares," in Silver and Ursini, *Horror Film Reader,* 119.
4. Chris Rodley, ed., *Cronenberg on Cronenberg* (London: Faber and Faber, 1992), 58.
5. Fisher, "Horror Is My Business," 74.
6. Truffaut, *Hitchcock,* 73.
7. "Interview with Hideo Nakata, Specter Director," Kateigaho International Edition, Winter 2005, accessed July 10, 2010, http://int.kateigaho.com/win05-/horror-nakata.html.
8. Ibid.

Chapter 17

1. Melinda Corey and George Ochoa, *The Man in Lincoln's Nose: Funny, Profound, and Quotable Quotes of Screenwriters, Movie Stars, and Moguls* (New York: Fireside, 1990), 188.

Chapter 18

1. Martin Heidegger, "'The Origin of the Work of Art,'" from Lectures 1 & 2," in David E. Cooper, ed., *Aesthetics: The Classic Readings* (Oxford: Blackwell, 1997), 234.
2. Michael Schredl, "Nightmare Frequency and Nightmare Topics in a Representative German Sample," *Eur Arch Psychiatry Clin Neurosci* (March 14, 2010) [epub ahead of print].

Bibliography

The American Heritage Dictionary of the English Language. 3rd ed. Boston: Houghton Mifflin, 1992.

Bloom, Harold. *The Anxiety of Influence: A Theory of Poetry.* New York: Oxford University Press, 1973.

Boone, Andrew R. "Prehistoric Monsters Roar and Hiss for Sound Film." *Popular Science Monthly* 122, no. 4 (April 1933).

Bordwell, David, Janet Staiger, and Kristin Thompson. *The Classical Hollywood Cinema: Film Style & Mode of Production to 1960.* New York: Columbia University Press, 1985.

Brody, Meredith. "We Killed 'Em in Chicago." *Film Comment* 23, no. 1 (January 1987): 68–75.

Brosnan, John. *Movie Magic: The Story of Special Effects in the Cinema.* New York: New American Library, 1976.

Brunas, Michael, John Brunas, and Tom Weaver. *Universal Horrors: The Studio's Classic Films, 1931–1946.* Jefferson, NC: McFarland, 1990.

Carroll, Joseph. *Literary Darwinism: Evolution, Human Nature, and Literature.* Florence, KY: Routledge, 2004.

Carroll, Noël. *The Philosophy of Horror, or Paradoxes of the Heart.* New York: Routledge, 1990.

Cioffi, Frank. *Freud and the Question of Pseudoscience.* Chicago: Open Court, 1998.

Clark, Mark. *Smirk, Sneer and Scream: Great Acting in Horror Cinema.* Jefferson, NC: McFarland, 2004.

Clarke, Alastair. *The Faculty of Adaptability: Humour's Contribution to Human Ingenuity.* Cumbria, UK: Pyrrhic House, 2009.

Clemens, Valdine. *The Return of the Repressed: Gothic Horror from the Castle of Otranto to Alien.* Albany: State University of New York Press, 1999.

Clover, Carol J. *Men, Women, and Chain Saws: Gender in the Modern Horror Film.* 1992. Reprint, Princeton: Princeton University Press, 1993.

Corey, Melinda, and George Ochoa. *The Man in Lincoln's Nose: Funny, Profound, and Quotable Quotes of Screenwriters, Movie Stars, and Moguls.* New York: Fireside, 1990.

Dawkins, Richard. *The Selfish Gene.* 1976. Reprint, Oxford: Oxford University Press, 2006.

Dendle, Peter. *The Zombie Movie Encyclopedia.* Jefferson, NC: McFarland, 2000.

Derry, Charles. *Dark Dreams 2.0: A Psychological History of the Modern Horror Film from the 1950s to the 21st Century.* Jefferson, NC: McFarland, 2009.

Eagleton, Terry. *Literary Theory: An Introduction.* Minneapolis: University of Minnesota Press, 1983.

Edelstein, David. "Now Playing at Your Local Multiplex: Torture Porn." *New York Magazine,* January 28, 2006, http://nymag.com/movies/features/15622/.

Edison Kinetogram 2 (March 15, 1910): 3–4.

Everson, William K. *Classics of the Horror Film.* New York: Citadel Press, 1974.

Field, Syd. *Screenplay: The Foundations*

of Screenwriting. 3rd ed. New York: Dell, 1984.
Fischer, Dennis. *Horror Film Directors, 1931–1990*. Jefferson, NC: McFarland, 1991.
Fisher, Terence. "Horror Is My Business," in Silver and Ursini, *Horror Film Reader*, 67–75.
Freedman, Jonathan L. *Media Violence and Its Effect on Aggression: Assessing the Scientific Evidence*. Toronto: University of Toronto Press, 2002.
Freeland, Cynthia A. "Feminist Frameworks for Horror Films." In *Film Theory and Criticism: Introductory Readings*, 6th ed., edited by Leo Braudy and Marshall Cohen, 742–63. Oxford: Oxford University Press, 2004.
Gottlieb, Carl. *The Jaws Log*. 30th anniversary edition. New York: Newmarket Press, 2005.
Harrington, Curtis. "Ghoulies and Ghosties." In Silver and Ursini, *Horror Film Reader*, 9–19.
Hays, Matthew. "A Space Odyssey." *Montreal Mirror* 19 (Oct 23–29, 2003), http://www.montrealmirror.com/ARCHIVES/2003/102303/film1.html.
Heidegger, Martin. "'The Origin of the Work of Art,'" from Lectures 1 & 2." In *Aesthetics: The Classic Readings*, edited by David E. Cooper, 229–243. Oxford: Blackwell, 1997.
Hirsch, Jr., E.D. "Objective Interpretation." In *Validity in Interpretation*, 209–44. New Haven: Yale University Press, 1967.
Huesmann, L. Rowell, Jessica Moise-Titus, Cheryl-Lynn Podolski, and Leonard D. Eron. "Longitudinal Relations between Children's Exposure to TV Violence and Their Aggressive and Violent Behavior in Young Adulthood: 1977–1992." *Developmental Psychology* 39, no. 2 (2003): 201–21.
Huss, Roy, and T.J. Ross, eds. *Focus on the Horror Film*. Englewood Cliffs, NJ: Prentice-Hall, 1972.
Hutcheson, Francis. *Thoughts on Laughter and Observations on 'The Fable of the Bees' in Six Letters*. 1758. Reprint, Bristol: Thoemmes, 1989.

"'The Innocents': Scared? You will be..." *Independent*. June 8, 2006, accessed July 1, 2010, http://www.independent.co.uk/arts-entertainment/films/features/the-innocents-scared-you-will-be-481537.html.
"Interview with Hideo Nakata, Specter Director." *Kateigaho International Edition* (Winter 2005). Accessed July 10, 2010. http://int.kateigaho.com/win05/horror-nakata.html.
Jones, Ernest. *On the Nightmare*. 1931. Reprint, New York: Liveright, 1951.
Keesey, Pam. "*The Haunting* and the Power of Suggestion: Why Robert Wise's Film Continues to 'Deliver the Goods' to Modern Audiences." In Silver and Ursini, *Horror Film Reader*, 305–15.
Kendrick, Walter. *The Thrill of Fear: 250 Years of Scary Entertainment*. New York: Grove Weidenfeld, 1991.
King, Stephen. *Danse Macabre*. 1981. Reprint, New York: Berkley Books, 1983.
LoBrutto, Vincent. *Stanley Kubrick: A Biography*. New York: Donald I. Fine Books, 1997.
Lovecraft, H.P. "Herbert West: Reanimator." Accessed July 2, 2010, http://www.dagonbytes.com/thelibrary/lovecraft/reanimator.htm.
Lovejoy, Arthur O. *The Great Chain of Being: A Study of the History of an Idea*. 1936. Reprint, Cambridge, MA: Harvard University Press, 1982.
MacDonald, Scott. "Theory of Knowledge." In *The Cambridge Companion to Aquinas*, edited by Norman Kretzmann and Eleonore Stump, 160–95. Cambridge: Cambridge University Press, 1993.
Maltin, Leonard, ed. *Leonard Maltin's Movie & Video Guide*. 2004 edition. New York: Signet, 2003.
Maltin, Leonard, ed. *Leonard Maltin's 2011 Movie Guide*. New York: Signet, 2010.
Manguel, Alberto. *Bride of Frankenstein*. London: British Film Institute, 1997.
McCarty, John. *Splatter Movies: Breaking the Last Taboo of the Screen*. New York: St. Martin's Press, 1984.

McIntee, David. *Beautiful Monsters: The Unofficial and Unauthorised Guide to the Alien and Predator Films*. Surrey, UK: Telos Publishing Ltd., 2005.

Miller, Alan S., and Satoshi Kanazawa. *Why Beautiful People Have More Daughters*. New York: Perigee, 2008.

Mock, Douglas W. *More than Kin and Less than Kind: The Evolution of Family Conflict*. Cambridge, MA: Belknap Press, 2004.

Morris, Gary. "Sexual Subversion: The Bride of Frankenstein." *Bright Lights Film Journal* 19 (July 1997), http://www.brightlightsfilm.com/19/19_bridel.php.

"The Motion Picture Production Code of 1930 (Hays Code)." ArtsReformation.com. Accessed July 3, 2010, http://www.artsreformation.com/a001/hays-code.html.

Nagel, Thomas. *The View from Nowhere*. Oxford: Oxford University Press, 1989.

O'Neill, Michael J., Betty R. Lawton, Mariana Mateos, Dawn M. Carone, Gianni C. Ferreri, Tomas Hrbek, Robert W. Meredith, David N. Reznick, and Rachel J. O'Neill. "Ancient and continuing Darwinian selection on *insulin-like growth factor II* in placental fishes," *Proceedings of the National Academy of Sciences*, 104, no. 30 (2007): 12404–9.

Paglia, Camille. *Sexual Personae: Art and Decadence from Nefertiti to Emily Dickinson*. 1990. Reprint, New York: Vintage Books, 1991.

Peary, Gerald. "Missing Links: The Jungle Origins of King Kong." 1976. Revised 2004; accessed February 28, 2010, http://www.geraldpeary.com/essays/jkl/kingkong-1.html.

Price, Vincent. Foreword to *The Horror Film: A Guide to More Than 700 Films on Videocassette*. Evanston, IL: CineBooks, 1989.

Punter, David. *The Literature of Terror: A History of Gothic Fictions from 1765 to the Present Day*. London: Longman, 1980.

Rockoff, Adam. *Going to Pieces: The Rise and Fall of the Slasher Film, 1978–1986*. Jefferson, NC: McFarland, 2002.

Rodley, Chris, ed. *Cronenberg on Cronenberg*. London: Faber and Faber, 1992.

Rorty, Richard. *Contingency, Irony, and Solidarity*. Cambridge: Cambridge University Press, 1989.

Rorty, Richard. "Nineteenth-Century Idealism and Twentieth-Century Textualism." In *Consequences of Pragmatism (Essays: 1972–1980)*, 139–59. Minneapolis: University of Minnesota Press, 1982.

Sackett, Susan. *The Hollywood Reporter Book of Box Office Hits*. New York: Billboard Books, 1990.

Sarris, Andrew. "Notes on the Auteur Theory in 1962." *Film Culture* 27 (Winter, 1962/63): 1–8.

Scanlon, Paul, and Michael Gross. *The Book of Alien*. London: Titan Books, 2004.

Schredl, Michael. "Nightmare Frequency and Nightmare Topics in a Representative German Sample." *Eur Arch Psychiatry Clin Neurosci* (March 14, 2010) [epub ahead of print].

Silver, Alain, and James Ursini, eds. *Horror Film Reader*. New York: Limelight Editions, 2000.

Skal, David J. *Hollywood Gothic: The Tangled Web of Dracula from Novel to Stage to Screen*. 1990. Reprint, New York: W.W. Norton, 1991.

_____. *The Monster Show: A Cultural History of Horror*. 1993. Reprint, New York: Penguin Books, 1994.

_____. *Screams of Reason: Mad Science and Modern Culture*. New York: W.W. Norton, 1998.

_____. *Vampires: Encounters with the Undead*. New York: Black Dog & Leventhal Publishers, 2006.

Sobchak, Vivian. *Screening Space: The American Science Fiction Film*. 2nd ed. New Brunswick: Rutgers University Press, 1997.

Swales, John M. *Genre Analysis: English in Academic and Research Settings*. Cambridge: Cambridge University Press, 1990.

Truffaut, François, with Helen G. Scott.

Hitchcock. Rev. ed. New York: Touchstone, 1985.

Truffaut, François. "Une certaine tendance du cinéma français." *Cahiers du Cinéma* 31 (January 1954).

Tudor, Andrew. *Monsters and Mad Scientists: A Cultural History of the Horror Movie*. Hoboken, NJ: Wiley-Blackwell, 1991.

Twitchell, James B. *Dreadful Pleasures: An Anatomy of Modern Horror*. 1985. Reprint, New York: Oxford University Press, 1988.

Webster's II New College Dictionary. 3rd ed. Boston: Houghton Mifflin, 2005.

Wood, Robin. *Hollywood from Vietnam to Reagan*. New York: Columbia University Press, 1986.

———. "An Introduction to the American Horror Film." In *Movies and Methods*, vol. 2, edited by Bill Nichols, 195–220. Berkeley: University of California Press, 1985.

———. "Neglected Nightmares," in Silver and Ursini, *Horror Film Reader*, 110–27.

———. "Return of the Repressed." *Film Comment* 14, no. 4 (July-August 1978): 25–32.

Worland, Rick. *The Horror Film: An Introduction*. Malden, MA: Blackwell Publishing, 2007.

Young, Elizabeth. "Here Comes the Bride: Wedding Gender and Race in 'Bride of Frankenstein.'" *Feminist Studies* 17, no. 3 (1991): 403–37.

Zillmann, Dolf, and James B. Weaver. "Effects of Prolonged Exposure to Gratuitous Media Violence on Provoked and Unprovoked Hostile Behavior." *Journal of Applied Social Psychology* 21, no. 18 (1999): 1517–23.

Index

Numbers in **bold italics** indicate pages with photographs.

Abbott and Costello Meet Frankenstein (1948) 114
The Abominable Dr. Phibes (1971) 26–27, 40, **43**, 59–60, 121, 159, 176
About Schmidt (2002) 198
Academy Award 147–48, 198–99
acting 180, 194–200
action movie 7, 12, 112–14
Adams, Julia (Julie) **172**
The Addams Family (TV series) 146
adrenaline rush theory 7
aesthetic evaluation 83, 96
aesthetics 201–3
alien 109–10, 162, 165
Alien (1979): alien 9, 33–34, 52, 134, 165, 170; final girl 59; influences on and of 134–**35**, 136, 182; science fiction film 109–10; structure 41
Alien vs. Predator films 135
Aliens (1986) 105, 113–14
The Alligator People (1959) 52, 161, 197, **202**–3
The Amazing Colossal Man (1957) 167
American International Pictures 131
An American Werewolf in London (1981) 136, 177
Amicus Productions 133
Anaconda (1997) 164
Andrews, Dana 194
Aquinas, St. Thomas 1–2, 6, 9, 12–13, 18–19, 28–29, 202
Archibald, William 132
Argento, Dario 134, 182
Aristotle 2, 6, 9, 13, 15, 114
Army of Darkness (1993) 191
Arness, James **111**
Assault on Precinct 13 (1976) 184
The Astronaut's Wife (1999) 67
Attack of the 50 Ft Woman (1958) 167
Atwill, Lionel 196
The Aztec Mummy see *La Momia azteca*

Baclanova, Olga 184
The Bad Seed (1956) 31, 34, 68, **75**, 133, 159
Badejo, Bolaji **135**
Baker, Rick 177
Band, Richard 136
Barrymore, Drew **138**–39
Basket Case (1982) 167
Bates, Kathy 148 180, 198–**99**
Bava, Lamberto 183
Bava, Mario 127, 131, 133, 139, 182–83
Beals, Jennifer 93
The Beast from 20,000 Fathoms (1953) 164
the beautiful 13–14
Beery, Wallace 147
Beethoven, Ludwig van 201
being 12–13
Bentley, James **8**
Berridge, Elizabeth **50**
The Best Years of Our Lives (1946) 11
Beyond Re-Animator (2003) 138
The Birds (1963) 36, 164, 188–89
The Black Cat (1934) 65, 122
Black Friday (1940) 156
Black Sabbath see *I tre volti della paura*
Black Sunday see *La Maschera del demonio*
Blackburn, Richard 180
Blade Runner (1982) 109
Blair, Linda **25**, 148, 169
The Blair Witch Project (1999) 140, 175
Blatty, William Peter 147–48
The Blob (1958) **29**–30, 33, 178
The Blob (1988) 178
Blood and Black Lace see *Sei donne per l'assassino*
Blood Feast (1963) 18–20, 57, 133
Bloom, Harold 118
The Body Snatcher (1945) 127
Bond, James 12, 112
The Bounty (1984) 198
Bowie, Les 179
Bradley, Doug **166**

Index

Braindead see *Dead Alive*
The Brain That Wouldn't Die (1963) 104, 156
Bram Stoker's Dracula (1992) 11, 14, 69–70, 115, 147, 169, 176, 179
Breen, Joseph 145, 149
The Bride (1985)
Bride of Chucky (1998) 93–**94**
Bride of Frankenstein (1935) 122; bride 31, 87–89, 156, 174; direction 192–93; evaluation 83–**84**, 85–96; Frankenstein monster 5, 14, 35, 85–87, 89, **206**–7; Pretorius 87, 160, 170; structure 44–45
Bride of Re-Animator (1990) 93, 95, 138, 156
Bride of the Gorilla (1951) 93
Bride of the Monster (1955) 93, 95
The Brides of Dracula (1960) 67, 93–95, 194, 197
British Board of Film Classification 144
The Brood (1979) 69, 186
Browning, Ricou 197
Browning, Tod 120, **182**–84
Brunas, John 89
Brunas, Michael 89
The Burning (1981) 57
Burroughs, Edgar Rice 124
Burstyn, Ellen 148
Burton, Richard Francis 124

Cabin Fever (2003) 35, 52, 67, 69, 164
The Cabinet of Dr. Caligari (1919) 120
Campbell, Bruce **156**
Campbell, Neve 139
Candyman (1992) 16, 157, 171
Capote, Truman 132
Captain Kronos — Vampire Hunter (1974) 173
Carpenter, John 133, 176, 184–85
Carrie (1976) 43–44, 79, 133, 167, 169–70
Carroll, Joseph 79
Carroll, Noël 1, 6, 10, 39
Carson, Shawn **50**
Casino (1995) 200
Cassell, Sandra **32**
The Cat and the Canary (1927) 132
Cat People (1942) 33, 54, 126–27, 161, 163
Cat People (1982) 127
Catch-22 (1970) 198
The Champ (1931) 147
Chaney, Lon 120–**22**, 176, 183, 195–96
Chaney, Lon, Jr. 162–**63**, 195–96
Chang (1927) 124
Chapman, Ben 197
charity 69
Chicago 119, 171
children *see* youth
Child's Play (1988) 94, 166
Chinatown (1974) 198
Christine (1983) 136
A Christmas Carol (novella) 157
cinematography 25, 173–75
Clayton, Jack 132

Clennon, David 185
Clive, Colin 21, 192–93
Clover, Carol J. 7, 59, 149
Cloverfield (2008) 58, 175
Collet-Serra, Jaume 82
Combs, Jeffrey 137
The Company of Wolves (1984) 111
computer-generated imagery (CGI) 162, 178
Conan Doyle, Arthur 124
conservatism 63–69, 71, 78, 81
contamination 67
Conway, Tom 126
Cooper, Merian C. 124
costume 170–71
Cotten, Joseph 59–60
Count Dracula see *Nachts, wenn Dracula erwacht*
Count Yorga, Vampire (1970) 153
Cox, Courteney 139
The Craft (1996) 166
Crampton, Barbara 137
Crane, Richard 197, **202**
Craven, Wes 133, 139
The Crawling Eye (1958) 178
The Crazies (1973) 67, 161, 164, 192
The Crazies (2010) 161
The Creature from the Black Lagoon (1954) 24, 31, 167, 170, **172**–73, 197
The Creeping Unknown see *The Quatermass Xperiment*
Creepshow (1982) 164
crime film 111–12
Cronenberg, David 133, 186–87
Cross, Harley 97
Cujo (1983) 136
Curry, Tim 171
The Curse of Frankenstein (1957) 127, 187–88
The Curse of the Cat People (1944) 127
Curse of the Demon (1957) 54, 194
The Curse of the Werewolf (1961) 187
Curtis, Jamie Lee **113**
Cushing, Peter 21, 104, 160, 188, 196

Dargis, Manohla 170–71
Dark Castle Entertainment 82
Dark Water (2002) see *Honogurai mizu no soko kara*
Dark Water (2005) 158, 190
Davis, Geena 97
Dawkins, Richard 117
Dawley, J. Searle 119
Dawn of the Dead (1978) 57, 104, 174, 176, 191–92
Dawn of the Dead (2004) 154
Day of the Dead (1985) 11, 64, 67, 176, 191–92
The Day the Earth Stood Still (1951) 110
Daybreakers (2010) 154
DDB *see* deformed and destructive being
Dead Alive (1992) 138

Index

Dead and Buried (1981) 57
Deadgirl (2008) 142, 173
Deathdream (1972) 117
deformed and destructive being (DDB): attack 24, 26, 39–41, 45; defined 12; ethics 61–62, 71; knowing 18–27; profile (traits) 28–37; stardom 194–200; taxonomy 151–**52**, 153–67; *see also* being; deformity; destructiveness; monster
deformity 9–14; deformity-destructiveness causal chain 9, 12, 57; display 53–55
delight 5, 16, 49
Demme, Jonathan 148, 181
demon 1, 9, 28, 110, 165–66, 205; *see also* Satan
Demon Seed (1977) 166
DeNiro, Robert 54–55, 200
The Descent (2005) 140, **177**
destructiveness 9, 11–12, 14; display 55–57
Devil *see* demon, Satan
The Devil Doll (1936) 171
The Devil's Commandment see I Vampiri
The Devil's Rain (1975) 65
Diary of the Dead (2007) 191
Dickens, Charles 158
Die Hard (1988) 12, 112
directing 181–93
Dirty Harry (1972) 181
Dr. Jekyll and Mr. Hyde (1908) 119
Dr. Jekyll and Mr. Hyde (1932) 122, 147, 180
Dr. Jekyll and Sister Hyde (1972) 64
Dr. Phibes Rises Again! (1972) 60
Dr. Terror's House of Horrors (1965) 28, 133
Doctor X (1932) 125, 196
Dog Soldiers (2002) 105
Dolores Claiborne (1995) 198
Donovan's Brain (1953) 156
Dracula (1931) 30, 53, 63, 122, 130, 143–**45**, 178, 183
Dracula (1958) see *Horror of Dracula*
Dracula (novel) 118, 120
Dracula A.D. 1972 (1972) 65
Dracula — Prince of Darkness (1966) 36, 179
Dracula's Daughter (1936) 31
Drag Me to Hell (2009) 69, 142, 191
Drake, Frances **49**
Dressed to Kill (1980) 171
Duel (1971) 134, 181
The Dunwich Horror (1970) 136

Eagleton, Terry 72
Ebert, Roger 149
Edelstein, David 55
Edison Company 119–20
editing 175–76
Eight Legged Freaks (2002) 165
elements, essential *see* essential elements of horror films
Enemy from Space see Quatermass 2
Englund, Robert 180, **186**, 196–97
entrance of the DDB 40
epistemology 18–27
essential elements of horror films 47–60
ethics 61–71
evaluation, aesthetic *see* aesthetic evaluation
Event Horizon (1997) 135
Everson, William K. 54, 148–49
evil child *see* youth
The Evil Dead (1983) 136, 190–91
Evil Dead II (1987) 138, **156**, 191
evolution 13–14, 203–4
evolutionary psychology 34, 37
The Exorcism of Emily Rose (2005) 165–66
The Exorcist (1973): Academy Award 147–48; demon **25**–26, 28, 31, 169; direction 181; evil child 68–69; possession film 165–66; ratings system 133, 146; teaser and frisson 42–43
Exorcist II: The Heretic (1977) 58
The Eye (2002) see *Gin Gwai*
The Eye (2008) 156
Eyes Without a Face (1960) see *Les yeux sans visage*

The Faculty (1998) 162
Famous Monsters of Filmland 1, 146
fantasy 110–11
Farmiga, Vera 75
Farrow, Mia **66**
Field, Syd 38
Fiend without a Face (1958) 178
Fifth Symphony (musical composition) 201
final battle 23, 25–26, 39–41, 45
Final Destination (2000) 30, 166
final girl 59, 135, 139, 149
Fisher, Terence 129–30, 187–88
Five Easy Pieces (1970) 198
Five Million Years to Earth see *Quatermass and the Pit*
The Fly (1958) 10, 21, 64, 96–**97**, 109, 161
The Fly (1986) 115, 138; direction 186–87; monster 10–11, 26, 35–36, 96–**98**, 99, 161; origin of monster 21, 64, 102, 109; structure 40–41
The Fly II (1989) 83–85, 96–104, 162, 197
Focus on the Horror Film (book) 149
The Fog (1980) 184
For Love of the Game (1999) 191
Foran, Dick **195**
Forbidden Planet (1956) 109–10, 134, 139
form 9, 13
Foster, Jodie 148
Fox, Megan 33, **65**, 180
Frailty (2002) 70, 166
Francis, Freddie 132
Franco, Jess 130
Frankenstein (1910) 119–20
Frankenstein (1931) 3, 122, 145; conservatism 63, 65; direction 192–93; Franken-

stein, Henry 21–22, 24, 173; monster *10*–*11*, 14, 42, 54, 85–86, 118, 157; science fiction 109–10
Frankenstein (novel) 118, 136
Frankenstein and the Monster from Hell (1974) 104
Frankenstein Meets the Space Monster (1965) 52
Frankenstein Meets the Wolf Man (1943) 23, 36
Frankenstein: The True Story (1973) 134, 157
Freaks (1932) 122, 167, **182**–84
Freedman, Jonathan L. 55
Freeland, Cynthia 74
The French Connection (1971) 181
Freud, Sigmund 62, 126, 173, 189
Friday the 13th (1980) 197
Friday the 13th films 136
Friday the 13th Part VI: Jason Lives (1986) 138
Friday the 13th Part VII: The New Blood (1988) 197
Fried Green Tomatoes (1991) 198
Friedkin, William 148, 169, 181
Fright Night (1985) 136, 139, 153
frisson 41–44
Frogs (1972) 164
From Beyond (1986) 138
From Dusk Till Dawn (1996) 66
Fuhrman, Isabelle 75–**76**
Fulci, Lucio 134, 182
The Funhouse (1981) 47–**50**, 53, 56–59, 69, 121, 189

Gale, David **137**
Garasu no nô (*Sleeping Bride*; 2000) 190
Gargoyles (1972) 134
Garland, Beverly **202**
gender 31–33
genre 107–16
German Expressionism 120, 122
ghost 10, 28, 35, 110, 157–58, 205
Ghost Actress see *Joyû-rei*
The Ghost Breakers (1940) 154
Ghostbusters (1984) 107–8, 114
Ghosts of Mars (2001) 184
The Ghoul (1933) 122
giallo 182
giant 109–10, 127, 164–65
Giger, H.R. 134
Gin Gwai (*The Eye*; 2002) 156
Ginger Snaps (2000) 31, 140, 161, 163
The Girl Who Knew Too Much see *La ragazza che sapeva troppo*
God 9, 13, 65, 70, 92–93, 166, 202–3
Godzilla, King of the Monsters see *Gojira*
Gojira (*Godzilla, King of the Monsters*; 1954) 11, 13, 31, 110, 125, 127, 164, 170
Goldblum, Jeff **98**
Goldfinger (1964) 108

Goldman, William 138
goodness 12
Gordon, Stuart 136–38, 140–42
The Gorgon (1964) 167, 187–88
Gottlieb, Carl 39
Grand Guignol 118–19
Grant, Cary 188
The Great Chain of Being (book) 10
The Green Slime (1968) 178
Gremlins (1984) 167
Gritos en la noche (*The Awful Dr. Orloff*; 1962) 131
Grizzly (1976) 164
Gunga Din (1939) 112
Gwoemul (*The Host*; 2006) 165

Haggard, Henry Rider 124
hair 169–70
Halloween (1978) 133, 136, 139, 172–73, 175–76; crime film 112–**13**; final girl 59, 135; Myers, Michael 15, 21, 36, 158–59, 169, 184; unmarried sex 66
Halloween II (1981) 36, 56
Halloween IV: The Return of Michael Myers (1988) 138
Hamlet (play) 158
Hammer Films 21–22, 127–131, 133, 174, 178–79, 187–88
Harrington, Curtis 158
Harris, Marilyn **10**
Harry Potter (film series) 110
The Haunted Palace (1963) 136, 166
The Haunting (1963) 127, 157, 174
Haute tension (*High Tension*; 2003) 140, 159
Hedison, Al **97**
Hedren, Tippi 189
Heggie, O.P. **206**
Heidegger, Martin 201
Hello Mary Lou, Prom Night II (1987) 138
Hellraiser (1987) **166**
Helm, Brigitte 88
Henderson, Saffron 97
Henry: Portrait of a Serial Killer (1990) 159
Herrmann, Bernard 136
Hess, David A. **32**
The Hills Have Eyes (1977) 21, 63, 169, 173, 185, 198
Hilton, Violet and Daisy 184
Hirsch, E.D. 72
Hirst, Damien 203
history of horror film 117–42
Hitchcock, Alfred 24, 56, 108, 164, 188–89
Hodder, Kane 197
Homer 124
homosexuality 87, 91, 160
Honogurai mizu no soko kara (*Dark Water*; 2002) 31, 158, 190
Hooper, Tobe 133, 189
Hope, Bob 154
Hopkins, Anthony **148**, 198

Hopper, Dennis 189
The Horror Chamber of Dr. Faustus (1960)
  see *Les Yeux sans visage*
horror defined 5
Horror Express (1972) 173
Horror of Dracula (also known as *Dracula*;
  1958) 36, **128**–130, 170, 173, 187
The Host see *Gwoemul*
Hostel (2006) 31, 36, 55, 104–5, 140, 159
Hostel: Part II (2007) 31
The Hours (2002) 199
House of Frankenstein (1944) 85
House of Wax (1953) 196
House of Wax (2005) 171
The House of the Devil (2009) 65, 142
How to Steal a Million (1966) 111
Howards End (1992) 198
The Howling (1981) 136
Hudson, Kate 170–71
The Human Centipede (First Sequence)
  (2009) 142, 149
humor 52–53
The Hunchback of Notre Dame (1923) 120
hybrid 161–63

I Drink Your Blood (1970) 69
I Know What You Did Last Summer (1997)
  69, 139
I Married a Monster from Outer Space (1958)
  110
I Spit on Your Grave (1978) 23, 33
I Walked with a Zombie (1943) 127, 154
I Was a Teenage Werewolf (1957) 131
In the Mouth of Madness (1995) 184
indie 108
Ingagi (1930) 125
The Innocents (1961) 127, 131–33
Invasion of the Body Snatchers (1956) 52,
  67–**68**, 110, 117, 162, 181
The Invisible Man (1933) 42, 65, 122, 160,
  178, 192–93
The Invisible Man Returns (1940) 61
The Invisible Ray (1936) 47–**49**, 53, 56, 58,
  160
Island of Lost Souls (1933) 122, 161, 163
Isolation (2005) 65
It! The Terror from Beyond Space (1958) 110,
  135, 165
It's Alive! (1974) 69

Jackson, Peter 138
J-horror (Japanese horror) 182, 190
James, Henry 132
Jason X (2002) 115–16, 123, 197
Jaws (1975) 115, 133, 135, 173, 179; action
  film 112–13; direction 181; epistemology
  21, 23; nightmare 205; shark 10, **22**, 31, 34,
  52, 164; structure 38–39
Jeepers Creepers (2001) 33, 63, 167, 173
Jennifer's Body (2009) 33, **65**, 114, 180

Jesse James Meets Frankenstein's Daughter
  (1966) 108
Jones, Ernest 7
Joyû-rei (*Ghost Actress*; 1996) 190
Julian, Rupert 121
Jurassic Park (1993) 108

Karloff, Boris **10**, **49**, **84**–85, 89, 105, 118,
  157, 182, 192, 195–97, **206**
Keaton, Camille 23
Kendrick, Walter 149
Kerr, Deborah 132
Kerr, Frederick 192
Kerry, Norman 121
Kidman, Nicole **8**–9, 30, 199
Kill, Baby, Kill see *Operazione paura*
The Killing (1956) 111
King, Stephen 136, 138, 149
King Kong (1933) 21, 122–**23**, 124–26, 165,
  194; Kong 15, 33, 35, 42, 122–25; sound
  effect 169
King Kong vs. Godzilla see *King Kongu tai
  Gojira*
King Kongu tai Gojira (*Kong Kong vs.
  Godzilla*; 1962) 125
Kiss of Death (1947) 111
Klein-Rogge, Rudolf **88**
Kneale, Nigel 134
Knudson, Robert 148
Kubrick, Stanley 74, 181

Lanchester, Elsa **84**, 88
The Land That Time Forgot (novel) 124
Langenkamp, Heather **186**
The Last Exorcism (2010) 166, 175
The Last House on the Left (1972) **32**–33, 55,
  69, 117, 133, 185
Låt den rätte komma in (*Let the Right One
  In*; 2008) 58–59
Lee, Christopher 19, 36, **128**–30, 178–79,
  188, 196
Leigh, Janet 56, 139, **176**
Lemora, a Child's Tale of the Supernatural
  (1973) 31, 64, 180
Leprechaun (1993) 167
Leroux, Gaston 121
Let the Right One In (2008) see *Låt den rätte
  komma in*
Lewis, Herschell Gordon 57
Lewton, Val 126–27
Lewis, Jerry 109
Lewton, Val 54
LifeForce (1985) 189
Lincoln, Fred **32**
The Lion in Winter (1968) 198
Little Caesar (1930) 111
Little Rascals (series of shorts) 55
The Little Shop of Horrors (1960) 164, 198
London 124
London After Midnight (1927) 183

Lost (TV series) 200
The Lost Boys (1987) 153
The Lost World (1925) 124
The Lost World (novel) 124
Lovecraft, H.P. 136–38, 166, 184
Lovejoy, Arthur O. 10
Lugosi, Bela 19, 36, *49*, 53, 130, *145*, 195–96
Lusk, Norbert 144

M (1931) 122, 159
Macdonald, Shauna *177*
Mad Love (1935) 156
mad scientist 158, 160–61, 192–93
makeup 176–77
The Man with Nine Lives (1940) 105
Mann, Alakina *8*
March, Fredric 147, 180
Marsh, Carol 129
Martin (1978) 192
Mary Shelley's Frankenstein (1994) 54–55, 157, 200
La maschera del demonio (*Black Sunday*; 1960) 131, 182–83
masochism 5, 7
Mathews, Kerwin *112*
May (2002) 108
May, Mathilda 189
McCambridge, Mercedes 169
McCarthy, Kevin *68*
McCormack, Patty *75*
McQueen, Steve 178
meaning 72–74
media violence *see* violence, media
Meet the Parents (2000) 200
Méliès, Georges 119
metaphysical being 165–66
Metropolis (1927) *88*
The Midnight Meat Train (2008) 173
Mighty Joe Young (1949) 125
Miller, Jason 148
Misery (1990) 138, 141, 148, 180, 198
La Momia azteca (*The Aztec Mummy*; 1957) 155
monster defined 9, 12
Moore, Matthew 97
morality *see* ethics
Morris, Gary 90
Mortimer, John 132
mummy 31, 155
The Mummy (1932) 65, 122, 155
The Mummy (1959) 187
The Mummy (1999) 155
The Mummy's Hand (1940) 35, 155, 194–*95*
Munch, Edvard 139
The Munsters (TV series) 118, 146
Murder on the Orient Express (1974) 198
Murdoch, Rupert 103
music 176
musical 47
My Bloody Valentine (2009) 171

mystery 24, 26
The Mystery of the Wax Museum (1933) 10, 121, 125, 196

Nachts, wenn Dracula erwacht (*Count Dracula*; 1970) 130
Nagel, Thomas 5
Nakata, Hideo 190
Nanook of the North (1922) 124
Natali, Vincenzo 82
Near Dark (1987) 153
New York 58, 123–26
Newman, Chris 148
News Corporation 103
Nicholson, Jack *74*, 198–99
nightmare 7, 205
Night of the Lepus (1972) 165
Night of the Living Dead (1968) 57, 59, 105, 133, 136; cinematography 174; structure 45–46; zombie 26, 34, 36, 153–54, 191–92, 197–98
A Nightmare on Elm Street (1984) 35, 42, 185–*86*, 196
A Nightmare on Elm Street films 136, 157, 180
normal 20–23, 58–60
North by Northwest (1959) 188
Nosferatu (1922) 120, 130
The Nutty Professor (1963) 109

O'Bannon, Dan 134
O'Brien, Willis 124–25
O'Connor, Una 192
Ôdishon (*Audition*; 1999) 141, 173
Odyssey (poem) 124
Ogle, Charles 119
The Old Dark House (1932) 171, 192
The Omen (1976) 34–36, 50–*51*, 59, 68, 133, 175
The Omen 666 (2006) 52, 65
Operazione paura (*Kill, Baby, Kill*; 1966) 166, 182
O'Quinn, Terry 200
Organizm (2008) 65
Orphan (2009) 69, 75–*76*, 77–82, 142, 149, 159
Oscar *see* Academy Award
Osment, Haley Joel 199
The Other (1972) 68
The Others (2001) *8*–9, 30, 55, 121, 133, 157–58, 199
Owens, Patricia *97*

P2 (2007) 173
Paranormal Activity (2009) 54, 142, 175
Paris 118–119, 121
Peck, Gregory 50–51, 56
Peel, David 194, 196–97
Perkins, Anthony 168
Pet Sematary (1989) 65, 154

phantasm 19
The Phantom of the Opera (1925) 9, 30, 120–22, 175–76
The Phantom of the Opera (1962) 187
Phantom of the Paradise (1974) 121
Philbin, Mary 121
The Physical Impossibility of Death in the Mind of Someone Living (artwork) 203
Pierce, Jack 85, 88, 118, 176
Piranha 3D (2010) 67, 178
The Plague of the Zombies (1966) 154
Plan 9 from Outer Space (1959) 84–85
Planet of the Vampires see *Terrore nello spazio*
Poltergeist (1982) 65, 189
Predator films 135
The Premature Burial (1962) 172
Price, Vincent 1, **43**, 59–60, 169, 196
Prince of Darkness (1987) 184
Production Code 42, 66, 133, 144–46
production design 171–73
Prom Night films 136
Psycho (1960) 59, 63–64, 171; Bates, Norman 9, 30, 53–54, 198; conservatism 63, 66; crime film 112; direction 188–89; shower scene 25, 56, **176**; slasher film 131, 133, 139
Psycho II (1983) 198
Psycho III (1986) 198
Psycho IV: The Beginning (1990) 198
psychological theory of horror film 7–8
psychology 204–5
psychopath 158–61
Pulp Fiction (1994) 108
Pumpkinhead (1988) 167
purpose 5–17, 72, 83, 107–8

Quatermass and the Pit (U.S. title *Five Million Years to Earth*; 1967) 127, 134, 173
Quatermass 2 (U.S. title *Enemy from Space*; 1957) 127
The Quatermass Xperiment (U.S. title *The Creeping Unknown*; 1955) 127

Rabid (1977) 67
La ragazza che sapeva troppo (*The Girl Who Knew Too Much*; 1963) 182
Raiders of the Lost Ark (1981) 12
Raimi, Sam 136, 190–91
Rain, Jeramie **32**
Rains, Claude 178, 192–93
Randolph, Jane 126
ratings system 133
Raw Meat (1972) 173
Rea, Stephen 140
Re-Animator (1985) 57, 107–8, 114, 136–**37**, 138, 140–41, 154, 156
Reazione a catena (*Twitch of the Death Nerve*; 1971) 182
Red Eye (2005) 185–86
Reed, Oliver 48, 59
Repulsion (1965) 174

reputation 143–50
The Return of the Living Dead (1985) 53
The Return of the Vampire (1943) 117
Richardson, Lee 100–**1**
Ring (1998) see *Ringu*
The Ring (2002) 67, 102, 140, 157, 174, 177, 190
The Ring Two (2005) 81, 178, 190
Ringu (*Ring*; 1998) 67, 102, 140, 190
RKO 122, 125–27
The Rocky Horror Picture Show (1975) 108, 171
Romero, George 57, 115, 133, 191–92
Rorty, Richard 2, 6, 75
Rosemary's Baby (1968) 33, 36, 65, **67**–68
Rue, Betsy 171
Russell, Kurt 184

sacrilege 64–66
St. Thomas Aquinas see Aquinas, St. Thomas
'Salem's Lot (1979) 134, 189
Sarsgaard, Peter 75
San Francisco (1936) 66
Sarris, Andrew 72
Satan 50–51, 62, 65, 69, 165–66, 175, 179, 183; *see also* demon
Saturday Night Live (TV series) 86
Savini, Tom 176
Saw (2004) 55, 140, 159
Scalps (1983) 57
Scanners (1981) 186–87
Scary Movie (2000) 139
Scheider, Roy **22**
Schoedsack, Ernest B. 124
Schreck, Max 130
Schreiber, Liev 52
science fiction 108–10
Scream (1996) 63–64, **138**–139, 185
The Scream (painting) 139
screenplay 179
Sei donne per l'assassino (*Blood and Black Lace*; 1964) 139, 182
Selig Polyscope Company 119
Selznick, David O. 124
serial killer 11, 14, 158–61, 205
The Serpent and the Rainbow (1988) 185
setup 40
Seven (1995) 159
The Seventh Victim (1943) 127
The 7th Voyage of Sinbad (1958) 110–**12**
sex, unmarried 66–67
Seyfried, Amanda 180
Shadowlands (1993) 198
Shakespeare, William 158
She (novel) 124
Shelley, Mary 45, 88, 119, 127
The Shining (1980) 8, 73–**74**, 75, 136, 157–58, 174, 181, 199
Shivers see *They Came from Within* (1975)
Show Boat (1936) 192

Shusett, Ronald 134
The Shuttered Room (1967) 48, 59
Siegel, Don 181
significance 72–75
Signs (2002) 66
The Silence of the Lambs (1991) 59, 179, 181; Buffalo Bill 102, 171, 173; crime film 112; Lecter, Hannibal 53–54, *148*, 198; structure 41, 43
Silver, Joel 82
Simon, Simone 126
A Simple Plan (1998) 191
Siskel, Gene 149
The Sixth Sense (1999) 11, 31, 121, 140, 157–58, 179, 199
Skal, David J. 121
The Skeleton Key (2005) 170–71
slasher 1, 57, 63, 66, 133, 135, 138–39
Sleeping Bride see *Garasu no nô*
Slumber Party Massacre (1982) 194, 197
Smith, Cheryl 180
Smith, Kent 126
Sneak Previews (TV series) 149
Sobchak, Vivian 110
society 150, 205–7
Son of Frankenstein (1939) 35, 63
Son of Kong (1933) 125
sound effect 25, 168–69
Spacek, Sissy *44*
special effect 177–79
Species (1995) 162–63
Species films 135
Spider-Man (2002) 191
Spielberg, Steven 134, 164, 181
Spivack, Murray 169
splatter film 57
Splice (2010) 82, 142
Spoorloos (*The Vanishing*; 1988) 172
Sssssss (1973) 161
Star Wars (1977) 109, 134–35, 196
Star Wars: Episode II: Attack of the Clones (2002) 196
Star Wars: Episode III: Revenge of the Sith (2005) 196
Steele, Barbara 183
The Stepfather (1987) 159, 200
Stephens, Harvey *51*
Sting 93
The Sting (1973) 148
Stoker, Bram 120, 128
Stoltz, Eric 97, 197
The Stone Tape (1972) 134
Straight, Beatrice 132
Strange, Glenn 197
The Strange Case of Dr. Jekyll and Mr. Hyde (novella) 118; film versions, 161–63
Stribling, Melissa *128*
structure of horror film 38–46
Stuck (2007) 64, 140–42
subversion 71, 79, 81

Superman (1978) 109
suspense 24, 26
Suspiria (1977) 134
Suvari, Mena 140
Swales, John 107
symbolic theory of horror film 7–8
sympathy for DDB 15, 49, 52; for normal 52, 58–60

Tally, Ted 148
Tandy, Jessica 189
Tarantula (1955) 109–10
taxonomy 151–*52*, 153–67
teaser 42–45
technique 168–80
teleology *see* purpose
Terms of Endearment (1983) 199
The Terror (1963) 198
Terrore nello spazio (*Planet of the Vampires*; 1965) 134, 182
The Texas Chain Saw Massacre (1974) 133, 170–71, 174, 189
The Texas Chain Saw Massacre 2 (1986) 189
Them! (1954) 109, 127
Thesiger, Ernest 87, 192–93
They Came from Within (also known as *Shivers*; 1975) 67; 133–34; 186
They Live (1988) 184
The Thing (1982) 136, 165, 184–85
The Thing from Another World (1951) 109, *111*, 127, 134, 139, 165
The Thing with Two Heads (1972) 9
30 Days of Night (2007) 154
This Gun for Hire (1942) 111
Thomas *see* Aquinas, St. Thomas
Tilly, Jennifer *94*
Titanic (1997) 198
To Kill a Mockingbird (1962) 50
Tokyo 11, 31
torture porn 1, 55, 149
Tourneur, Jacques 126
Tower of London (1939) 108
I tre volti della paura (*Black Sabbath*; 1963) 182
Tremors (1990) 164
Truffaut, François 72
Turistas (2006) 140
The Turn of the Screw (novella) 132
20th Century-Fox 103, 132, 134
28 Days Later (2002) 67
Twilight (2008) 16, 115, 147
Twitch of the Death Nerve see *Reazione a catena*
Twitchell, James B. 1, 146
The Two Faces of Dr. Jekyll (1960) 187
2001: A Space Odyssey (1968) 109
Two Thousand Maniacs! (1964) 63, 133, 176
Tyler, Tom 194–*95*, 196–97

The Unborn (2009) 69
undead 10, 151–58

Underworld (2003) 153
The Unknown (1927) 183
Universal Pictures 1, 10, 21, 120–22, 146, 174, 176, 178
unmarried sex *see* sex, unmarried
Urban Legend (1998) 139

Valentine, Elizabeth R. 145–46
vampire 9, 11, 12, 14, 28, 67, 110, 153–54, 205
I vampiri (*The Devil's Commandment*; 1956) 127
Vampyr (1932) 122
Van Helsing (2004) 162, 178
The Vanishing see *Spoorloos*
Van Vogt, A.E. 135
Videodrome (1983) 186
Village of the Damned (1960) 68
Villella, Michael 194, 196–97
violence, media 55
The Voyage of the Space Beagle (novel) 135

Walas, Chris 102
War of the Worlds (1953) 165
Warner Bros. 82, 147
Waterloo Bridge (1931) 192
Watts, Naomi 178
Waxman, Franz 89
Weaver, Sigourney 135
Weaver, Tom 89
werewolf 10, 11, 67, 110, 161–**63**, 205
Werewolf of London (1935) 122, 126, 161
Wes Craven's New Nightmare (1994) 185
western 12, 47
Whale, James 85, 192–93
What Ever Happened to Baby Jane? (1962) 141, 199

White Zombie (1932) 154
Wicked Stepmother (1989) 199
The Wicker Man (1973) 67
Willard (1971) 164
Williams, Caroline 189
Williams, John 23
Williamson, Kevin 139
Willis, Bruce 31, 140, 199
Winston, Stan 134
The Witches of Eastwick (1987) 199
The Wizard of Oz (1939) 110
Wolf (1994) 199
Wolf Creek (2005) 63, 140
The Wolf Man (1941) 21, 52, 63, 126, 162–**63**, 169
The Wolfman (2010) 62, 162, 168, 198
Wood, Robin 20, 59, 86
Woods, James 184
Worland, Rick 9, 110
Wray, Fay 33, **123**, 194
Wrong Turn (2003) 63
Wynter, Dana **68**

Les Yeux sans visage (*Eyes without a Face; The Horror Chamber of Dr. Faustus*; 1960) 55, 131
You Only Live Twice (1967) 12
Young, Elizabeth 90
Young Frankenstein (1974) 86, 118
youth 67–69; children 75, 77–82

Zombi 2 (*Zombie*; 1979) 134
zombie 10–11, 28, 36, 67, 110, 153–54, 205
Zombie see *Zombi 2*
Zombieland (2009) 114–15
Zuniga, Daphne 102

www.ingramcontent.com/pod-product-compliance
Ingram Content Group UK Ltd.
Pitfield, Milton Keynes, MK11 3LW, UK
UKHW041948140426
5217IPUK00014B/697